Ought, Reasons, and Morality

Ought, Reasons, and Morality

The Collected Papers of
W. D. FALK

With a Foreword by Kurt Baier

Cornell University Press

Ithaca and London

First published 1986 by Cornell University Press.

International Standard Book Number 0–8014–1784–8
Library of Congress Catalog Card Number 85–22436
Printed in the United States of America
*Librarians: Library of Congress cataloging information
appears on the last page of the book.*

*The paper in this book is acid-free and meets the guidelines for
permanence and durability of the Committee on Production Guidelines
for Book Longevity of the Council on Library Resources.*

To Jeanette,

my children, and stepchildren

Contents

Foreword

David Falk's ideas were a powerful direction-setting force behind some of the important shifts that occurred in ethical theory between the 1940s and the 1970s. Falk taught—and taught very successfully—on three continents, first at Oxford in the 1930s and 1940s, then at Melbourne in the 1950s, and finally in this country, at Syracuse, Wayne State, and Chapel Hill, reaching a wide and diverse audience, by no means merely philosophers or academics. The publication of these essays, among them five never previously printed, is therefore most welcome. This collection makes it possible to trace the development of Falk's central theses, to explore their fruitful application in the solution of many classical problems, such as that of how reason can move us to action and that of whether it must always be rational to be moral, and to note his ethical preoccupations, soon to be shared by more and more ethical theorists. Indeed, what has struck me most as I reread these essays—and what I feel sure will strike others—is how much better his thought has stood the test of time, how much closer the problems he raises are to ours, and how much less dated his essays are in terms of methodology and commitment to philosophical styles than those of the best-known (perhaps because most frequently and passionately refuted) of his contemporaries. The freshness of much of Falk's work is probably explained partly by the fact that he was never a 'schoolman', never a wholehearted logical positivist, Wittgensteinian, or ordinary language philosopher. But the most important part of the explanation, I would guess, is that his thinking about ethics is informed by his wide and deep knowledge of the history of social, including political and economic, thought. In his lectures at Oxford (which I had the privilege of attending in 1949

[9]

and 1950) he usually examined the central moral, political, and economic ideas of Rousseau, Hume, Smith, Kant, Hegel, and Marx. Such historical comparisons of vastly different approaches to moral and social practices cannot but help one identify deep and persistent ethical patterns and problems, which stem not merely from fashion or from the idiosyncrasies of a particular ethical approach, and suggest fruitful methods for their explanation and solution. (A fine example of the explicit use of such historical comparisons is "The Age of Reason," but all the essays in this volume at least implicitly draw on them.)

This, of course, is not the place to attempt a critical examination of Falk's views in their rich and complex detail, but readers may welcome a brief overview of the main topics discussed in the collection. They can be formulated in three major and closely interrelated questions, taken up in most of these essays: How exactly is duty related to motivation? What role can reason play in solving practical problems, including moral ones? Exactly what makes a reason a moral one? It hardly needs emphasizing that all three of these topics are central in the most recent discussions of theoretical ethics, and there is no doubt that Falk's arguments have been influential in setting the agenda for these current investigations.

The first of these problems and the one with the widest ramifications concerns the relation between duty and motivation. Falk assumes, as do many others, that one cannot have a duty to do something unless one is able and has sufficient reason to do it. If one did not have sufficient reason to do whatever is one's duty, one could sometimes ask why one *ought* to do it and get no answer. And if having a sufficient reason did not also always give one a sufficient motive, then one would sometimes be unable to do one's duty and so be excused from doing it, even when one had a compelling reason to do it. Philosophers in the classical tradition from Plato to Butler overcome this difficulty by making two assumptions. One is psychological: that all persons desire only their own good. The other is ethical: that it is incumbent on ethicists to show that in doing one's duty one necessarily promotes one's good. These two together guarantee that one always has a sufficient reason and motive to do whatever is one's duty. As is well known, H. A. Prichard thought that this solution to the "motivational problem about duty" rested on a mistake. He did not believe that duty was necessarily tied to interest, and he thought that the conviction that it had to be was based on the psychological mistake of thinking that all persons desired only their good. Prichard's alternative solution was to postulate a desire to do one's duty. Falk argues, cogently, that this answer presents Prichard with an insoluble difficulty. For Prichard, like most moral philosophers, holds what Falk calls an "externalist view of 'ought' or 'duty' " (" 'Ought' and Motivation," p. 33), that is, a view to the effect that having a duty is being subject to external demands whether by a deity, by one's society, or simply by what is 'called for' or 'required by' the situation one is in. The difficulty is that, on this Prichardian view, one may be confronted by a conflict between duty and interest, and it must remain an open question whether one *ought* to do what is one's externally imposed duty or what would promote one's best interest, for Prichard "is not prepared to hold that the sense of duty, even dispositionally, must always be everyone's strongest motive" (ibid., p. 31).

In the essays in the first section, Falk pursues the ramifications of this difficulty and effectively shows its surprisingly far-reaching implications. As Falk sees it, the heart of the difficulty is that we want to say both that the "very fact of a duty entails all the motive required for doing the act" (ibid., p. 29) and so "morality needs no external sanction," but also that it does need such a sanction, that whether we have a sufficient motive or reason for doing our duty is contingent upon our other desires and motives. Falk's own ingenious solution consists of two moves. The main move is to adopt an 'internalist' account of duty, asserting a conceptual connection between having a duty and being dispositionally motivated to act accordingly. On this view, no external demand can be one's duty unless one is dispositionally motivated to satisfy it. The second move is to divide the task of practical guidance into two parts: an objective part which provides the person to be guided with relevant facts, those that constitute dispositional motives and that would incline the person to act in certain specific ways if he were apprised of them and appropriately attended to and appreciated them. The second part is a task for the person to be guided: after acquainting himself with all the relevant facts he must fully appreciate or 'mind' or 'dwell on' them or 'chew them over.' For this reason, learning a fact that is *saddening news* is in important ways different from learning a fact that is a *guiding reason*. "One cannot receive the saddening news without being saddened by it; one can learn about a guiding reason and not be guided by it" ("Action-Guiding Reasons," pp. 89–90). "A known reason is not something to straightaway pounce on one; it seems rather something available to pounce, sometimes almost poised to pounce, something that would pounce if only one did what is necessary to let it" (ibid., p. 91). "One may have to *take* guidance from reasons because the guidance they can *give* is there only for the *taking*" (ibid.). This solution to Prichard's

problem is developed in considerable detail, and Falk uses its implications to throw light on many other problems (the most important
being weakness of will). I think it fair to say that Falk's discussions of
ought and *motivation* have done more than anyone else's to transform
ethical discussions of duty, obligation, and ought. Not only do moral
philosophers now feel compelled to take sides on the issue of internalism versus externalism, conceived in much the way he does, but,
despite some notable holdouts, most have followed him into internalism.

On the second topic, the role of reason in solving practical problems,
Falk's views emerge out of his struggle on two opposite fronts. Against
rationalism (and against the skepticism that flows from "the disappointment of misplaced expectations" generated by rationalism ["Moral
Perplexity," p. 256]), he insists that reason is not always and not simply
a matter of calculation and deduction or even experiment. "Moral
reason is not that of the scientist or mathematician, whose 'reason'
has in our time become the paradigm of all reason. One's proper
choice is not found under the microscope or by calculation, but it can
be found" (ibid., p. 259). As he put it, in 1956, in the idiom of the
1980s: "One should not think that where there is no argument there
can be no conversation" (ibid.).

His other battle is against the emotivists and prescriptivists with
whom he can agree that guidance by reason is guidance by reasons
but cannot agree that that means merely the presentation of facts and
that "one starts 'oughting' where reasons fail one" ("On Learning
about Reasons," p. 71) "because reasons, in addition to their cognitive
nature, have conative-affective effects" (ibid., p. 73, quoting from Stevenson's *Ethics and Language*). Against this emotivist account of guidance by reasons Falk insists that reason-learning is not exhausted by
fact-learning. For although, in giving Smith a reason, one cannot do
more than tell him facts that are relevant to his practical problem,
Smith may then know these facts, yet not know *that* they are reasons
for him, that is, facts relevant to his problems. In one sense he has
been told what is a reason, but in another sense, he has not: for in
telling Smith that fact, "one had not engendered in him the conviction
that he had a reason, or enough of one, in what one had taught him.
He still had to work his own passage to this conviction" (ibid., p. 78).
Logic and science give us exaggerated expectations about the guiding
powers of practical reason. "What everyone hopes for as a guide are
rules by which to settle all cases, applicable with ease, and in the same
way to everyone alike. Instead, what we have available is a procedure,
calling on many and fallible qualities of mind; a procedure which
yields some broad and fairly obvious answers, but which for the rest

leaves us to puzzle things out for ourselves, with a margin for error and disagreement too wide for comfort" ("Moral Perplexity," p. 260). In another essay, "Action-Guiding Reasons," Falk spells out, in great detail, his development of this Sidgwickian version of self-guidance by practical reason.

Whatever one may in the end decide about Falk's conception of practical reason, there can be no doubt that he has shown the crucial importance of reason in practical including moral matters and has exposed fatal weaknesses in both of the two rival conceptions of practical reason which had occupied center stage for so long.

The third problem Falk took up concerns the delineation of morality. As we have seen, for him, being guided by reason is tantamount to being guided by reasons. Similarly, being guided by morality is tantamount to being guided by *moral* reasons. As he sees it, the problem therefore is to determine what makes reasons *moral*. He found the reliance many of his contemporaries placed on the ordinary use of 'morality' quite misguided, for in his opinion that ordinary use works with two different criteria, the formalist and the nonformalist, which tend to come apart.

The formalist criterion represents reflective, mature morality as "practice which the due exercise of knowledge and reflection makes mandatory by making it reflectively compelling" ("Morality, Form, and Content," p. 234) or in a nutshell, "the general practice of conscientiously ought-abiding living" ("Morality, Self, and Others," p. 230), which requires the conscientious surveying of the relevant facts and conscientiously minding them or chewing them over. The material criterion, by contrast, represents reflective mature morality as doing what is "socially beneficial and a matter of active social concern" (ibid.). This duality of criteria raises in acute form the problem of what is truly moral, for "the rational and autonomous mode of life overlaps, but no longer necessarily coincides, with the moral mode of life as conceived from the point of view of the social interest" (ibid., p. 231). Usage is little help. For one thing, it leans both ways, although it "backs the nonformalist more than the formalist" (ibid., p. 230). In any case, usage can only determine the current use of the word 'morality'. It cannot solve our problem. For, Falk concludes, we then would have to "grant that 'morality' on this level is demoted from its accustomed place of being the sole and final arbiter of right and wrong choice" (ibid.). What would be chosen by the material (social) criterion may not, then, be chosen by "autonomous noncoercive reason." And Falk makes it clear that the highest respect is owed to reason when it is autonomous and noncoercive.

Again Falk has worked at, and succeeded in, bringing this problem to our consciousness. Whether or not we agree with his account of what it is to be guided by reasons or by moral reasons, whether or not we agree with his account of "autonomous noncoercive reason" as that form of reason which deserves the highest respect, it seems we cannot afford to ignore the problem he has done so much to force on our attention.

There is, of course, a great deal more to praise about these essays beyond their central themes; for instance, the deeply informed, perceptive, and illuminating historical pieces, which I have had to ignore. But I feel I cannot ignore Falk's contribution as a philosophical friend, which almost always meant a sympathetic yet relentless critic. Falk and I were colleagues in the Department of Philosophy at Melbourne University in the 1950s, and we met regularly for long and at times heated discussions. The dialogue between "In" and "Out" in "Morality, Self, and Others"—no mystery here about who is "In"—captures some of the highlights of our disagreements. Wherever Falk taught, he conducted many of his philosophical investigations not in the quiet and safety of his study but in animated or even fervent conversations with colleagues, friends, and students. The lucidity and elegance of his writings is the result of a long process of clarification and simplification achieved through having to explain his ideas to, and defend them against, acute discussion partners of very different backgrounds and convictions. I would guess that among the most challenging, intense, and stimulating, though by no means the last of these interchanges (Stephen Darwall's recent book *Impartial Reason* testifies to the persistence of this influence to the present day), were those that occurred when Falk was at Wayne State during the late 1950s and the 1960s. His most frequent discussion partners at that time were his immediate colleagues Hector Castañeda and George Nakhnikian at Wayne State and Charles Stevenson, William Frankena, and Paul Henle, his close neighbors at Ann Arbor, where he often visited. I would guess that their writings of that period (see, for example, A. I. Melden, ed., *Essays in Moral Philosophy* [Seattle: University of Washington Press, 1958], and Hector-Neri Castañeda and George Nakhnikian, eds., *Morality and the Language of Conduct* [Detroit: Wayne State University Press, 1963]) exhibit not only the impact of Falk's published work but also his persuasive personal influence.

These essays deserve to be read widely, not only because when they first appeared they were well ahead of their time or because they helped to shift our ethical concerns in more profitable directions but because they are rich in moral observations and insights that have not yet been fully mined. They are an important chapter in the recent history of ethical theory, but like all good philosophy, they will continue to figure in future chapters of that history.

KURT BAIER

Pittsburgh, Pennsylvania

Preface

The essays collected in this volume were written over a period of years during which I was teaching moral and political philosophy at Oxford (England), at Melbourne (Australia), and since 1963 at the University of North Carolina at Chapel Hill. The essays raise different issues but have a common theme. The issues raised concern the nature of reflective morality, its autonomous status, the internality of its norms, the truth value of its propositions, the problem of self and others, and the analysis of such fundamental concepts as reasons, ought, and value. The common theme is in a resistance to identifying with any one of the interpretive fashions that have ruled moral philosophy and value theory in my time; whether the intuitionism of H. A. Prichard or W. D. Ross, the prescriptivism of Charles Stevenson and R. M. Hare, or the conventionalism of Kurt Baier. Instead, I have been exploring the feasibility of a rational empiricism which has empirical affinities with Hume and rational affinities with Kant, which is 'naturalistic' without committing the naturalistic fallacy, and which treats values as 'objective' without treating them as absolute.

Most of the essays have been published before. They were written, at long intervals, for special occasions, and apologies for their frequent overlap are in order. The encouragement of colleagues, friends, and former students was needed to overcome my qualms about publishing the collection. For their solicitude, I owe special thanks to James Rachels and to my friend Kurt Baier, with whom I have had the privilege of joining in friendly philosophical combat over many years. I also express my gratitude to William Frankena and the late Charles Stevenson for their sympathetic regard for my work and their support for my move late in life from Australia to this country. My thanks also go to the Department of Philosophy at the University of North Carolina, Chapel Hill, to Maynard Adams and my other distinguished colleagues, to a succession of keen graduate students, and to Claire Miller, our indefatigable administrative assistant, for having given me an environment in which to prosper for these last twenty years. Warm thanks are also due to Bradley Goodman for his always willing and understanding editorial assistance.

W. D. FALK

Chapel Hill, North Carolina

PART ONE

REASONS, GOOD, AND OUGHT

[1]

'Ought' and Motivation

I want to consider an argument put forward by the late Professor H. A. Prichard in his lecture "Duty and Interest"[1] as it raises issues of wider interest. The argument occurs in the second half of his lecture, where Prichard attributes to popular moralists and philosophers a view which to him seems paradoxical. The view has been widely held and is well exemplified by Bishop Butler; whether it should also be attributed to Plato I shall not be concerned to discuss.

The problem is briefly this. Moralists in the past have been preoccupied with showing that a person who does his duty will, in doing so, also advance his personal good. This would be understandable if they thought that only acts which advance someone's good could be duties, for then we could never know we ought to do an act unless we were convinced of its good consequences for ourselves. But there are moralists, like Bishop Butler, who, as Prichard agrees, consider this view as obviously false. They grant we can have duties on other grounds than that an act would promote our own good, e.g., on the ground that an act will be one of beneficence or of keeping faith; but in spite of this, they remain worried by the problem of a necessary connection between duty and personal good. Thus Butler finds it necessary to supplement his conviction of the irreducible authority of conscience by an attempt to prove that whenever conscience bids us do some act on its own account and regardless of our own good, in fact, and contrary to appearances, our own good will always be served,

First published in *Proceedings of the Aristotelian Society* 48 (1947-48):492–510, © The Aristotelian Society 1948. Reprinted by courtesy of the Editor.
1. H. A. Prichard, "Duty and Interest," in Wilfrid Sellars and John Hospers, *Readings in Contemporary Ethical Theory* (New York: Appleton-Century-Crofts, 1952).

or at least not be harmed, by our doing it. Now according to Prichard these attempts to prove a connection between duty and personal good where the duty itself is not thought to depend on this connection seem paradoxical: we cannot but view them with the suspicion that "the real question is not so much whether they are successful, but whether they ought ever to have been made"; and I myself share this feeling. But why should they never have been made? Prichard's answer to this question, an answer accepted by Sir David Ross in the *Foundations of Ethics*, is my reason for returning to the problem, for I feel it still does not meet the real point. The trouble, I think, does not lie principally in the psychological errors of his opponents as alleged by Prichard: it lies deeper, in a persistent uncertainty shared by moralists and ordinary men about the relation to motivation of the very use of such words as 'ought', 'duty', 'obligation'.

According to Prichard the exponents of a connection between duty and interest in the above sense are concerned to meet a perplexity of ordinary life. They must be judged by their success in meeting it. People commonly take it for granted that, when it is their duty to do some act, they have also a reason or motive for doing it, in some sense even an especially stringent one. But for many there comes a time, particularly when some personal interest seems at stake, when they feel troubled by doubt or in need of reassurance; and in this mood they turn to the moralist with a request: "Exhibit to me," they say in effect, "the reason or motive sufficient, even at cost to myself, to induce me to do what I ought, but don't want to do; for though I grant the duty, I see no such reason, and maybe there is none, or none sufficiently strong; and no one can do anything unless he has a sufficient reason for doing it, and knows what it is!" Here what is asked for is a 'justification' in terms of motive for them doing some act whose moral obligatoriness is not questioned and the psychological possibility of moral conduct is made dependent on its success. How is the moralist to deal with this? He may either deny the legitimacy of the request— by denying that moral conduct requires a reason or motive sufficient or otherwise—or else he must show how it can be satisfied. The search for a connection between duty and interest is an attempt to do the latter. It is granted that the questioner has a real ax to grind: that when he has a duty it is still an open question whether he will also have a motive; but he is told that the facts, psychological and otherwise, will be found to dispel his doubts. It so happens that when he ought to do an act he will also, and in spite of contrary appearances, always be promoting his own good by doing it, and his own good is in fact what he desires to promote. He is therefore always in error when, while acknowledging a duty, he pleads absence of a motive.

But, tempting as this reply has seemed to many, Prichard's misgivings are justified. For if this were the only answer the connection between duty and motivation would be much looser than we commonly expect it to be. If the questioner were overlooking no more than a connection between duty and self-interest, some may be right in denying that they had a motive sufficient for doing what they ought, since even if general, the connection could not be proved necessary; and in fact the exceptions would be likely to prove to be the rule.

But the chances of success apart, the reply seems altogether out of place, since it rests on the assumption that moral conduct can have none but interested motives. It implies that "morality needs a sanction"; that "to stimulate a man into doing some action it is not merely insufficient, but useless to convince him that he is morally bound to do it, and that, instead we have to appeal to his desire to be better off." But, in fact, we believe that morality needs no external sanction: that the very thought that we morally ought to do some act is sufficient without reference to any ulterior motive to provide us with a reason for doing it; and we consider that strictly moral, i.e., morally good conduct is activated by no other motive than that provided by this thought. The reply offered by the exponents of a connection between duty and interest therefore fails altogether to meet what must be the questioner's fundamental error.

In what then does his error consist? According to Prichard, in a psychological oversight, a failure to notice within himself the existence of disinterested desires, and among them a desire to do acts simply because he ought to do them. The exponents of a connection between duty and interest fail to refer him to this, because they are themselves blinded by a psychological dogma, the belief that a person's own good is the one and only rational motive to action. But once the psychological facts are recognized for what they are, no difficulty remains in dealing with the request for a motive where a duty is acknowledged in a way that will account for our ordinary moral convictions. This is how Prichard summarizes his conclusion: "For, if we admit the existence of a desire to do what is right, there is no longer any reason for maintaining as a general thesis that in any case in which a man knows some action to be right, he must, if he is to be led to do it, be convinced that he will gain by doing it. For we shall be able to maintain that his desire to do what is right, if strong enough, will lead him to do the action in spite of any aversion from doing it, which he may feel on account of its disadvantages."[2]

The strength of this view lies in that it can explain how the man

2. Ibid., pp. 485–86.

who acknowledges a duty to do some act may be provided with a motive for doing it, even at cost to himself, purely by the conviction that he ought to do it. To this extent, Prichard seems to account for our ordinary convictions more adequately than the rival doctrine. All the same, I think, he still does so to a far smaller extent than may at first sight appear. In fact, I shall argue that if, as he contends, a psychological oversight is all that accounts for the questioner's doubt of a motive for acting as he ought, some persistent features of our ordinary moral convictions, far from having been accounted for, will have to be discarded.

But before turning to these difficulties, some consideration must be given to what the demand for a motive or reason, as a condition of anyone's ability to act, amounts to. Among the confusions attending the use of words like 'motive' and 'reason' one arises from the habit of speaking of both thoughts and desires as motives for actions. The motive is described as being constituted by an impelling thought *or* desire. According to Prichard, there is here a distinction without a difference, as a motivating thought implies a purpose which it motivates, and a purpose is what someone desires to attain. The point, he says, needs stressing on account of a distinction between 'having a motive' and 'desiring', introduced by Kant. For, according to Kant, we have in the thought that we ought to do some act a motive for doing it: but, 'having a motive' does not here entail 'having a desire'; and when we act from the motive, we shall do so with the aid of an effort of will and against desire or inclination rather than from them. It seems plain to Prichard that Kant is here drawing an artificial distinction, presumably under the influence of his conviction that desire is always for some pleasurable experience, which would exclude the possibility of a desire for doing one's duty for its own sake. But the difficulty disappears with the abandonment of the latter view. We shall then say, with Kant, that we have in the thought that we ought to do some act a motive for doing it, and equate this with saying that we possess a desire to do our duty for its own sake or a 'sense of duty'. To convince a man that he has a motive for doing his duty must therefore consist in convincing him that he desires to do it; and when he comes to act, under the influence of this motive he will be acting from desire pure and simple as he would under the influence of any other motive.

But, whatever the merits of Kant's contribution, the problems involved here are more complex than Prichard presents them. For we use 'having a motive' in different senses, and in neither of them, though for different reasons, does it seem appropriate to equate 'having a motive' with 'desiring'. In order to avoid misunderstandings, I must here state what I take a 'reason' or 'motive' to mean. In the sense relevant to this discussion, a reason or motive is a moving or impelling thought, the thought of that for the sake, or in view, of which, some act is done; and I myself see no intelligible alternative to saying that it 'moves' or 'impels' in the sense that it functions as a cause of actions, in the conventional sense of cause as an antecedent implying a consequent by a rule of invariable connection. I should, therefore, describe a motive as a *causa rationis*, a mental antecedent which, when attended to by a person, and in otherwise comparable conditions, will invariably be followed by an orientation of his organism toward the action thought of, in a way which, except for the intervention of distractions, countermotives, and physical impediments, will terminate in the action itself. Such a thought may be said to constitute simply a reason or motive, if, when attended to by itself alone, it thus causally implies action; and a sufficient reason or motive when, in addition, it persists in doing so even in view of opposing motives in the situation. Now, that someone has a motive may be used in either an *occurrent* or a *dispositional* sense; for 'he is being impelled (or caused) by the thought of some act to do it', or 'he would, if he dwelt on it, be impelled (or caused) by the thought of some act to do it'. The motive may be his either actually or potentially and reflectively so. The differences between these two uses are considerable, and each is differently related to 'desiring'. In the first use there is a connection, though none as close as Prichard presents it. Actually 'to have a motive to do some act' and 'desiring to do it' would here mean the same if 'desiring' were used simply for 'being impelled'. As a rule, however, it is used not for 'being', but for 'feeling' impelled. But to say we feel impelled to do some act functions (so it seems to me) as a composite statement, asserting that we are impelled and that we have perceptual evidence of our being so, evidence derived from sensations which we take to arise, under the influence of a motivating thought, from the orientation of our organism toward an overt action. To say that someone desires to do some act would therefore go beyond saying that he had a motive or was impelled, even if, whenever anyone were impelled to action, he also felt desire; but in fact people are often impelled to act under the influence of a motivating thought without noticing any desire at all.[3] There is no harm if in ordinary speech we refer to desires as well as impelling thoughts as the motives or causes of actions: but consistently, not even impulses, let alone desires, should be called causes, since our having an impulse is not the cause of our acting, but

3. In fact, the incidence of felt impulse, or desire, seems to depend on the extent to which the passage of motives into action is obstructed by psychological or physical impediments. We feel desire in proportion as our impulses are in difficulties.

the very fact of our being caused to act; and in referring to desires in this way we are confounding in part at least our perception of the operation of a law of motivation with the operation of this law itself.

But if, in the occurrent sense, there is at least a close connection between 'having a motive' and 'desiring', in the dispositional sense there is none whatever. Here a person is said to have a motive when the thought of some act (either as such, or as having some property or effect) is *capable* of determining him to do it; and that someone would be made to do some act if he dwelt on the thought of it in no way entails that he is being made, or desires, to do it. On the contrary, while dispositionally he may have the stronger reason for doing one act, another may be all that he is desiring. Prichard entirely ignores this latter use though it is the one that bears primarily on his argument. There would be no point in making the questioner realize that he had a 'sense of duty' in the occurrent sense: that he thought he desired only his own good but that really he desired to do his duty. For in the occurrent sense, for someone to have a motive strong enough for doing some act is for him to be subject to the operation of a law implying action; and a law cannot be said to depend for its operation on anyone's knowledge that it is operating. The questioner's failure to realize that, in the occurrent sense, he had a motive could no more prevent him from acting under its influence than the realization that he had it could assist him.[4] In fact, it is in the dispositional sense only that it makes sense for people to claim that their ability to do some act depends both on their *having* sufficient cause for doing it and their *realizing* that they have it and in what it consists. For a sufficient reason which exists dispositionally only will not actually function as a cause as long as the thought that constitutes it is not being dwelt upon; and if anyone wanted to make it function as a cause, he would first have to realize that he had it and what it was. He would then, in the knowledge of the reason which dispositionally he has for doing the act, have a means for determining himself to do it.

Instead of refusing to follow Kant, Prichard should therefore have agreed with him to the extent that the man who does not desire to act as he ought, and on this account questions his ability to do so, could still be shown that in the very thought that he ought to do the act, he had dispositionally a motive for doing it, so that if he tried he would induce himself to do it. Moreover, Prichard should have acknowledged that if a man induced himself to act under the influence

4. We cannot occurrently have a motive without knowing it in the sense that we are acquainted with the thought that moves us, but this is not to say that we shall also know *that* it is moving us.

of such a motive he would not be acting simply from desire, or inclination, as the motive thought would here not function as a cause unless the agent had enabled it to do so.

I shall now turn to the difficulties which I said attach to Prichard's solution of the questioner's doubt. Here it is noteworthy that, sharply as Prichard censures his opponents, he agrees with them on one underlying assumption. Like them he holds that the man who while granting a duty doubts he has also a motive has a real ax to grind: there is no convincing him that he has a motive except by considerations additional to those which already convince him that he has the duty. The case of the exponents of a connection between duty and interest plainly rests on this assumption, but, only less obviously, so does Prichard's. For by convincing a man that he has a duty we are not on Prichard's view providing him with a motive in the sense that to convince him of the first consists in convincing him of the second, or of anything that necessarily entails the second. We are doing so in the sense only that in a suitably constituted person, the conviction of duty, when he attends to it, will incidentally also function as a motive, while itself being the conviction of something else, of what exactly Prichard never states, but presumably of some nonpsychological fact inherent in the situation confronting the agent. Correspondingly when we speak of morally good conduct, we cannot on this view strictly say that it consists in actions conditioned solely by the fact that it was our duty to do them. For what would be moving us to action would not be a motive implicit in the very fact of duty itself but a motive constituted by the thought that we had the duty, and existing apart from and additionally to the fact of duty. The point is candidly admitted by Ross, "An act's being our duty," he says, "is never the reason why we do it," for "I did the act simply because I knew, or thought it to be my duty, and because I desired to do it, as being my duty, more than I desired to do any other act."[5]

This being so, it should be allowed that Prichard shares his opponent's view that morality needs a sanction, admittedly a more respectable one. For we imply that morality needs a sanction whenever we say that merely on account of the fact that we ought to do some act we have not yet any incentive sufficient for doing it; and that, whether we shall have the latter or not, will depend on conditions distinct from and additional to the former. It is merely a corollary of this, though an important one, that on Prichard's view no less than, say, on Butler's, our doing what we ought to do needs a 'justification' additional to that which we express by saying that we morally ought to do it. For

5. W. D. Ross, *Foundations of Ethics* (Oxford: Oxford University Press, 1939), p. 227.

there is a sense in which we may be said to justify to ourselves some act which, on some grounds, we are averse from doing by seeking to assure ourselves of a reason sufficient for doing it. In ordinary speech, we are seeking, in this sense, a justification when we ask with respect to some act, "is there, when I come to think of it, any real need for my doing it at all, or one strong enough, considering the cost?" using here 'is there any real need' for 'is there any reason, at least potentially and reflectively, sufficiently compelling to make me do it?' To ask this sort of question, even when we grant that an act would be morally justified, being the one we morally ought to do, must on Prichard's view be permissible without involving the questioner in any absurdity; for no answer to a question of this sort would as yet be entailed by the questioner's conviction that he morally ought to do the act. Indeed, far from being absurd it would be pertinent for people to ask this question; for on occasions when they do not actually desire, or desire sufficiently, to do some act which they grant they morally ought to do, or when they find themselves in a reflective state of mind, their very capacity to act morally will depend on the answer to it. Rather than object to Butler, Prichard should therefore have agreed with him on the principle that "in a cool hour" we will not be able, when our own good seems at stake, to do what we grant we morally ought to do, unless we can find in addition some 'nonmoral' justification of our doing it. He should consistently have objected only to Butler's insistence on seeking this justification in an interested rather than a disinterested motive. Nor finally does Prichard, any more than Butler, show that the attempt to prove a 'real need' for moral conduct must always succeed. There may always be some who can maintain without absurdity and as a plain matter of fact that, though admittedly they are morally bound to do some act, at the same time there is no real need or sufficient reason whatever for them to do it. Hence whether the questioner is in error or not is not a question that affords of a general answer. The question is an open one, and each case has to be treated on its merits.

In a way all this seems plausible enough. The suggestion that we can refer the questioner, sometimes at least, to the thought of duty itself as a motive accords with our ordinary moral convictions, more so, at any rate, than the view that we can refer him to none but interested considerations, and the conclusion seems unavoidable that whether we shall be able to do so must turn on a question of psychological fact. But somehow, if its implications are considered, Prichard's solution still falls short of expectations: it makes the connection between duty and motivation less close than sometimes at least we are wont to view it. For it is a fact about ordinary moral thinking that no less persistent than the conviction that morality needs some sanction is its opposite, that it needs no sanction whatever: that somehow the very fact of a duty entails all the motive required for doing the act; and anyone who, rightly or wrongly, adheres to this conviction will take exception to Prichard's solution. He will object to the question of motive being made separate from and additional to that of duty: to its being treated, when a person is said to have a duty, not as a foregone conclusion, but as an open question, turning on a benevolent dispensation of providence in the shape of a singular psychological disposition. Certainly Kant, whose freedom from vulgar errors Prichard holds in such esteem, would not have countenanced this solution. To Kant the very existence of a duty was inseparable from the existence of a motive, and anyone who had a duty could, solely on this account and at whatever cost to himself, determine himself to do it if he tried. And if we consider the implications of the opposite view, it is only tempting to sympathize with Kant. It seems paradoxical that moral conduct should require more than one kind of justification: that having first convinced someone that regardless of cost to himself he was morally bound to do some act we should then be called upon to convince him as well that he had some and some sufficiently strong reason for doing this same act. "You have made me realize that I ought, now convince me that I really need to" seems a spurious request, inviting the retort "if you really were convinced of the first, you would not seriously doubt the second." And even supposing we granted that to justify an act morally and to justify the same act in terms of motive were distinct, we would still be hankering after a necessary and not merely a contingent connection between the two. We would feel it was paradoxical for anyone ever to be right in saying that, though regardless of some personal sacrifice he ought to do some act, because of the sacrifice and in spite of the duty, he, though others might, had no manner of sufficient reason for doing it. We should readily grant him a lack of motive only in the occurrent sense: that he may have a duty without actually having any, or any strong enough, impulse or desire to do the act. At the back of these hesitations lies the conviction that, if anyone has a duty, that he has it is inseparable from the existence of some real check on his freedom to act otherwise; a conviction which entails that the connection between duty and motivation is too close to be merely contingent. Whether and how this conviction can be sustained is another matter; but plainly Prichard does not account for it.

Some reflection of these unacknowledged difficulties in Prichard's position is found in his failure to deal convincingly with a problem which, he points out, may be said to present him with an "insoluble difficulty." If doing our duty, he says,[6] depends on a special desire, then someone may hesitate between the desire to do one act because it is his duty, and another because it would be for his own good. Such conflict we normally resolve by means of a choice, resting on our eliciting a preference between the alternatives; but to do the same with the conflict between the act we ought and the act it would be for our interest to do feels inappropriate. Prichard seeks to explain this by saying that in the case of duty and personal good the objects of the conflicting desires are incommensurable, there being "no comparable characteristic of the two alternative actions which will enable us to choose to do the one rather than, or in preference to, the other"; and he concludes that the way of resolving conflict does here consist, paradoxical as it may seem, in a 'deciding' that is *sui generis* and in no way rests on choice. But this argument is unconvincing. No doubt the objects of the conflicting desires are here incommensurable, but so are the objects of other desires (as of the desire to spare myself pain and the desire to preserve my life) between which we allow choice to be possible; and in fact there is logically no reason why choice should depend on the commensurability of the objects between which we are undecided. For if choice rests on the eliciting of a preference between two incompatible courses of action, there is logically no reason why, if put to the test, the thought of one act should not prove impelling by comparison even to the exclusion of the other act, even though, why it did so was inexplicable and not dependent on any common quality which the one act possessed in greater measure than the other (e.g., that the one should give more enjoyment than the other); and therefore, if it were for no other than the reason put forward by Prichard, there would logically be no bar whatever to our treating the conflict between duty and interest as an open question to be solved, one way or another, by eliciting a preference between them. Nor otherwise, is it clear by what means a person should here seek by 'decision' to escape from the dilemma of irresolution. The only alternative, apart from random choice as by tossing a coin, would it seems be for him to wait for the one motive to get the better of the other on its own; but though with luck we sometimes come to be decided in this way, we could hardly here be said to have decided, in the sense of our having made any active contribution toward it. But none of this is to say that our feeling of inappropriateness of a choice between duty and interest must be groundless. On the contrary, this feeling would be justified on one assumption not considered by Prichard: on the assumption referred to before that our very thinking

6. Prichard, "Duty and Interest," p. 486.

that we ought to do some act already entails that, by comparison, we have a stronger reason in the circumstances for doing it than any other. For it would then follow that whenever we acknowledged one act to be our duty, whether by comparison we had a stronger reason for doing this act or another conducing to our own good, would, *ex hypothesi*, be no longer an open question. Our indecision would here be of a special irrational kind: it would persist although the means for rationally resolving it were already at hand; and to pretend that the resolution of indecision still here depended on our making a rational choice would imply the absurdity of treating as open a question to which, whenever we asked it, we implicitly acknowledged that we knew the answer already. But if this is the explanation, and logically no other seems possible, it is plain why Prichard cannot offer it. For he is not prepared to hold that the sense of duty, even dispositionally, must always be everyone's strongest motive.

The nature of Prichard's dilemma will now be clear. He must on his premises present the conflict between duty and interest as an open question, so that consistently it should allow of resolution by way of rational choice in the same manner as the conflict between any other alternative actions. At the same time, he cannot resist the feeling that a rational choice would here be spurious, a feeling, however, which has no justification except on an assumption which, though a persistent ingredient of ordinary moral thinking, he is nowhere prepared to make. He is caught up at this point by the intrusion of a view of the connection between duty and motivation whose implications he cannot either accommodate or entirely reject. And the dilemma seems a real one. For neither position can be easily surrendered, neither that morality needs some additional psychological sanction, nor that what sanction it requires, it necessarily carries with it, and short of surrendering the one or the other there seems no getting away from the dilemma.

A problem like this does not arise without some deep-seated confusion, and my object in the remainder of this essay will be to trace this confusion to its source. I shall suggest it has its origin in uncertainties and contradictions in the common use of words like 'ought' or 'duty', in an unnoticed juxtaposition of meanings each of which entails a different relation to motivation; and I shall try to bring out these ambiguities of language and the confusions of thought that underlie them.

What Prichard supposes words like 'ought' or 'duty' to be used for cannot be clearly stated because he considers them unanalyzable. But this much is beyond doubt, that he holds them to refer to some non-psychological objective fact, a special feature of the situation confronting an agent. His general outlook at any rate is in line with similar contemporary views, such as C. D. Broad's or Ross's, according to which 'someone ought' or 'has a duty' means that an act of his and the 'situation' would in some way be complementary to one another, so that we can say either an act of his is 'called for' or 'required' by the situation or would be 'fitting' to the situation. Views like these seem the modern descendants of traditional views of a more full-blooded but in essentials similar kind: that a person's subjection to moral law consists in his subjection to demands to do or to forebear made on him by a deity, or society, or a confused mixture of these; and that his actions would be right or wrong in proportion as they conformed to this standard. For, whatever their differences, there is this much in common between all such views. They presuppose, not unnaturally, that when someone 'ought' or 'has a duty' he is subject to some manner of demand, made on him without regard to his desires; and they imply that this demand issues essentially from outside the agent: that, whether made by a deity or society or the 'situation' (if this means anything), it has an objective existence of its own depending in no way on anything peculiar to the agent's psychological constitution. Now, the view that morality needs some sanction is a traditional associate of all views of this kind and indeed their natural corollary. If 'I ought' means 'I am from outside myself demanded to do some act', whether by the will of another, or more impersonally by the 'situation', there will then be no necessary connection for anyone between having the duty and being under any manner of real compulsion to do the act. For no one really need do any act merely because it is demanded of him, whether by a deity or society or the 'situation', but only if, in addition, he finds within himself a motive sufficient for satisfying the demand. Inevitably, therefore, at least in a 'cool hour', moral conduct will require a twofold justification: people will want to be assured not only that some act is their duty, but also that they really need to do it: and only the latter, and not merely that the act is their duty, would constitute an incentive for doing it. Thus, the problem would in some manner be solved if the claimant could be shown to demand only acts conducing on balance to the agent's own good, either in this life or in the next, or to some social good which the agent has at heart; or else we must postulate, as Prichard does, an endowment of human beings with a singular love for complying merely for its own sake with the demands on them of some external claimant strong enough, if need be, to overrule all concern for human good.[7] But also, whether people will be capable of such a

---

7. For *ex hypothesi* the motive for the act which is one's duty must here be thought

desire, and if so sufficiently, must here remain an open question. For to say that the thought of any act can function as a motive is to assign to it a causal property which only experience can tell whether it will have. But provided the externalist view of 'ought' or 'duty' is consistently adhered to, we should not hesitate to accept this implication; and if we still feel that the claim of duty must necessarily be an overriding one, but have on other grounds no reasons to support this feeling, it should be dismissed as a prejudice, founded most likely on a wishful expectation of a preestablished harmony between the existence of moral demands and of reasons for people to comply with them.

I should add that for Butler morality needs a sanction for somewhat different reasons, for according to him a duty does not consist in a demand on people of some external claimant, but of a demand arising from within their psychological constitution. People have duties because the thoughts of some acts will, if they contemplate the nature of these acts, raise an affection toward, or away from them, which by its 'authority' is superior to all competing impulses in the situation. A duty therefore is here not a demand dissociated from any human end or purpose; on the contrary, that someone has a duty does here entail that he has some motive, or that the act is an end for him. But it does not entail that the motive will be a sufficiently strong one, for Butler insists that the moral impulse derives its authority from a superiority in quality or kind, and not essentially in strength. To this extent the moral compulsion is divorced, as before, from people's natural capacity to do the act, and in consequence, at this point, the problem of a sanction must once again rise. The person who thus ought to do an act, even at apparent cost to himself, may rightly ask for a reason strong enough to induce him to do it; and there is here no other remedy but to explain away the conflict between duty and personal good as illusory. But once more, if Butler's use of 'ought' or 'duty' is strictly adhered to, there are no grounds on which to reject this implication merely because we should like to think of the claim of duty as necessarily overriding. If a duty can be thought of as constituted only by a 'higher' but not necessarily dispositionally stronger compulsion to action there is no ground on which we can deny it assistance from being 'at least not contrary' to our 'lower' nature.

What then does explain the persistence of the conviction that all these accounts fall short of expectations? It is, I think, that we apply to them, without noticing, a standard foreign to them, but implicit in

---

as independent of any relation to human good, and, in case of conflict, as its rival, since to any extent to which the latter were thought to matter, the act would no longer be done for a purely moral reason.

still another use of 'ought' or 'duty' which may be called the purely formal motivation sense. For there is a habit of speech according to which, when a person asks, "need I really, or have I, if only dispositionally, a sufficiently strong reason for doing this act?" he might as well have said, "should I or ought I really to do this?" the latter expression being in fact the more colloquial. This substitution could have been made whenever the previous discussion turned on the justification by motive of a person doing some act which he granted he morally ought to do. For we could also have presented him as asking, "why should I, or ought I to do the act which I morally ought to do?"; and if he had been using the second 'ought' in, say, some externalist sense he would not have been asking a spurious question. He would have been using the first 'ought' in a motivation sense as referring to the question of whether, at least dispositionally, there was some sufficient motive or compulsion for him to do the act which he morally ought to do. In fact, whenever in any externalist sense a person ought to do some act, the further question of whether in the motivation sense he ought to do this same act can still always be asked; but equally, the latter question could be asked by anyone who had no use for duties in the externalist sense at all: who did not believe in a deity to make demands, who found the objective requirements of the 'situation' too nebulous an expression to be meaningful, and who refused to call the demands on him of society moral imperatives. For even he might still wonder whether some act which he actually did not desire (say, assisting another in need), or which he was actually averse to on account of its implications (say, some personal sacrifice) was not one which, on its own account and in spite of all, he had dispositionally an overriding reason for doing; and his natural way of expressing this puzzlement would be to ask whether, though he did not want to, he ought not to do it. Now, this motivation use of 'ought' is important for our problem, for it would have all the implications demanded by the expectation of a necessary connection between ought and motivation. The 'ought' here would express nothing other than a certain relation between a person's dispositional and occurrent motives: that though occurrently he had no impulse or desire to do an act or none sufficiently strong, dispositionally he was under an effective and overriding compulsion to do it. A duty here would potentially carry with it all the sanction required for doing the act; and the need for postulating a special disposition to be moved to acts on account of their being duties would have disappeared. Nor would we here allow that the questioner who while acknowledging a duty requested in addition a motive had a real ax to grind, even if his own good was at stake. His very request would be absurd, since what he was overlooking was not some matter of psychological fact, but the logical implications of his saying that he had a duty. What might be called the 'purist' view of the connection of 'ought' with motivation would be justified, but only because of the special meaning assigned to the term. It is worth remembering that Kant, who insisted most on the purist view of the connection, insisted also on a use of 'ought' in a purely formal motivation sense. Modern deontologists overlook that Kant would have rejected offhand their view of duty as an objective requirement of the situation, as he did reject the view of duty as consisting of the demands of a deity, or of some inward compulsion of a special quality. For he objected to anything being called a moral imperative with regard to which a person could still ask whether the act required of him was one which, in a motivation sense, he really ought to do, i.e. in Kant's language, whether the act was one which rationally a person would be necessarily and unconditionally determined to will; and he insisted on 'ought' or 'duty' being used for nothing but the very fact itself that rationally a person would thus be made to will an act. Kant's very definition of 'ought' therefore makes it a tautology that anyone who has a duty has, on this account alone, a reason, though not necessarily an impulse or desire, sufficient for doing the act; and Kant thus dispenses with a 'sense of duty' in the shape of any singular and contingent psychological disposition.

But while such a use of 'ought' would explain the purist view of its connection with motivation, before any conclusions can be drawn from this use it requires further clarification because of all uses of 'ought' this one has been explored least. Kant alone has attempted to give an account of it, and though this account deserves closer attention than it commonly receives, it is notoriously difficult and not free from faults. What is more, there is a deep-seated prejudice among contemporary moralists, hardened into the dogma of the 'naturalistic fallacy', which commits them to disregard this use as a fortiori irrelevant to any discussion of 'ought' in a moral or normative sense. For, in what I have called the motivation sense, 'ought' statements would be about a certain kind of psychological fact, about the person who ought having dispositionally, though not occurrently, a compelling motive for doing an act; and, so it is laid down, no moral or normative statement can be analyzed without residue into any kind of statement of psychological fact. This is the view of those who regard moral or normative statements as being about some objective requirement of the situation, but also the view of their positivist critics. Professor Stevenson, in *Ethics and Language*, is emphatic on this point. The alternative to saying that normative language is about some 'supersensible' fact cannot be that it is about some psychological fact, but must be, insofar as it is normative, that it is not about any fact at all. Thus we have the further complication that of the one use of 'ought' which could explain the habit of connecting it necessarily with motivation, contemporary moralists are agreed that, if they were to grant it at all, it would have no significance within moral or normative discourse.

This is not the place to deal fully with this situation, but to conclude my argument, I shall show that the motivation use of 'ought' bears at least a sufficient resemblance to what ordinary usage expects of a normative term for it to qualify for entrance in the general competition for recognition. It would probably be agreed, as a general characteristic of normative language, that it can function, in a manner peculiar to itself, in the direction of people's volitional attitudes and actions; and by this standard, beliefs, arguments, and inquiries about dispositional as opposed to people's 'occurrent' motives, and among them about 'ought' in the motivation sense, should be granted their places in any unprejudiced consideration of normative discourse, as they are prominent among the tools employed either when we seek to change other people's behavior, or try to direct our own. In fact, the denial of this seems to me the chief weakness of a writer otherwise as observant as Stevenson. For his contention that normative language *expresses* imperatives intended to function in the direction of conduct, but is in no way *about* imperatives capable of functioning in this manner, is bound up with the other contention that the arguments or inquiries employed in discourse concerned with the direction of volitional attitudes are never *about* these attitudes, dispositional or otherwise, but only about nonpsychological matters of fact, like the properties or effects of some course of action. But though all this applies sometimes, to contend it applies always is an oversimplification. The case of personal deliberation, where a person seeks escape from the dilemma of conflicting desires, alone bears this out. For we often organize our release from indecision by seeking an answer to a question such as "Should I do x rather than y?," "Which of the two would I prefer?," "Which by comparison would I want more?"; and the inquiry which answers a question of this kind, like the question itself, is about, not indeed an occurrent psychological state, but a dispositional one, our own state of motivation as it would be on condition that we had carried out some further mental operations. Among these, no doubt, the articulation of our beliefs about the competing acts would take first place, but to clarify our beliefs concerning them would neither be one with the primary inquiry we are carrying out, nor often be the only consideration relevant to it. For often even the fullest clarification of the properties of competing acts will leave us only more tantalized than before; and decision will then depend on some further mental operation, on eliciting a preference between the alternatives in the light of the properties attributed to them, an operation which will also yield the answer to the original question. Even without fuller analysis this will serve to illustrate how personal deliberation may involve a specific inquiry into a hypothetical psychological state whose function it is to aid a practical decision. Correspondingly, statements concerning the likely outcome of such an inquiry may play a part in interpersonal discourse intended to effect change in the attitudes of others. A may say to B, whom he considers to be undecided, "I think by comparison you would prefer x to y," inviting him thereby to go through the mental operations, which, if fulfilled, A thinks would prove his statement true. A would here be trying to change B's attitudes with the aid of a statement about B's dispositional attitudes, and with a view to converting B not to a change of attitude desired by A himself, but to one appropriate to B. A's statement would here be a quasi-normative statement, on account not of its emotive but of its descriptive meaning.

I am calling such statements and inquiries quasi-normative to stress that, though they essentially function in the direction of volitional attitudes, they are not about any 'ought', but a hypothetical 'want'. But this only seems to confirm that no normative significance should be attached to 'ought' statements in the motivation sense. For they have been described as being about someone having dispositionally a reason for doing an act, and, it may seem, any such statement, even if about an overridingly strong reason, can as well be said to be about what someone would want, or want most. Unless, therefore, 'ought' statements can be distinguished, as a species of statements about dispositional motives, from statements about merely dispositional 'wants', the objections to allowing them to be called normative would seem justified. Prichard once objected on this very ground to Kant's hypothetical 'ought', as it would express no more than that someone would want to do one thing for the sake of another he desired, and thus could not properly be called an 'ought' at all. Nevertheless, ordinary speech insists here on saying 'ought' rather than 'want'. Someone who is divided in his feelings toward some act tends to ask, "would I on the whole want it or not?" but someone undecided about adopting the means for some end will not ask, "what would I want?" but "what ought I to do?" He will say that as he wants to get to London by 10:30 he will, even if it means rising early, have to take the 8:40, and not that on the whole he will want to take it: that if he wills the end, he must will, and not merely would will the means. A statement like this is also about a dispositional motive: it says of a person that he would want an act, but it adds that he also must, or would have to, want it. What this addition consists in has proved an elusive question, but I think Kant does here offer a clue when he says that any 'ought' (whether 'hypothetical' or 'categorical') expresses a rationally necessary or objective determination of a person's will—though I shall not insist that in taking from Kant what I think is the correct clue I am interpreting him correctly. I take him to call 'necessary' what no trying will alter, or what is invariable, and 'rationally necessary' or 'objective' what would not be altered or varied by reason, or by mental operations. A rationally necessary or objective willing in the case of the hypothetical 'ought' would then be a willing, or an impulse to action, which a person would have if he both acquainted himself with the facts (with what end he desires and the means to and implications of attaining it) and tested his reactions to them, *and* which he would have necessarily, i.e., unalterably by any repetition of these mental operations. Someone who thinks he would *have* to do some act will therefore think (and plainly no more than a probability judgment would here apply) he has dispositionally a reason for doing it that can satisfy some further test: the test of all the operations capable of affecting his attitude toward the act having been carried to an ideal limit, thus exhibiting to him an 'objective' attitude, likely to be most adapted both to the realities of his situation and to his own dispositions. The conception of such a test is not itself an abstraction from any psychological fact, but is the product of reflection on the range of our capacity to control, by means of mental operations, our volitional attitudes, an *ideal construction* developed from procedures familiar to us from experience; and the reasons why we should sometimes wish to apply this test are not far to seek. We habitually do so when we think there is, or might be, a threat of opposition between our occurrent and dispositional motives, as when, on their own account, we do not desire, or are averse, from adopting the means to some desired end. We then wish to be assured that the dispositional reason is at least one from which even further inquiry would not help us to escape; and it is also in this very situation that we view that we have such a reason as an 'ought' or imperative, as what we apprehend in it is an ideally inescapable check on our freedom to act otherwise. A motivation 'ought' thus expresses the reasonableness of a course of action for someone who is not actually feeling reasonable about it. According to Kant, there is a further division within the motivation 'ought' into a conditional and an unconditional or absolute 'ought': but, though Kant is right here in principle, I do not think the division can be made to turn on the distinction between empirical and a priori. The crucial point is simply that not every motivation 'ought' does as yet express a completely conclusive reason for doing an act. If an act must dispositionally be willed only on account of some other end which is desired, whether it also must or can be so willed in every respect would still be an open question; for it may still apply that this end itself need not or could not, on consideration, be willed, either on its own account, or on account of the implications of pursuing it in a given situation. A conclusive reason would be one with regard to which no further question could be asked: which was thought rationally unavoidable on account of the act itself (or on account of some other end thought rationally unavoidable in itself), and rationally, in the given circumstances, unavoidably stronger than all opposing motives. An 'ought' embodying such a reason would be 'absolute' in the sense that, in relation to given circumstances, it was *formally complete*; and it is when such an 'ought' is identified with a moral 'ought' or duty that the connection of duty with sufficient motivation becomes logically necessary.

Enough has been said to show that there is a case for the purely formal motivation use of 'ought' and that an analysis of normative language interested in its function in the directing of volitional attitudes is too narrowly conceived if it ignores statements and inquiries about it. Writers like Stevenson are, no doubt, right that 'you ought' is often used to express a speaker's recommendation to another to change his attitudes to those favored by the speaker himself; and argument here, because there is no normative assertion to prove or to disprove, can amount only to 'support' of the speaker's aim by *any* change of belief in the hearer suitable to the speaker's purpose. In fact, this use most likely marks the beginnings of normative language, as it still permeates our habits of speech in the 'ought' we first hear in childhood, or in that of social convention, or of political or commercial propaganda. But where A's 'you ought' *expresses* his subjective recommendation, or command to B, 'I ought' for B *states* the fact that he is so recommended or commanded. The use of 'ought' for a requirement from outside is only the reverse of its subjective recommendation use. But surely some, when they reach mental maturity, become resistant to the appeal of this 'ought' and the reasoning that 'supports' it. They oppose to it the question whether, in the motivation sense, they really ought to do what another expresses to be his wish. They are interested in other people's emotive noises to the extent only to which perchance they might also embody an objectively valid recommendation for them. In fact, in dealing with them, if someone wanted to influence their volitional attitudes, he would most likely fare better if rather than express, and support, a subjective recommendation he did, from the start, state, and try to prove, an objective one.

For anyone familiar with the objective motivation use of normative language is apt to resent its subjective recommendation use in relation to himself, for he will be tempted to regard an analysis of normative language in terms of the latter alone to be about its abuse rather than its use, meaning by 'abuse' here more than a subjective recommendation against using it.

I can now conclude my argument. Our problem arose from Prichard's failure fully to justify the conviction that the thought that an act is a duty provides a motive for doing it. Prichard cannot on his view of 'ought' allow for more than a contingent connection between 'ought' and motive, while he makes claims which implicitly presuppose a necessary one; and in this confusion he reflects a pervading tendency of ordinary moral thinking. People very commonly combine a view of 'ought' as a requirement from outside, or an inner compulsion of a special quality, with adherence to a purist view of its connection with motivation, not so much as long as they view the moral law as the demand of a deity or of social convention, but once they think of it as somehow objectively grounded in the nature of things. They tend to sympathize with the questioner's request for a motive, but they will not be satisfied with any merely contingent answer, even if shown that no other is available on their premises. The explanation of this confusion must be in an ambiguity in their use of moral language. There would not be so common an insistence on the purist view of the connection of duty with motivation, if, whatever people profess, they never used 'ought' in the purely formal motivation sense; and the chances are that in the moment of moral doubt and decision they are thinking in these terms. When called upon to decide here and now which act to do they consider which act they have from within themselves the most conclusive reason for doing; and they then no longer think of being morally bound as an external requirement but as an ideally inescapable inner entanglement, a dictate of conscience. But the confusions here are deep-seated. Historically, what most likely was first called a moral injunction or prohibition was some external demand complied with habitually. The habit of reasoned choice grows more slowly, and even where reasoned choice rather than habit operates, its nature and range remain imperfectly understood. The external and internal uses of 'ought' remain undifferentiated and are imperceptibly juxtaposed and confused. There may be an unnoticed switch from the use of 'ought' from the one to the other, from a divine command, or requirement of others, to a dictate of conscience, or, when the more sophisticated speak the language of objective 'claims', an alternation between a nebulous externalist and an internalist interpretation of one and the same thing. In fact, the purist view of the connection of 'ought' with motivation nearly always makes its appearance, if only by the acceptance of some of its implications, as in the conviction that morally good conduct is open to anyone who acknowledges a duty; but by force of habit, and perhaps for fear of its empiricist and subjectivist implications, this view is constantly blended with some externalist and nonpsychological conception of 'ought'. Plainly, confusions like these must give rise to the dilemma indicated before, a dilemma which is as much Prichard's as it is common to ordinary moral thinking, except where moral skepticism has cut the knot. The exponents of a necessary connection between duty and interest, people feel, try wrongly to placate the questioner, but no satisfactory vindication of this feeling is forthcoming. For what answer is appropriate to the questioner's doubt depends on the meaning attached to his admission that he ought to do the act. On an externalist view of 'ought' his request is legitimate and in need of some factual answer; on a purely formal motivation view his very request is absurd; and where both views are confusedly held no answer can satisfy. There is no saying whether morality needs a sanction or not as long as there is confusion about what to call a moral duty.

Nor, once the confusions have been uncovered, can the matter rest here; for we cannot avowedly use 'moral ought' both for an external and an internal state of affairs, as if a man might have one but not another moral duty in respect of the same act. In using moral language we mean to denote something that, when known, can conclusively serve to direct what we do, and we cannot obey two masters. Analysis therefore reveals not so much a failure to distinguish between normative facts of different kinds, confusedly referred to by the same name; but ultimately a lack of clarity and decision about what fact would most nearly correspond to our intentions in the use of moral language, and which words like 'ought' and 'duty' should be made to denote. Nor could a person, aware of a capacity of reasoned choice and intent on using it, easily agree to a use of these words for any demand on him that still left him to ask whether he also had a formally sufficient reason for doing the act; and the only use of them free from this shortcoming would be for the very fact itself that he had such a reason. The present stalemate in ethics between an obscurantist objectivism and an avowed skepticism rests on a failure squarely to face this issue.

[2]

Goading and Guiding

I

Some years ago, it was said, "we are now happy about ethics." The thanks were due to the emotive theory. There are signs now of a more reflective mood. The new therapy has revived the patient, but he is still too unlike his once boisterous self. What then has gone wrong?

Hume said of moral judgments that they "are supposed to influence our passions and actions, and go beyond the calm and indolent judgments of the understanding." Much of the merit of the modern approach lies, I think, in the development of his observation. What is stressed is the similarity between moral and other kinds of prescriptive speech. "You ought not to smoke here" is more like "Don't smoke here" than like "Smoking is expensive here." It is typically said for direction, as a way of telling someone to do something; not just for *instruction*, 'calmly' as a piece of gossip or information. We cannot say "you ought" and deny that we meant to influence, or be surprised at having said something evocative. Hence we shall not get to the bottom of moral speech unless we treat the study of it as part of a study of language as an instrument of persuasion and practical direction, rather than one purely of the dissemination of knowledge.

Observations like these have given a fresh impulse to inquiry; and so far so good. But there are bigger claims; they are also said to entail a new solution. 'You ought to' plays a practical role like 'do'; hence it also shares its logical properties; it is another and specialized way of

Reprinted with permission of the publisher from *Mind* 62 (April 1953):145–71.

using the imperative mood. There are good reasons why this suggestion should have been welcomed. Ethical theory of the recent past has culminated in what to many appears a dilemma. If moral statements were to assert moral truths, these would allow in principle only two interpretations: such as are 'naturalistic' and false, and such as are nonnaturalistic and, except to the initiated, mystifying. To me, this disjunction is neither unambiguous nor convincing. But, if accepted, it may well appear a dilemma; and the emotive theory has the merit of evading it without having to deny it. Its welcome has been proportionate to the hope of relief it raised. But this welcome would not be justified purely on the ground that if true the theory would dispose of an embarrassment. It will not dispose of anything unless it is true; and the test for this must be in its conformity with linguistic usage. This conformity is being claimed for it; I shall try to show on insufficient grounds.

I shall press here only one point. It is not contended that moral statements are *simply* imperatives. Stevenson calls them "quasi-imperatives," stressing that they are different from ordinary ones. And this is as well, for plainly 'you ought to' has at best a similar use, not the same use as 'do'. "You ought not to smoke here" cannot be replaced by "anyway, don't" without a drastic change of tune. But, then, is it safe to say that 'you ought to' *is* only a special way of saying 'do'? Surely not, unless the dissimilarities have been scrutinized as well as the resemblances. What is the special work which 'you ought to' does and 'do' does not do? There is evasion on this point, covered by remarks about the dangers of pressing language too hard. But language, though flexible, is not without definite shapes which pressing, and only hard pressing, can reveal; and there can be no assurance that 'you ought to' is logically like 'do', unless the dissimilarities have been pressed and shown to be irrelevant to the issue. The emotive theory lies open to attack on this point.

It may be said, "but we are agreed 'you ought to' tells someone to *do* things, and not just *about* things; what else then should it be but a way of saying 'do'?" It often seems that there is implicit reliance on this. If 'you ought' serves to change 'attitudes', that it should also serve to impart some elusive species of moral belief is treated as a plain case for Ockham's razor. Yet might 'you ought to' not also play its practical role not by being a kind of ordering but the communicating of a special evocative truth? This alternative receives scanty consideration; there are even suggestions that it can be in principle ruled out. I shall try to show that complacency on this point is as unjustified as on the previous one.

II

As a preliminary, two slogans need disposing of which have all too easily gained currency.

One is that moral statements cannot be assertions, since we are agreed to call them 'normative', and a normative statement is one like "keep off the grass," one which gives an order, 'prescribes a norm'. This short way with dissenters turns on an unsettled point of language. One can grant that 'normative statement' tends to suggest 'statement that prescribes a norm'. But the term is not one of ordinary language, and there are no settled rules for using it; and it is certain that if there were no other use, there would be no general agreement about using it of moral statements. In fact, it is obvious how it has been used in the past. Moral statements have been treated as an analogue of statements *reporting* that some law is in force, the sort of statements *about* the state of the law that are made by solicitors, jurists, and legal commentaries; they were called 'normative' in the sense of a 'statement about a norm, or prescription'. And this is a defensible alternative to the use of 'normative statement' for one which *issues* a prescription, or *enunciates* a law, like the statements found in legal statutes or public notices. The point of the present controversy is whether moral statements are more properly conceived as being in type like a 'normative' statement in the one or in the other sense. This issue cannot be prejudged by reference to the unsettled usage of a technical term.

Confusions of greater interest are contained in another argument. 'You ought to', it is said, cannot be an assertion about a kind of law because of its admitted practical role. It serves to tell others to *do* things; hence it does not serve to tell them *that* something is the case, whether the state of some law or anything else. Professor W. H. F. Barnes, in a paper on ethics without propositions, has made the point by asking rhetorically "how *can* a statement both assert a fact and prescribe a norm?" It is assumed that it is plain that it cannot. And, in a sense, this is correct. One can ask: what is the *point*, the characteristic objective, of a prescriptive utterance, a command, entreaty, warning, admonition? It is proper to reply, to induce people to *do* things, and *not* to tell them a story; to be evocative, and *not* to be informative. In this sense, a statement used to 'prescribe a norm' is obviously not one used to 'assert a fact'. But also, this is trivial, and to let the matter rest here misleading. One could not say either that 'to fish' *is* 'to sit by the water holding a rod'; for the point about fishing is not this, but to try and catch fish. But one could not use this as an argument to show that one cannot both fish and sit by the water holding a rod. On the contrary, the latter, though it *is* not to fish, may yet be the way we fish, or part of the way, or one way among others. The same applies when one says that to speak prescriptively *is* not to tell a story. This does not entail in the slightest that one cannot speak prescriptively by way of telling a story, or that this cannot be part of how it is done, or be one way among others.

In fact, quite evidently, the contrary is the case. It is commonly said that orders are not used to tell that something is the case, and certainly "get out" is not meant to *state* a fact. But "I want you to leave" may also be an order; and, among other things, it uses as a means of being evocative a statement about the speaker's wishes. An order becomes 'unconvincing', among other things, when we think the speaker is untruthful or in error in what he communicates about his wishes. Orders in the imperative mood do not of course make *statements* about the speaker's wishes; and they are the paradigm of an utterance which is purely prescriptive without being assertive. But the imperative mood is only one way of giving orders, a point too commonly overlooked; moreover, orders in the imperative mood rely also, as a rule, on communicating some matter of fact. "Leave me alone" is not *saying* "I want you to leave me" but we use it to *convey* this, by the use of descriptive terms together with a conventional grammatical sign, as surely as if we had said it. A story may be told by hinting at it, as well as by expressly stating it; and the imperative mood is, among other things, a conventional formula for giving a hint.

Moreover, it is one-sided to refer to orders as the only way in which we can prescribe to others. "You will burst if you don't stop eating" is not an order; but it may do the work of "stop eating." In either case, you cannot complain that you had not been warned. But "you will burst if ... " obviously relies for being a warning on making a statement of fact. As a warning, its point is to influence, and not to tell a story; but also it is the type of warning that depends for effect primarily on telling a deterrent story and on having it believed. A statement like this may be as manifestly evocative in tone and manner as an order, but it aims at 'changing attitudes' only by way of 'imparting beliefs'. One can ask, "what did it say?" and "was it true?"

The case is of special interest for our problem. For plainly there may also be warnings which rely for effect on a statement *about* a prescription. "Smoking is forbidden here" may be used to restrain a fellow traveler, as well as "you are making me cough," or "don't." Here the state of some law is reported, not, however, for information, as in a lecture on railway by-laws, but for direction, as a way of telling someone to stop doing something. A report on anyone's order or plea may be so used. Father's "don't be home after ten" will be a prescription, manifestly evocative in purpose and manner. Mother's "father says don't" may report this, and the reporting may be no less prescriptive and in purpose and manner manifestly evocative. So far then from it being the case that a statement cannot both be prescriptive and assert a fact, it may well be *prescriptive by way of asserting a fact about a prescription*; and if orders can perform a practical role, so can reports about them.

The new observations about the evocative character of saying "you ought" should not therefore lead to premature conclusions. They may imply that "you ought not to smoke here" is a way of saying "don't"; but they need not. They could also be compatible with the traditional view that it is a way of saying "smoking is forbidden here." All that they demand is that moral speech should be accounted for in a way that explains how it has the preeminently prescriptive capacity which its use exhibits. The candidates are to be looked for either in a specially evocative way of speaking, or in a way of saying something specially fit to be evocative. Whether the case for the one or the other is the stronger must depend on further considerations.

III

If one were to treat the matter purely as one of tracking down a quarry from the traces left by it here and there, how should one proceed? There is, I think, an approach which has not yet sufficiently been tried out. We are agreed that 'you ought to' is prescriptive; we are in doubt whether it is so after the manner of 'do', or 'the law says'. Both forms are, or may be, used to direct others, but they differ in type; 'do' goes about directing others in one way, 'the law says', or 'you are making me cough' in another. The differences extend to the logic, the methods, and the evocative attitudes typical of each form.

These differences have not passed unnoticed; they are referred to in recent discussions as the differences between 'nonrational' and 'rational' methods of persuasion. But they have not been explored sufficiently, and there has been bias in the treatment of 'rational methods' as largely a way of 'supporting' nonrational methods of persuasion by other means. With a clearer view of these two types of approach it will become possible to locate more reliably the place of moral speech on the logical map.

Let me illustrate what I mean. If one says "do," "please do," "I want you to," "I should be glad if you did," one will not deny that one is telling or asking someone to do something; and this is one type of evocative address. But if one merely says pointedly, "smoking is forbidden here," or "heavy smokers die early," and the other retorts, with a touch of indignation, "are you telling or asking me to stop?" then one *might* reply, "not at all, I was merely pointing out a fact, I was making no demand." But the denial would be thin. It would be met by "surely, you were not saying this merely to let me know, but to make me *do* something." And the fair reply would be "well, then, I was *indirectly* telling or asking you to do something; but still not straightout or directly." One would have used an evocative address, but of a different type.

The two types may be referred to respectively as 'direct' and 'indirect' performances of telling or asking. The first comprises most, though not all, speech in the imperative mood and any other statement which can be said to be a way of *straightout* making a demand. The other comprises any statement, used evocatively, on which one can comment by saying, "I was not directly telling or asking you to do anything, I was merely saying so and so." The distinction is logically basic to prescriptive speech and cuts across its grammatical forms. The imperative mood is not always used for a direct telling or asking; it is not in 'my advice is, do this', or in 'take ten eggs'. Mrs. Beeton is not telling us to cook, but how to cook; and to make recommendations is incompatible with making demands. Conversely, all three of 'I want you to go', 'your bus is about to leave', 'if you don't leave, I shall show you the door', use a statement of fact or prediction, and all may be prescriptive. But the first, as a rule, tells directly, and is used like 'go'; the second tells indirectly; and the third, a threat, is characteristically in between the two.

Furthermore, there are striking differences in detail. A policeman may warn, "parking is forbidden here," or order, "I want you to move on." One would say that one complied with the warning 'because of what was said', with the order 'because one was told to'. People are good at indirect pleading when they are apt at convincing others; good at direct pleading when they know how to speak with firmness, charm, or pathos. One would call someone rude, disobedient, or disobliging if 'do stop smoking' met with no response; but not rude, only perverse, weakminded, or difficult to convince, if 'heavy smokers die early' met the same fate. There is some measure of coercion in every direct telling or asking, even the mildest 'please'; one feels one is being *goaded* into responding. But coercive intention can be denied of every indirect plea; the speaker can claim that he is only trying to *guide*, not to *goad*; he is not himself doing the urging, he is only 'letting the facts speak' for him. "I am not saying 'go', only your bus is about to leave"; "not saying 'don't play with matches', only people burn their fingers if they do"; "not saying 'don't drive so fast', only it is against the law."

One will bring up one's children quite differently whether one favors the one or the other approach. Their comparative merits, as ways of directing other people, are a matter for debate among educationalists, moralists, and politicians.

Here are tests that should help to settle to what family of utterance 'you ought to' belongs. Is it compatible, or not, with the disclaimer 'I am not telling or asking you to, I am only saying you ought to'? Can one say 'you ought to' and claim one is only seeking to guide, not at all to goad? Does one comply because it was said impressively, or because one was convinced of what it said? Would one be in tune in calling someone rude, disobliging, or disobedient for being deaf to having been told 'you ought to'? Or should one only call him hard to convince, perverse, or weakminded? Tests like these should be of use. They will still not be enough to run down what exactly 'you ought to' is used to do. They will only show whether in type it does the work of a direct or indirect telling, is more like 'do', or like 'the law says'; and it is certain that, whichever of the two it resembles more, it does not exactly do the work of either, but one peculiar to itself. But there would have been a methodical narrowing down of the direction for further inquiry.

I shall take up the question of these comparisons in the last part of this essay. My first and main concern must be with the two prototypes and the contrast between them.

IV

What is it to be directly prescriptive? In the first place, what is the method? It has been referred to as 'nonrational' and contrasted with the 'rational method' of persuading by telling an evocative story. But this is too simple. Direct pleading *may* be entirely 'nonrational' in its methods, but it is not so as a rule, only in marginal cases. 'Shoo' if said to drive away the cat, or 'attention' on the parade ground, are orders that don't rely on telling any story. The cat could not grasp a story, the well-drilled soldier need not. Effect is sought here not by using speech to relate something evocative, but to make an evocative noise: one to which, one hopes, cats are constitutionally ill-disposed, and to which soldiers have been drilled to respond as the 'mere word of command'. But the more usual forms of direct pleading do not rely purely on the act of speaking and its manner. 'I want you to go', we have noted, states a fact, and 'go' signalizes what 'I want you to go' states. The speaker relies on a communication being understood and believed; and the same applies to threats or bribes which may support direct pleading. They either state or hint at matters of fact calculated to be evocative.

It is characteristic of direct pleas that, threats and bribes apart, what they put forward for persuasion are the speaker's own wishes, and never an impersonal fact like 'your bus is about to leave'. But the mere fact that they voice our wishes does not make them directly prescriptive either. I may say "I want you to stay," and add, "but please I am not telling or asking you to, and don't feel committed by my saying so; just bear it in mind." Here I have voiced my wishes persuasively but divested my doing so of being directly prescriptive.

What makes pleading direct is not therefore that it never relies on telling a story calculated to be evocative, but that this is never *all* that it relies on. Characteristically, when one is anxious to get one's way, one troubles to *voice* one's wishes, even when thinking them known. *That* one voices them, one thinks, will add to the impressiveness of the known fact one is voicing; and there is a familiar excuse for inaction in saying, "I guessed your wishes well enough, but after all you did not say so." The force of an asking is in the saying, not only in what is said.

Much combines to make speaking impressive. I have mentioned the evocative impact of sounds; and no less hypnotic in effect may be gestures, facial expressions, and the whole impact of the speaker's personality. A telling or asking is more impressive in person than over the telephone or by letter.

Moreover, in addition to the story told and the mechanics of telling it, there is the force of the story that transpires from the telling. Saying, "I want you to" is something one does to influence someone; it is the display in action of the same desire one reports. The speaker is not, and could not, be saying that it is this: a statement cannot be used to comment upon itself. The speaker cannot report that he is ordering or asking in the same words in which he does so. But the story of one's purpose in speaking can transpire; the hearer can piece it together from one's tone of voice, the fact that one volunteers one's wants, the circumstances in which one does. One is not thought to have made a request when one says, "I want you to," or "do this" in answer to a question about one's wishes. Any prescriptive utterance thus tends to manifest something about one's own mood and concern in speaking; and in direct pleading one relies for effect on what one's speaking makes manifest as much as on what it says.

Furthermore, merely because one has spoken, others will find it harder to resist one. One has shown one's hand and courted rebuff, created a situation which others may be too timid, too softhearted, or too embarrassed to resist. One has committed them by what one is *doing* to give consideration to more than what one is *saying*.

Finally, some of these effects can also be bettered deliberately. One can vary the direct force, and the suggestiveness, of one's voice or bearing, or wear down others by sheer persistence. Direct pleading can be a skill, if not an art.

All this makes it direct. The act of relating one's wishes, complete with what it both says and shows about itself, its manner, and the situation it creates, is one's act of telling or asking; and persuasion is made dependent on the whole act: directly on what one is *doing* and not merely indirectly on what one is *saying*. Hence the way people explain their compliance with direct pleas: 'because one was told to'; not just 'because one was told something'.

Hence also the catch in asking in relation to an order, "what did he tell you about?" and "was it true?" This does not apply to a saying whose persuasive significance on the whole is in what it is trying on, not in what it is trying to say. But the present fashion is to oversimplify this. There is generally something which, in giving an order, is meant to be believed and understood; and this part can be challenged apart from the rest in the ordinary way. "I don't ever want you to set foot in this house again" by "I don't believe you; you don't speak the truth, or don't know your own mind"; "I want you to buy me a horse" by "what do you mean, a toy horse or a real one?"; "I want you to lend me your brains" by "don't talk nonsense." It depends partly on what is said in the ordering whether an order is 'convincing' and 'clear'; and hence also whether it will be effective. Only this need not be all. Even an order expressed in terms which are unconvincing may carry weight by the sheer force of the giving.

More consideration must be given to the most telling feature of direct pleading, its peculiar coerciveness. Even the mildest 'please' and 'if you don't mind' seem intent on dragging someone where he had not intended to go; and, in complying *purely* on the ground of someone's pleading, one says, "I did it, but not at all voluntarily, only because I was asked to." One may, of course, buy a child a toy not because of his asking, but thinking it anyway a good thing for him to have. A telling or asking coerces only if one is made to yield by its own method of persuasion. But the method is intrinsically coercive and contrasts with others which seek to make people do things, but not otherwise than 'voluntarily'.

This brings up the distinction between 'rational' methods and the 'nonrational' methods of direct pleading. Persuasion by 'rational methods', it is said, is 'purely by reason' and not coercive. But when are methods 'rational' and when not? Direct pleading surely also provides reasons for doing things; orders, threats, bribes are referred to as supplying them. Why then not here speak of 'rational methods'?

The point is partially met by distinguishing 'reason' from 'cause'. One speaks of a 'reason' where one can ask for the consideration which induced someone to do something; but not all behavior has reasons. A shout makes one flinch, but it is the cause of one's flinching, not the consideration which induced one to flinch; and direct pleading partly *causes* behavior directly by what it does. One may succumb to the policeman's voice or bearing not from any considerations, but like the snake obeying its charmer. This much, direct pleading is the continuation of violence by other means. It is coercive in the sense of controlling others while bypassing, if not paralyzing, any voluntary contribution to their own behavior.

But direct pleas are not always or entirely obeyed in robot fashion. They are also obeyed for reasons supplied by themselves; by what the speaker says and shows about his wishes and mood, the situation he otherwise creates, and by threats and bribes, and compliance for such reasons is no enforced reflex. 'Ten days in jail if you keep resisting' will make one come 'off one's own bat' rather than be dragged. Surely, this is to yield to 'rational' methods, and 'voluntarily'.

There is a sense in which one persuades by 'rational methods' when one purely adduces or proffers a reason. This is *not* what 'I want you to leave' does. Instead of merely *adducing* a persuasive circumstance by what it says, it *imports* one into the situation by what it does. It does not *proffer,* it *creates* a reason. Threats and bribes, though less obviously so, do the same. 'If you don't leave, I shall show you the door', 'if you do, you can take what you want' does in form proffer a reason. It has the air of being indirectly prescriptive. 'I am not telling or asking, am I? I am merely saying so and so'. But the air is spurious, for the reason which is proffered is also imported. The situation would not contain it independently, as a preexisting feature; it only will for the speaker's deliberate intervention.

Compared with having force used on one's body or nervous system, to yield to put-up incentives is to yield to 'rational methods' and 'voluntarily'. But, in another use of these terms, this would be a travesty of the facts. A child is not taking its medicine 'purely of its own accord' if only because it was offered a sweet or threatened to have to go without it; nor would this be the occasion to boast of how amenable to 'reason' it was. Had it taken the medicine on the ground that it would do it good, this would have been a different matter. Here, what is meant by 'rational methods' is to persuade purely by adducing reasons which preexist in the nature of the act and its circumstances; and by 'acting of one's own accord' to act purely from the consideration that there are such reasons. And, in this sense, telling, asking, threatening, or bribing are the negation of using rational methods and a way of making people do things otherwise than of their own accord. One does not wait for them to consider a case on its merits, either because one knows there is no case, or does not trust them to appreciate it, or is just impatient to get results. Instead, one creates a case to goad them along, giving them a sense of unfreedom in succumbing. This unfreedom consists in dependence in action on the deliberate intervention of another's will; its contrary is 'doing things freely', not here in any absolute sense, but simply in the sense of depending in action not on anyone else, but purely on considerations relating to the merits of the case.

Not all *goading*, however, is *coercing*. One is goaded, or coaxed, when one is offered a bribe or a tempting deal. But no one can claim that he was coerced by bribery. This is reserved for threats and direct pleas. The point is, the yoke of being goaded may be borne willingly or not; and this involves another sense of 'voluntary' cutting across the two distinguished already. What is done to obtain something wanted is said to be done 'voluntarily' or 'willingly'. Such is the time-honored case of the sailor throwing his goods overboard to lighten the ship. There is no paradox in saying that he acted purely voluntarily (on the merits of the case alone, not just under captain's orders), and yet not at all voluntarily or willingly, only under compulsion. Actions from put-up incentives may bear these same traits. A bribe solicits action for the sake of obtaining something wanted; a threat for the sake of avoiding something unwanted. Hence when bribed one responds willingly to being goaded; when threatened, unwillingly. A threat adds insult to injury. It makes one act otherwise than of one's own accord and for no more than the avoidance of a *trumped-up* unpleasantness. Hence bribes only seduce and corrupt; threats coerce and break the will.

All direct pleading tends to coerce in this way, though with varying insistence. This is plain of tellings which rely for a great part on threats, but it applies also to askings which do not. An asking does not coerce like a threat by holding out a future unpleasantness to be avoided, but by creating a present one to be got rid of. One is called on to comply to escape a quandary put up for one: either to pay ransom, and be badgered no longer, or to make oneself unpleasant. The coercion one yields to is only less patent, but often more insidious, than that of any straight telling.

It has been said that the typical purpose manifested by prescriptive speech is to reach 'agreement in attitude'. One speaks in the first place to make others favor what one oneself desires, to get one's own way with them. I think that, as an account of the typical objectives of *all* prescriptive speech, this is either too vague to be of use, or, if taken at its face value, a travesty of the facts. But it does describe direct pleading. The evocative attitude it manifests is one of 'getting one's own way'.

Actually, in its full sense this notion is complex. It suggests that someone is trying to gain some purely personal or at least capricious end; that he should be 'goading in aim'; and also an attitude of readiness to gain his end by a liberal use of means, by 'goading in method'. Plainly, much direct pleading is carried out fully in this spirit; it is the characteristic note one often senses in it. But there are variations on the theme. An asking does not display the same evocative attitude as a telling even if they are both goading in their aim. It is self-limiting in its attitude toward the means, and correspondingly in its insistence on gaining the end: one shows that one is restricting oneself to using some means and not others (not threats or shouts), or is ready to withdraw in some circumstances (if one were to cause avowed inconvenience, as in 'please, if you don't mind'). Some direct pleas, again, may display an uncompromising determination to be goading in method while not being goading in aim. A parent who firmly orders his offspring about may claim he is not doing it for a purely personal or capricious end. Still, all direct pleading is getting one's own way at least by being goading in method; and, frequently, by being goading in aim as well. Nor should the last cause surprise. Direct pleading is exactly suited to the role. It is not restricted to preexisting incentives. It can liberally create them and pile them up to enforce any end, however purely personal or capricious. It is the open and natural method for the purpose, with no need either for making bones about it.

V

What is it, by contrast, to be indirectly prescriptive? In most ways, the reverse. One pleads indirectly when one puts forward a fact for consideration, like 'your bus is about to leave'; and the fact must belong to the situation as it is, and not be one of one's own importing. 'If you don't leave, I shall show you the door' resembles an indirect plea, but is none. Moreover, an indirect plea relies *purely* on what it says, on 'letting' the facts speak for themselves; and not also on being a 'telling'. It is a telling, and manifestly so. But it is not effective directly by being a telling, or by showing itself to be one; but indirectly by the story it tells. It is always in place to ask of an indirect telling "what did it say?" and "was it true?"

One may state one's own wishes, just as a feature of the situation to be borne in mind; one will then voice them without making a direct plea. But this is exceptional. 'I want you to' is normally part of a direct pleading and will be so, unless one desires otherwise and takes special steps. One would have to say, "don't take this as a request," "don't do anything merely because I say so; only if you want to of your own accord," "just bear the fact in mind"; and one must take care not to spoil one's words by one's deeds, as by an insistent, pathetic, or agitated tone of voice. Otherwise, one will still be taken to be asking.

But as a rule one relates something impersonal of concern to others. Indirect pleading is the way to widen one's persuasive appeal beyond saying "I want"; and, what is more, this widening of appeal is not logically possible except through pleading which is indirect. No one expects one to put forward one's wishes not 'tellingly', but just for consideration; if one does, it is one's own choice. But one is expected not to put forward impersonal facts, except purely for consideration. To add to "your bus is about to leave" "this is not to urge you to go, only to remind you" invites "naturally, I should expect so."

This is not to say that impersonal facts may not be related in a deliberately evocative or pleading manner, and the plea succeed on this account. People often put them forward not at all intending to give others the chance to be influenced purely 'by a reason', and to act of their own accord alone. They want to be able to appeal to impersonal facts with the aid of the same methods of goading by which one can aid the stating of one's wishes. The point is not that this cannot be done, but that there is an incongruity in doing it. The test is that a too emphatic speaker can here be held up for inconsistency; and an obstinate hearer can pretend that no more surely *could* have been intended than the proffering of a reason. "Your bus is about to leave," you say firmly, ill-disguising a desire to see the last of me. "Not yet, in another hour," I can reply uncooperatively; or "never mind, I need not hurry, there are more buses later"; and you cannot rightly call me rude or disobliging for this. Or, if you do, referring to the pleadingness of your speaking, I can say, "but surely, considering what you *said,* this was neither here nor there. Why not be honest, and tell me to go straightout." People sometimes act on an admonition or warning not because the reasons were convincing, but quietly taking a hint, or being browbeaten by firm speaking, But one cannot reasonably expect this, or insist on it; nor should one here say that these were sufficient grounds for yielding.

Why is there a logical bar to stating impersonal facts 'tellingly', but not one's wishes? Because in the first case, what is said, and what is done by the saying, diverge in their influence; in the other they converge.

'I want you to go' puts forward one's wishes and shows and exercises them in the speaking. What is shown makes what is said more impressive, for it confirms and amplifies it; what is done by voice or manner is consistent with the purpose stated and shown. The hearer is subjected to influences all of a piece; if ready to yield to one, he will yield to all unless told not to.

'Your bus is about to leave' puts forward a fact other than one's wishes; and it gives one to understand that this fact alone is to count as incentive. To be precise, this is not *said*. Persuasive statements of this form *state* nothing except a fact about the situation. They don't state what would be a distinct proposition, *that* the fact is sufficient to provide a reason. But this goes without saying. The story is manifestly told to persuade. Hence the speaker must wish to claim that it provides a reason and a decisive one; for otherwise why tell the story, or this story and not another? The hearer can certainly take him up on what he *said* as much as on what he *implied*: dispute the facts, or grant them and add "but this is no reason." And the speaker can expect the hearer to consider that much, but no more.

This is why any impersonal plea is logically indirect. A prescriptive statement manifests the speaker's concern; but the speaker's concern is here irrelevant to the fact on which persuasion has been openly made to turn. The hearer is not committed to consider it, since he was not invited to; nor could he do so without deserting the point openly at issue. An impersonal plea is a challenge to be influenced only by what is said about a feature of the situation and suggested about it providing a reason. It is met to all intents when both claims are considered, and as adequately by their honest acceptance or rejection. The speaker cannot therefore grumble if no heed was given to his own persuasive concern, which was shown but not mentioned. He has staked success on asserting something evocative and impersonal; it is not then either here or there that the assertion should have been made evocatively. In any appeal to impersonal reasons, as distinct from direct pleading, the manifestly prescriptive purpose of the utterance does *not* logically figure as an instrument of persuasion.

Nor again would it here be consistent for the speaker even to *try* to be effective by a deliberately evocative manner. To be goading in method is to exercise one's wish for someone to do something. To exercise it when one has also put forward one's wishes is all of a piece; to do so for good measure when openly inviting someone to accept some impersonal fact as a good and sufficient reason is so to mix persuasive methods as to make nonsense of both. One can try to put up impersonal facts and not 'let them speak for themselves', to turn impersonal pleading into the continuation of direct pleading by other means; but one cannot do so consistently. It invites the protest, "what are you after? trying to give me a reason for doing this? or badgering me into doing it? you can't have it both ways." Nor is it any more becoming, instead of mixing the two methods, to let them succeed each other. "You will cut your tongue with the knife, dear." "No, this is the blunt one." "Well, anyway put it down" won't endear one to an intelligent child. It shows that the first plea had been insincere or that one was just being muddled.

Where *goading* is a plain incongruity, impersonal pleading is confined to its own method, which by contrast I may call *guiding*. To influence by guiding is to influence without compulsion. One is not creating an evocative situation; one is merely using the situation as it is. One is trying to make others do only what they will acknowledge they have independently a reason for doing. While goading is intrinsically detrimental to producing actions 'purely on the merits of the case', and 'of people's own accord', guiding is intrinsically and purely in aid of producing such actions.

All this affects the evocative attitudes appropriate to this form of pleading. 'Get out' and 'your bus is about to leave' cannot *both* be simply 'aiming at agreement with one in attitude', 'bringing you round to favoring what I favor', 'getting my own way with you'. In their ordinary meaning these descriptions fit direct but not indirect pleading. If they were meant to cover both, they would have to mean something different in each case.

For one thing, the ordinary notion of 'getting one's own way' carries the suggestion of *forcing* one's will on others; one is familiar with sensing the note of this being intended and tried in direct pleas. But the note is absent from an indirect prescription. One is being beckoned to do something in 'your bus is leaving' as in 'get out'; but here with no suggestion of dragging or harrowing and with a note of deference to oneself as someone able to appreciate reasons and quite unanxious to do things otherwise than of his own accord. To be addressed guidingly bears no resemblance to being addressed goadingly; and if it does it shouldn't.

Moreover, to be trying to get one's own way suggests that one is after some *purely* personal end; and this too is inconsistent with indirect pleading. This is not because one may not be both guiding in method and goading in aim. Commercial advertisers notoriously, but if moderately honest, quite properly guide to goad by making evocative observations about their wares. The point is rather that the goading aim is perforce here qualified by the means chosen. Indirect pleading is intrinsically less well adapted to gaining purely personal ends than direct pleading. One is at the mercy of coincidence. There *need* be no reasons for others to do what one wants them to do for reasons of one's own; and even if one thinks there are, one is still dependent on finding them appreciated. At best, therefore, guiding as a method is suited only to a goading severely self-limited in aim: to try to make others do as one wants them to do, but no further than within the limits in which they are ready to do so for reasons of their own. 'Dentex will keep your dentures clean' shows someone intent on persuading for gain; but one takes it that he is not after more than can be achieved by leaving us free to buy only when we believe him and need to. And not only is this in a restricted sense only to 'try and make others fall in with one's own ends'; it cannot be *purely* called this at all. For there is another side to it: it is also to 'try and make others fall in with what would be an *end for them*'. Wherever guiding is used as a method, persuasion has an other-regarding orientation: looking at actions from other people's point of view, trying to make others do what they would want, or would have an incentive to do, if they were not ignorant or obtuse. And where one is guiding to goad one is still trying to make them act as one wants *oneself* only by means of trying to make them act as they would want *themselves*. Surely then not all prescriptive speech aims purely and typically at bending the hearer's attitudes to those of the speaker. This language is more than misleading. It implies disregard of what is an outstanding characteristic of prescriptive speech: that it may have a dual orientation, egocentric as well as centered on others. It can serve both to make others favor what we favor and to aid them in learning to favor what *they* do not favor but would, or might, for independent and acknowledged reasons of their own.

In fact, on occasions, the last may be the one and only object of prescriptive speech. Instead of *guiding to goad,* one may just be *guiding to guide.* I may give you the news about the timetable not to get rid of you without having to say so, but purely from a concern that you should not get into trouble for being late for supper. One may put facts to people purely so that they should not act rashly or in ignorance. The wheel here comes round full circle, and prescriptive speech loses the last vestige of an egocentric objective. To refer to its object one would have to say, "I am putting this to you, not to see you influenced by it for a personal reason; only to prevent you from acting rashly or in ignorance; or so that cogent reasons should prevail with you." None of this is *said.* One only says, "your bus is about to leave." But one would need words like these to explain one's persuasive attitude, or defend it against the charge of being purely interested.

And other words might be used as well. "I only want you to act sensibly, reasonably, rationally," "to show a rational attitude," "to do what the situation requires," "what it is desirable for you to do." All these notions present familiar difficulties. But there seems here a natural soil for them to grow in. *They cannot be dispensed with if one is to describe one's characteristic aim in persuading others by giving them reasons.* It is plain then that these terms cannot be only formulae of direct pleading, conventional trumpet-calls to press others into conformity with one's own attitudes. For they have a place in the description of the implicit intentions of a form of prescriptive speech which does not *use* them for persuasion at all, and has neither the aims nor employs the methods of direct pleading. One cannot call on prescriptive speech to account for them if they are needed, in some of its forms, to account for it.

Persuasion by rational methods has been treated as if it had none of these implications; and this raises a last point about it. The silence is due in some measure to a biased interest in its use in a special context: where it serves in support of 'nonrational' or direct methods of pleading. One says, "please take the evening off: come out with me. You need distraction; your work can wait." Here a direct plea is supported by observations of evocative fact. In this context, it certainly does not follow that the evocative observations will be made genuinely to 'guide'. They may be made not to guide but to misguide; they will serve their purpose as well if they successfully do the one or the other. In fact, evocative observations are a really useful tool for supporting direct pleading only if they are not used squeamishly. The facts as they are, or as one thinks them to be, need not be at all suitable for the purpose. But they can be taken in hand. One can allege that something is the case, knowing it is not; or quietly not mention what one knows is the case besides; or put forward what is the case knowing it would provide no good reason on dispassionate consideration. If Eve had said, "come on, eat," praising the apple knowing it to be rotten, and quietly ignoring the taboo, Adam would have fallen for all the wiles. The Eves are now joined by advertisers and politicians; and there are still Adams.

For an account of how *direct pleading is supported by evocative observations* it is therefore irrelevant whether they are used to guide or misguide, and the distinction can be suppressed. But this is not at all irrelevant to an account of *persuasion by rational methods*. It is not only significant that they can be used in either of two ways; what is more, only guiding and not misguiding can be properly described as using rational methods at all. One hesitates to say that an unscrupulous advertiser or friend is using 'rational methods' on one; or that persuasion by a deliberately misguiding story is properly called 'warning someone', or 'commending something'. Or else one will distinguish between using rational methods in form but not 'really'; and between an honest warning or recommendation and a lying one. The point is that misguiding is not a *variant* of guiding, but its *corruption*. It is goading in method dressed up as guiding; a form of speech which is not what it gives out to be. The lie is not only in misstating the facts; they may be correct as far as they go. It is in the false claim, implicit in mentioning the facts for persuasion, that they provide good and sufficient reasons for a doing. Where this claim is made dishonestly, or with wishful carelessness, just to make others think, or deceive themselves into thinking, that there is a good reason where there is none, pleading by evocative observations of fact does not aim at guidance; but it is not then either *persuading by rational methods.*

Recent discussions have bypassed or suppressed these distinctions by falsely treating the original and the fake under the same name.

VI

I shall now return to moral speech and try to locate its place on the logical map of prescriptive speech. There are two diametrically opposed prototypes. To which does 'you ought not to smoke here' or 'you ought to leave now' bear the greater resemblance? To 'don't smoke here' or 'smoking is forbidden here'? To 'leave now' or 'your bus is about to leave'?

There is often, no doubt, a resemblance to direct pleading. 'You ought to' may be said goadingly, crossly, entreatingly, peremptorily, insinuatingly, with the deployment of all coercive devices of a direct telling or asking.

But we have seen that whether in fact such methods are used does not decide whether an utterance is directly or indirectly prescriptive in *type*. The devices may have been used inconsistently; in spite of them, the utterance may logically be one to rely on saying something evocative and not on being a form of evocative speaking. Here tests from the grammar of direct and indirect pleading must be used; and by these tests 'you ought to' is more like indirect than direct pleading. I shall enumerate a few.

(1) If I crossly say, "you ought not to smoke here," you can say, "what are you trying to do? Tell me that I ought not to? or ordering me not to do it?" And I can answer apologetically, "sorry, I got excited; I am not telling or asking or begging you not to smoke here; I am only saying you ought not to."

(2) It is proper to say, "I complied with him when he said I ought to, because I was convinced what he said was right." If I said, "I just complied because he said 'you ought to' so firmly," one might remark, "Surely, this was not a very adequate reason."

(3) If I say, "you ought to," and you reply, "honestly, I don't see this at all, I don't think I need to," I shall feel, unless I can argue back, that my plea has been properly met and disarmed. I have said something calculated to be evocative and failed to carry conviction. I can say that you are 'difficult to convince', 'perverse', 'unreasonable'; but not 'how rude', 'how disobliging' of you to refuse me when I said 'you ought to' so firmly, so pathetically, or so nicely.

(4) 'You ought to leave now' is compatible with 'I have no personal interest in your going', I am not 'goading in aim', and 'I am not trying to coerce you in any way', I am not 'goading in method'. I am only trying to make you 'see reason', 'to make you act in accord with the realities of the situation', 'to aid you to act as you would of your own accord if you were not ignorant or obtuse'. Moral pleading can claim for itself to be guiding in both aim and method.

None of this one could say if it were a special formula for being *directly* prescriptive by speaking evocatively. All of it fits in with saying that it is a way of being *indirectly* prescriptive by asserting some evocative truth.

All, at any rate, but one thing. 'You ought to' is like 'the law says' or 'your bus is leaving' indirectly prescriptive in grammar; but otherwise it is not like either.

It is familiar ground that the analogy with 'the law says' cannot be pressed. 'The law says' reports that one is being addressed commandingly by someone, like 'captain's orders: everyone to throw his goods overboard'. But 'you ought to', if used to report anything, is not used to report on the deliverances of any moral captain. If it were, what was done purely because one ought to would be done regardless of whether one also had cause for doing it of one's own accord, for reasons purely in the nature of the act or its circumstances; it would, once again, be done purely because someone had spoken coercively, though not here the speaker himself but the agent whose command he is reporting. But usage suggests the opposite. What is done purely because one ought to, one tends to say, is done purely from considerations relating to the nature of the act and its circumstances; it is precisely not what is done purely because one was told to. Moral persuasion consists no more in *reporting*, as an incentive, a feature imported ad hoc into the situation by someone than in importing such a feature by 'telling' speaking. At the best one might say, as has been said, it consists in reporting that some doing is 'commanded' or 'demanded' by the nature of the act itself and its circumstances. But whatever it may mean to say this, it only underlines further the failure of the analogy with 'the law says'. 'Commands' or 'demands', in their ordinary sense, can issue only from persons capable of displaying their will impressively. Whatever 'the nature of the act and its circumstances' may be able to 'do', it is not this.

Is one to say then that 'you ought to' is more like 'your bus is leaving' than like 'the law says'? That it is used to persuade by reporting some evocative feature of the situation which naturally inheres in it? Strangely, this too has its difficulties. It is common ground that 'you ought to' cannot be said to report a feature of the situation of the same type as 'your bus is leaving'. If at all, it is said, it reports a 'nonnatural' feature, not a 'natural' one. But observations like these do not get down to the root of the difficulty. The trouble is not that 'you ought to' cannot be said to persuade by reporting as a reason for a doing the same *type* of feature of the situation as 'your bus is leaving'; but that what it reports does not seem to figure among the *reasons* put forward for any doing at all. One may put forward 'your bus is leaving' as an evocative feature of the situation; or, again, 'you are expected for dinner' as another such feature, either to add to the weight of the first, or in its place. But what about 'you ought to go now'? If it were also reported as a reason one would expect it to be put forward along with the others, either as an alternative or in addition to them. But, plainly, it is not. I do not try to persuade you to go (alternatively) by saying either "you ought to go" or "your bus is leaving"; nor would 'you ought to go' be on a par with 'you are expected for dinner', to be mentioned in addition to 'your bus is leaving' as a further feature of the situation to count toward going. The fact is 'you ought to' is not used to *replace or supplement* any of the features of the situation ordinarily put forward in persuasion by rational methods. On the contrary, it works only in *conjunction* with them. 'You ought to go now' is incompletely persuasive by itself. It needs support from 'your bus is leaving', or 'you are expected for dinner', or any other natural feature of the situation which may count as a reason for going, the same features in fact which one might also have brought to the hearer's notice without saying expressly that he ought to go at all. In order to make moral persuasion as effective as it might be one will mention *any* feature of the situation *whatever* which may count in the circumstances in favor of the doing which one is trying to induce; and only then will one add, if one does, "and so you ought." It follows that 'you ought to' is not used either to persuade by reporting some evocative feature of the situation which preexists in it. It is not one *among* the features put forward as counting toward some particular doing; it is said only once *all* of these have been enumerated, and, as one says, 'on the strength of them'.

The oddity of this conclusion needs stressing. 'You ought to' seems part of the machinery of persuasion by 'rational methods'; it is used when they are used, seems to share the grammar of statements doing this work, and, apparently, is persuasive in its effects. 'And so you ought to go' seems to clinch what 'you are expected for dinner' has begun. But also it seems a logically redundant part of this machinery. One persuades by rational methods when one gives reasons, reports those features of the situation likely to count in favor of a doing. And when *all* reasons have been given, one should expect, *all* that rational persuasion can *try* to do should have been *done*. What else but another reason could add persuasive force to the reasons already given? But 'you ought to' is said *after* everything to count as a reason has been enumerated. It seems persuasive and like adducing a reason, and yet it is not. It seems both to belong to persuasion by rational methods and not to be part of it. Odd as this may seem, it needs facing. The oddity is the logical turning point for the understanding of the special function of moral and similar types of speech.

It is tempting to account for this by once more falling back on the imperative view. Moral persuasion, it has been suggested, is not purely either by rational methods or by direct pleading, but by a mixture of both. 'You ought to' is a way of saying 'come on, do', which one is prepared to support by rational methods, or which one uses to support them. One says, "you ought to go, your bus is leaving": here it assists persuasion by reasons as a kind of imperative hors-d'oeuvre. Or one says, "your bus is leaving, and so you ought to go"; here it assists rational persuasion as a kind of imperative dessert. 'You ought to' is shown to belong to persuasion by rational methods without being part of it.

The suggestion is persuasive, but once again it won't pass the test of usage. It rests on taking it for granted that direct and indirect pleading can without hitch be used as *complementary* methods of per-suasion. But there are logical incompatibilities between these two methods; and they also rule out any account of moral persuasion as consisting, in essentials, in a kind of *mixed pleading*.

'You ought to', it is said, expresses the speaker's desire to make the hearer conform with the speaker's wishes. Reasons are adduced in practical support of a pleading of this sort. The whole broadly is 'moral persuasion'. But if so, there is no assurance here that *misguiding* won't be used as well as *guiding*. For it is not specified that the aim of adducing reasons need be any other than 'goading'; and misguiding may serve this aim as well as or better than guiding. It may equally suit the speaker to support 'you ought to' by a truthful and complete as by a deliberately distorted presentation of the facts. But then this is implicitly to define moral persuasion so as to make using 'rational methods' not a *necessary*, but only an *incidental*, part of it; and to make it comprise indiscriminately both scrupulous guiding and unscrupulous special pleading. And this plainly would be a travesty of the facts. Part of the common understanding of 'moral persuasion' is that it should be distinct from unprincipled goading; and it would not be necessarily distinct from this if its aim were to advance persuasive arguments simply for the sake of bending the hearer's will to the expressed will of the speaker.

Another example will underline this point. The notion of mixed pleading can be applied to aesthetics as well as to ethics. "This picture is good," "look at the coherence and assurance of the lines, the varied and balanced coloring, the unusual decorative design" can be taken as an invitation to the onlooker to share the speaker's sense of appreciation, followed up by deeds to get him into the right frame of mind. One may agree that the whole performance is correctly described as a way of trying to teach someone to appreciate something. But is it also correctly described as a way of first making the onlooker share the *speaker's* sense of appreciation? Surely, one needs a way of distinguishing between the manner appreciation is taught by a cunning dealer and by a conscientious critic. If the theory were correct, both would be equally intent on making us appreciate things in the way *they* happen to desire; and 'this is good' should have prepared us for an assault of this kind and nothing else, by expressing no more than 'come on, like it as I do'. In fact, one thinks, 'this is good' no less than 'you ought to' *entitles* one to expect guiding and not goading in its support: a scrupulous attempt at least to convert one to an attitude, as it might be in response to a truthful and comprehensive appreciation of the relevant facts. One may agree that both announcements are properly followed up less by *proving* to someone that something which he states is the case than by *converting* him to a novel attitude of appreciation, whether of a work of art or of a line of conduct. But the procedure is surely hitched on to the wrong bandwagon if one describes it as consisting in the ill-assorted companionship of the use of rational methods in the service of the intentions of a purely personal plea.

It is also plain that there would here again be a case for the hearer to challenge the mixing of the rational appeal with coercion. 'You are expected for supper', sandwiched in between 'do go' and 'so be gone' is open to be challenged by 'make up your mind, are you leaving it to me to decide for myself, or have you decided for me?' When the issue is pressed, one cannot insist on persuading by a mixture of telling and arguing. One either says, "all right, I am not arguing, I am telling you"; or one is ready to rely on arguing and to be done with telling.

There is one form of imperative speech which can be combined with persuasion by rational methods without being open to these objections; and it teaches a lesson of special interest. 'Do this' may be used in the sense of 'my advice to you is, do this'; it may express a *recommendation*. One might say, with some force, that this is what 'you ought to' is used to express. 'Do this', as advice, is not direct pleading, in spite of its grammatical form. One can say it, and deny that one is telling, or asking, or in any way trying to coerce; one is 'merely saying, my advice is, do this'; nor can one consistently take personal umbrage at having what was 'purely advice' rejected. It is also logically assured here that none but rational methods will be used in support. Advice can be 'good' or 'bad'; it has an implicit canon of achievement, defined in terms of what it is understood to set out to do. And this is purely to 'guide', to make people act as they would have valid and sufficient reasons for acting and not otherwise. 'My advice is, do this' can consistently be supported only by evocative observations of fact thought, and implicitly claimed, to constitute reasons of this kind; one cannot honestly say it without having formed an opinion concerning the facts of the situation all round, as well as concerning their relevance as reasons for the hearer. In fact, 'do this', as advice, may also be treated as the stating of an opinion to this effect. One can say, "my opinion is, do this" as if one were saying, "my opinion is that you have the best of reasons for doing this, the facts all round being so and so"; and one disarms advice by challenging either the facts or their alleged force as reasons. Hence 'do this', as advice, foots the bill of being an imperative expression necessarily, and not merely incidentally supported by 'guiding in method'. The imperative view would be free of inconsistencies if it claimed that 'you ought to' was used to express no more than precisely this.

But, if reduced to this, it would also then be too anemic to survive. 'Do', as advice, is effective not as a *plea* but as an account of the *opinion* it ventures. One follows advice when one thinks it sound, believing its claim that there are valid reasons for doing the thing suggested. One can give advice without stating this claim. 'Go; you are expected for supper' does not mention it. But, also, one might as well have explicitly made it, as certainly the hearer must take it to have been made for advice to be understood and to be effective as such. One might say, "go, there is the best of reasons, you are expected for supper"; and instead also "go, it's reasonable ...," or "it's what the circumstances require ... "; or again, to someone with hesitations, "go, it's what you ought to do. . . ." The last is here of a type with the others, and is no way of saying 'go' any more than they. 'Go, you ought to go' is no more just repetitive than 'go, it's reasonable to go'; what would be repetitive, though there would be a shade of difference, is 'you ought to go, it's reasonable to go'.

Last, one may give advice by using these expressions alone without the exhortative prefix 'go'.

The imperative view was called in to account for this type of expression. It turns out that the only imperative expression which would otherwise fit the requirements is one which for its description, and its effective understanding, presupposes an independent and descriptive use for the expressions which the imperative view had been devised to account for.

VII

It is outside the scope of this essay to argue the use of these expressions in detail. I have attempted no more than to locate their place on the logical map of prescriptive speech. And this place should by now be reasonably assured. 'You ought to', 'it is reasonable to', 'desirable to' are expressions belonging to prescriptive speech purely in its capacity to guide; and they are of a type *to answer the need for making its implicit intentions and functions explicit.* What tends to obscure this is that 'persuading by giving someone a reason' is an ambiguous notion. It may mean 'by stating a fact calculated to act as a reason' and also 'by stating such a fact *and* stating *that*, if considered, it will act as such a reason'. Prescriptive speech of the guiding type reaches a new level of concepts and propositions when it turns from purely stating persuasive facts to announcing the claim *that* they constitute reasons, 'good' reasons, 'valid' reasons, 'sufficient' reasons, 'reasons on the whole, or despite counterreasons'. No wonder 'it is reasonable', 'it is desirable', 'you ought to' are not *among* the reasons one puts forward for persuasion. What one puts so forward are the preexisting features of the situation; claiming *that* they are reasons is not to put forward a reason, but claiming that this is what one is doing. Nevertheless the explicit claim or reminder that something put forward as a reason is one seems to have a persuasive function of its own; something seems to be capable of turning on emphasizing 'and so you ought to go' after 'you are expected for supper' has been said. But how this is so is another story.

Much more needs saying to reach final conclusions, but the position which emerges may be characterized as follows. 'You ought to go', 'this picture is good' *state* something, the one something like *that* there would be reason for a doing if the facts of the situation were known and borne in mind; the other something like *that* there would be reasons for appreciation if the features of a work of art were all noted and attended to with discrimination. But the bare statement is vacuous here unless its claim is put to the test by a demonstration *ad oculos* not only *to* the hearer but *on* the hearer. What is more, it is not in order to *prove* what we say that we insist on the demonstration; but because we desire the hearer to have the benefit of *experiencing* what we claim. 'You ought to', 'this is good' are in this respect one of a type with 'you will like it if you try'. One does not say this just for information, but for *conversion*. One is making an objective claim, and the claim may be falsified or confirmed as things turn out. But one is not in the first place interested in what happens to the claim, but in that what was claimed should occur. 'You ought to go', 'this picture is good', followed up by relevant observations of fact, is an attempt *to teach someone to appreciate something*, a line of conduct, or a work of art. And 'teaching appreciation' is a type of activity of its own, different both from telling a story and from exhorting or preaching, though related to both. It shares with the first that it involves making an *objective claim* and with the second that it aims at *practical conversion*.

[3]

On Learning about Reasons

I

What is it to seek guidance from reason? One says that it is to seek it from knowledge. Knowledge, if of the right sort and properly before one, can redirect one's aims. But what sort of knowledge is this? What does the concept of a guiding knowledge imply?

Here one is tempted to speak with two voices. One may agree with Hume that the knowledge required and available for action guidance by reason is all knowledge of the case, of what one is doing or would do, of effects and causes. To 'reason' with the reckless motorist is to instruct him about death and injury on the road, with the nicotine addict to tell him about lung cancer or ulcers. Such instructions will be relevant insofar as they relate to matters of interest to those concerned; and if they do they are all that is required. Nietzsche said: "Do what you like, but know what you are doing." This is essentially Hume, at least in Book II of the *Treatise*. 'Reason' can make as much difference to conduct as knowing what one is doing can make to it; and nothing that is done in such knowledge can be called 'against reason' from the agent's own point of view, since what is done in light of such knowledge has been corrected by reason as much as it can be.

But there is also the pull of another view. Reason-guidance requires for a *first* step that one should know *what* one is doing, but it need not be *complete* with this step. In support one need only find as conceivable the following residual case: the man who is not lacking in knowledge, but whose conduct is still lacking in reason. Smokers and speedsters may persist after they have learned about lung cancer and death on the road. The doctor who gave the instruction, the expert who compiled the statistics, may be among them. And they need not be freaks of congenital unconcern either, so that one could say, "this was just not relevant information for them." There is an alternative description available: they may be people who are 'obtuse', 'impervious', 'who won't face facts', 'won't assimilate the facts which they know', 'won't learn or appreciate their lesson'. And one does not fail to assimilate or appreciate something that is of *no* relevance to one. Hence the conviction that knowing the facts may not be enough to make guidance by them complete. Some supplementary step may still be needed, one in aid of breaking the odd barrier of obtuseness. Moreover, there is the suggestion in language that here is a step which is once more cognitive, somehow involving a further apprehension beyond the facts of the case. One is tempted to say that the trouble with the impervious man is that he will not appreciate that because, as he knows, speeding endangers others, and he wants to avoid this, he *ought* to give it up; or that he will not appreciate, if he is too thoughtless to worry about others, that to injure them is what he *ought* to avoid on its own account, and that therefore he ought to give up what would lead to this. It seems that reminders of this form may have to complete guidance by the facts. Such reminders will involve some fact-supervening cognitive step and will be effective by somehow bringing home to people the lesson for choice of the facts before them.

Our headache is what to make of this supplementary step, and one way out, as we know, is to accept the fact while denying the interpretation. One will then agree that ought-language is the continuation of guidance by the facts by *other means*, but deny that it is its continuation by other *rational means*. 'And so you ought to', 'and so I ought to' supervene on the facts not by making a further truth-claim but by issuing an injunction. They continue guidance by the facts as the mild crack of the whip may sustain the use of sweet reason. 'Ought' and 'ought not' mark the intrusion into rational guidance of the thin end of a big stick. They are tools of language for the use of unreason in aid of reason. This solution has strong and varied backing, but it may still be treated as an issue.

This essay will bear on the issue, but only indirectly and in a general way. Nothing more will be said about 'ought' or any specifically moral language. But I shall remain concerned with the general question of the possible place in rational guidance of some fact-supervening cognitive step. I shall ask whether reference to some step of this logical type can be dispensed with in any full-account of rational guidance.

This question should be asked because of a line of thought which is at the back of much contemporary thinking on these matters. There may seem to be proof that no further cognitive step could assist rational guidance and still be part of it, and this on the ground that guidance by *reason* can also be described as guidance by *reasons*. There is, it is said, nothing really to choose between saying that there is a reason why someone ought to do a thing and simply saying that there is a reason for him to do it. In an account of guidance by *rational* means one may therefore bypass any mention of 'ought' altogether. One may simply say that one uses reason with others when all that one relies on for influence is convincing them of reasons; and that one uses reason with oneself if one seeks guidance from an adequate exploration of the reasons for or against one's alternative choices. New light is sometimes thrown on a conceptual problem when it can be transposed into another language key, and attention to reasons language is expected to have this effect. For it seems that one can now say with relief: "After all, then, rational guidance *must* be after the model of Hume. For the knowledge of reasons is of facts which are of interest, of this and of nothing more."

The premise of this view is correct: guidance by reason can well be described as knowing the reasons 'for' and 'against' in the case. But one may query the conclusion. The notion of guidance by reasons does not lead one straight back to Hume nor does it spare one from the need to recognize and explain some fact-supervening step-in-action guidance. This contention can be supported in two ways. The formal complexities of the language in which one mentions reasons provide a prima facie case, and a study of the concept of an action-guiding reason will explain why and how these formal complexities make sense.[1] In this essay I shall discuss the prima facie case.

II

First, I must discuss how guidance by reasons is understood on the above view. Three points need to be emphasized.

The first is that the reasons available are always some further specifiable feature of the action in question. All the reasons for or against doing anything are in some story that can be told about *it*; they are all reasons for doing one thing on account of some feature it has or some consequence it would involve.

The second point is that only such further features are fit to provide reasons which are in themselves a matter of actual interest to the agent concerned and are such that he would like or dislike or would wish

1. See W. D. Falk, "Action-Guiding Reasons," in this volume.

to seek or avoid them. Nothing therefore that may count as a reason for *one* need count as a reason for *everyone*, although some features may be more generally expected to provide reasons for most than others. 'This sherry is dry' will be a reason for drinking 'this' if and only if someone likes his sherry dry rather than sweet; 'this will endanger others' will be a reason against doing 'this' if and only if it so happens that someone would rather see others alive than dead. Only one exception to this rule is allowed: 'This will hurt others' may still count as a reason against doing 'this' even for someone not actually mindful of what he does to them, provided, say, that one can convince him that hurting others invites retaliation, which he wishes to avoid. But this is still to say that, whatever is the concluding term in a chain of reasons, the term that validates the rest must be some feature that happens to be of actual interest in itself to the person concerned.

The third point is that all the knowing and learning that guidance by reasons involves concerns the facts of the case. True enough, to learn about reasons or to teach them to others does not just come to the *same* thing as learning or teaching such facts. And it is obvious why. In learning a fact, one learns a reason only insofar as the fact is fit to provide one with a reason; and people who teach one reasons must therefore *accomplish* more than just teaching one a fact. Otherwise, having taught the fact, they may still meet the rebuttal: "But this is no reason for me, or not enough of a reason, or not the kind of reason you thought." It is said, however, though they must *accomplish* more, they need not *teach* any more. All the teaching and learning involved concern the facts, which are reasons. The only ignorance that needs curing, the only matter that can raise doubt or dispute, concerns the facts. One knows all that one needs to know about the reasons in the case when one has learned all about the facts which are there to provide them.

The alluring feature of this view is that it eliminates complications and deflates excessive expectations. Reason-guidance is simple in method and limited in scope. It is simple in method because 'practical' knowledge is just of the predictable implications of actions, of nice, hard, public facts. These facts hold the possible reasons for or against doing anything. There is no reference here to any *knowledge* supervening on the facts, and one may take it as demonstrable that there *could* be no room for it. Let us again consider the impervious speedster. He knows the facts, and given his ultimate interests, they must count as reasons for him; but he is not deterred. What more, then, could 'reason' conceivably do to discourage him? One might say: "You know the facts, and this is why you *ought* not to." But in saying this, no further *reason* would come to light. For 'you ought not to' is said only after the facts (or reasons) in the case have been enumerated and indeed is said 'on the strength' of *them*. And therefore how could 'and so you ought not to' or any similar observation be additionally persuasive by way of being additionally *informative*? To say that it could would be to assume what seems absurd: that for 'reason' to dissuade one from doing something, one needs to *know* more than the *reasons which are telling against doing it*. One can comprehend how 'you ought not to' may dissuade one further by 'telling one not to', but not by 'telling one any more'.

The other feature is that the view reduces the scope of rational guidance. It is an ordinary conviction that not only subordinate but also ultimate ends (and the relations between them) are in some measure corrigible by 'reason'. If the motorist does not actually care about what he does to others, so much the worse for him. It may still be intrinsically unreasonable on his part not to do so. But if rational guidance is only by *reasons*, these convictions cannot make sense. Hume said that it was "not against reason to prefer the scratching of my little finger to the destruction of the whole world." If one asked, "Why not?" there is nothing left to be said. Hence when one is confronted with the carefree motorist, one must bow to the inevitable. One must always conclude that when someone does not care, and there is no *further* reason why he should, there is *no* reason why *he* should. One may add once again, "but you ought to care about maiming others, just on its own account." But once again, if this is additionally persuasive, it cannot be so by being additionally instructive. One is saying only that he ought to care in default of being able to give him a reason for caring. One starts 'oughting' where reasons fail one, where there is nothing further informative to *say*, only something further persuasive to *do*. So in every way the argument leads back to Hume. If rational guidance is only by reasons, the sole means for promoting rationality in conduct is popular scientific education, statistics, and more statistics about the effects of speeding, smoking, bashing children, the use of vaccines, and the atom bomb.

John Wisdom remarks on the habit of philosophical arguments to proceed by impeccable reasoning from impeccable premises to questionable conclusions. This story has the authentic ring. It makes one feel: "It is more than true, it is obviously true. What more in the way of knowing *could* one require for action guidance than knowing the reasons 'for' and 'against' in the case? What more *could* this come to than knowing the facts to provide them?" And yet one may feel restive all the same. One is unwilling to accept education in the facts as the sure *and* sole prerequisite of rationality in conduct. The obtuse man would not be obtuse if he did not already know the facts. There is something which he will not see or appreciate, and what is this? Here is the ghost of a quandary which first pursued Aristotle in the guise of the incontinent man.

III

To explore the workings of this quandary one must attend to such notions as 'knowing a reason', 'learning about a reason', and 'teaching others a reason'.

Reasons, one says, are 'in' something which provides them. A reason against eating lobster would be 'in the fact that' lobster is indigestible; a reason against causing pain 'in' the very nature of what causing pain is. This is not to say that the reason is literally 'in' that which is said to provide it. Not the *event*, 'getting ill', will have dissuasive force, as the event 'eating lobster' will have 'ill-making' force, but the *knowledge* or *belief* that such an event will take place. One has a reason 'in' what one *knows* or truly *believes* about a thing; and there *is* a reason 'in a fact' about a thing only in the sense that there is a fact in the knowledge of which one would *have* a reason.

That someone knows a reason for or against some action may merely mean that he knows some prospective feature about this action which in effect is fit to provide him with a reason. He then knows *that* the action would have this feature, and in knowing this, he knows a reason. But this sense of 'knowing a reason' needs to be distinguished from another, namely, from knowing *that* one has a reason, and how much of a reason one has, in a fact one knows. These two are easily confused, much as they are distinct. In knowing *that* lobster is indigestible one need only *know a reason* in the sense of 'being acquainted with it', of 'having it available to one', of 'connaître', and not necessarily of 'savoir'. To realize, to appreciate, to admit to oneself, *that* one has a reason, and a weighty one at that, would then be a distinct and further matter. The distinction here is between 'knowing a case for or against doing something' and 'knowing that one has a case', between 'knowing a reason', and also 'knowing it for the reason which it is', between 'having relevant information' and 'knowing its relevance'.

To say that rational guidance proceeds by learning about reasons is not therefore unambiguous. The claim that one has taught someone a reason may be true in one sense and false in another. One convinced him of a relevant fact—so it is true; he did not grasp its relevance—so it is false. The same may apply to philosophical views on what knowing reasons or learning about them amounts to. Such views may seem obviously true by being true as an account of knowing and learning about reasons in one sense. Yet they may be debatable or false at the same time as a *complete* account. This applies, as will be shown, to the view under consideration.

IV

This view is interested only in providing an account of what it is to know and learn about reasons in the first sense. All that matters, if one is to receive guidance from reasons, is that one should be *acquainted* with them. That in addition one may have to appreciate *that*, and *how much*, one has reasons in what one knows is not considered a further part of the transaction. "The intellectual processes that attend ethical deliberation, are all concerned with matters of fact. The process of making an ethical decision is something more, of course, than the process of formulating factual beliefs, but this is simply because reasons, in addition to their cognitive nature, have conative-affective effects."[2] This comes to saying that acquaintance with the facts that provide reasons is all the distinctive 'knowing' that effective guidance by reason ever requires. In knowing about reasons in this sense one knows about them in every relevant sense. If this assumption is correct, the whole current view of the method and scope of reason-guidance follows.

One may feel that this assumption not only *is*, but *must* be, correct. It is not for nothing that it is so naturally made. Two factors explain this. One is in a common assumption about what a guiding reason is, namely, that it is an influencing or 'exciting' truth in the sense of a consideration which *will* influence, as far as it can, as soon as it is *known*. A known reason, in this case, either will influence, or not be a reason, or enough of a reason. And this will entail that acquaintance with the reasons must be all the knowing that effective guidance by them can require. For if what is known is a penny that *can* drop, it also *will* drop, or else it was not a penny that can.[3] The second factor lies in the temptation to take one's cue to what knowing about reasons amounts to from the learning and teaching that typically goes on in *interpersonal* dealings, and this is fashionable today. There is a primary interest in how one person can influence another rather than in how a person would go about directing himself. The teaching and learning that go on in this area consist largely of acquainting others with facts that provide reasons. The typical 'teaching' consists of 'giving' reasons, the

2. C. L. Stevenson, *Ethics and Language* (New Haven: Yale University Press, 1944), p. 133.
3. This view is plainly mistaken. See Falk, "Action-Guiding Reasons."

typical 'learning' of 'being given' them. And from here it is not far to assume that all that needs to be known about reasons is that which others can teach one in 'giving' them. People are considered only as receivers and givers of reason-information, each engaged in trying to bring 'reason' to the other, but never in the solitary endeavor of consulting reason for themselves. And then, that reason-learning comes to fact-learning and nothing more will again not only *seem*, but also *be*, a truism.

V

This last point needs expanding. I am saying that *teaching* reasons by *giving* them amounts to teaching facts, and this is a point of logical grammar. 'Teaching reasons by giving them' is logically geared entirely to 'acquainting people with reasons', 'making known to them', 'disclosing to them' what there is to provide them. When one asks another to give one a reason, all that one is asking him to *do* is to show one a relevant fact, and the other, once he has done this, has discharged his task. One is not also thereby asking him to help one determine the *relevance* of this fact as a reason. Even if one were slow to realize or to admit to oneself that the fact which others gave one was a reason, they could still claim that they had given one a reason and that one had *known* the reason all along, in the sense in which one had learned it by being given it. The only teaching in giving reasons relates to the facts in the case simply because nothing else is, in giving reasons, logically one's business. It is also easy to see why interpersonal dealings should be typically confined to this procedure. The most common ground why people do not act on the reasons in the case is their ignorance of what there is to provide them, and to cure this ignorance is all, or nearly all, that one person can hope to do for another.

Another question is why the only reasons which can be 'given' are *further* reasons, reasons in some fact about a thing. What logical bar really is there to giving reasons for a choice of things on their own account? This question deserves less casual treatment than it often receives. One suggestion is that one cannot be given a reason for, say, not causing pain as such, because there *are* only further and no intrinsic reasons for a change of attitude toward anything. And this is held on the ground that one *means* by a 'reason' something further specifiable: 'a reason, but not a reason in anything in particular' makes no sense. Some turns of speech bear this out. "What is your reason for being good to B?" may be answered by: "I have no reason, I simply want to." Here, 'I have no reason' means 'I have no special reason', 'no reason in particular'. It is used to ward off the imputation that one had. But 'reason' may be used more widely, too, as the example can also show. For why am I so anxious to ward off the imputation that I have a reason? Surely not to stress that I am acting blindly without *any* rhyme or reason to speak of, but rather to stress that what reason I have is no special reason, i.e., none which needs explaining. I am just doing a good turn for its own sake, just by dint of knowing what doing a good turn is. This is all my reason, but still it is plainly a reason. It is not, therefore, that there can *be* no purely intrinsic reasons. What one knows of the very nature of a thing may be said to tell for or against doing it no less than what further one knows about it. It is not, therefore, because there can *be* no intrinsic reasons that one cannot *teach* them by *giving* them or *learn* them by being *given* them.

What, then, is the trouble? The answer is that one cannot teach or learn what it is impossible to know any more than one can teach (or learn) what it is impossible not to know. The difference between further and intrinsic reasons turns on this last point. Let A know that this will cause pain and still be undeterred. Then there may be further reasons against causing pain of which he is ignorant, such as that causing pain invites retaliation, which one may disclose to him. But one cannot conceive how, knowing that this will cause pain, he could be ignorant of the *possible reason* against causing pain *as such*, and would have to have *it* disclosed to him. A purely intrinsic reason for doing a thing is in all and no more than is signified by the word for the thing. From the description of the case everyone who knows the language will know where to look for such a reason and what to find. To ask, "And what would be a reason against causing pain as such?" barely makes sense. To reply, "Well, causing pain is causing pain," is near trivial. And hence it is a truism that the only reasons to *give* are further reasons. 'To give reasons' is to acquaint, to make known, to disclose what there is to provide them, to cure ignorance of reasons in this sense. This can apply only to further reasons. One cannot be given a purely intrinsic reason because one cannot be given what one has already. 'That causing pain invites retaliation' is significant and can be news. 'That causing pain is causing pain' is near trivial and cannot be news to anyone.

This is not to say that intrinsic reasons can present *no* problem for knowledge, but only that what problem they can present is not one to be solved by 'giving' the reason. It is a problem in another logical dimension, one that arises only with the knowledge of the possible reason already in one's possession. The possible reason for not causing pain as such is always staring one in the face, but then, being preoccupied with oneself, one may fail to realize *that* it is. One is not aware, one will not acknowledge to oneself, *that* precisely that which one knows that causing pain is *tells against* causing it, and how much it does; that here is a consideration with power to deter one, if one took it to heart. One's problem here would be that *of appreciating that one had a reason in what had been available to one all along.*

The same applies to reasons for exercising an ultimate preference between one thing and another. Hume said that there could *be* no such reason, no reason for preferring the saving of the whole world to the scratching of one's little finger. But one *can have* reason for the choice of a thing as such. Thus surely one can have a reason strong enough to tell for its choice in *preference to something else.* Take someone frantic with anxiety about an impending amputation. He may feel that he would rather die than suffer the pain; but this is not to say that he may not have *reason* for suffering the pain rather than dying. What he knows that death involves may *tell* against dying even at the cost of suffering pain. But again, if one asked to be *given* a reason for suffering pain rather than death, no reason could be given. "Well, pain is pain, and death is death" is about all that one could say, and it is plain again why. The only intrinsic reason for avoiding death is in what one understands death to be; and the only reason for preferring its avoidance, even at the cost of suffering pain, rests once more in what one knows that death is while knowing also what it is to suffer pain. The possible reason for exercising an ultimate preference between one thing and another is always known to one in what one knows of the one and the other, and no question of 'being given' this reason can arise. What *may* arise is a question of *realizing* or not realizing *that* one has it.

It is plain now what sustains current views on reason-guidance. They are convincing by being the answer to the questions: *'How does one teach reasons by giving them?' 'How does one learn about them by being given them?'* In the nature of the case, this enterprise is confined to teaching people reason-providing facts, to curing their ignorance of what they are doing or planning, or to removing prejudice and stupidity on this score. The motorist learns about death on the road, the glutton about overeating, and everything that 'giving reasons' can do has been done. But not everything that effective guidance by the reasons in the case requires must have been achieved with this too. Knowing the reasons may require supplementing by knowing their relevance as reasons.

VI

On this matter I want to say that often it is enough for effective guidance that one should know the reason-providing facts. But sometimes more will be necessary. In addition to knowing about death on the road, the speedster may then also have to know, or realize, or acknowledge to himself, such things as the following: *that* he has reason nevertheless for avoiding it on its own account, and *that* therefore he has reason for avoiding what would lead to it; or again (where on special grounds he is all set on hurrying) *that* after all he has reason for not causing death in what he knows this to be even, say, at the cost of being late for dinner and incurring his wife's displeasure, knowing what this is, and *that* therefore . . . etc. To be acquainted with the reasons in the case will here be only the first step. To know, to be aware of, or to admit to oneself, perhaps against one's wishes, urges, or fears, the relevance of reasons for one *as* reasons would be a second and concluding step.

There is often no need for this second step. Someone overanxious about his health may be deterred by the bare recognition that what he is about to eat is indigestible. 'These toadstools are poisonous' will work this way with most or all, or would at any rate if it were just a matter of the plate before *them*. If the plate was their competitor's, and it was a matter of not giving it to him, the case might be different, but still perhaps not different enough seriously to raise an issue. One is sure without question, even if with a twinge of regret, that one had been given a sufficiently weighty reason. It is obvious that over a wide range of cases people are not influenced by the reasons in the case only because they do not know what there is to provide them (i.e., the facts), and to cure their ignorance will here be all that is needed to make their attitudes change.

The error comes, however, from generalizing from too few examples. Tell someone overjoyed at having been offered a well-paid post that he will be isolated and without professional contacts in the place to which he is going, when one knows from past experience that he thrives on such contacts. One has then disclosed to him a fact which may be a conclusive reason for refusing the post. Nevertheless, one's information, although not disputed as a fact, is ignored, and if challenged on his lack of response, the person concerned may then say things like "I was just obtuse. I felt so set on going because of the pay that at first I did not realize, perhaps did not even wish to realize, that your information held a reason against going after all." Or "It is not that I had not known from what you said that there is a reason against going, but I am not sure that this really is an important enough reason considering how much I want to be better off and I still must settle this before what you say could convert me." Or again, he starts bluntly by stating: "This is just no reason. I feel like being well off for once, and never mind whether I stagnate or not." And then on second thought: "But perhaps you are right after all; one has reason to prefer a full life to a full purse just on account of the nature of each alternative, and so confound you, although I hate admitting it, you have just given me a telling reason after all."

These instances bring out the ambiguity in the notion of 'convincing someone of a reason'. Had one at the outset convinced him of a reason or not? In a sense, one had: one had taught him what *was* a reason. But, in a sense, one also had not: one had not engendered in him the conviction *that* he had a reason, or enough of one, in what one had taught him. He still had to work his own passage to this conviction. And without this, knowing the reason was not here enough to correct his attitude. The impervious man's failing may be precisely that he will not realize that he has a reason, or how much of a reason he has, in the reason which he knows.

This is not one failing either, but a family of failings. It is least aptly described as a failure to 'know'. One may often quite well know that there are strong reasons against one's habits or plans, if 'know' is taken dispositionally as the capacity to affirm this correctly when the question arises. The trouble is that one will not also sufficiently *think* of what one knows. The smoker may avow: "Of course I *know* that I have every reason for giving it up. But then I don't *remind* myself of this at the right time"; or "I know, but I am loath really to *admit* it to myself"; or "I just don't manage to *appreciate the full weight* of the reason when my craving is uppermost." Such avowals show still further how little effect mere acquaintance with the reasons can have and that rational guidance by them may require much more. There is knowing the story of the reasons; there is also rehearsing this story to oneself at the right time and in the right way. Rationality in conduct owes much to knowing the right story, but it owes just as much to a regimen of telling to oneself the same old story all over again. Without this, one may have cured people's ignorance of the relevant facts, having enlightened and educated them, as much as is humanly possible, and still not have made them 'see reason'.

Blindness to this part of the story is due not least to fascination with the model of interpersonal dealings, with how *one* may use reason on the *other*, and *he* on *oneself*. All that will then be involved in rational guidance will be the dead exchange of information, giving reasons and being given them. The other half of the story covering the supervening judgments, reminders, and admissions of relevance concerning this information will remain obscure, for this is for the greater part a matter one settles for himself. We can take each other to reasons, but there is little we can do, even though it is not nothing, to make each other assimilate them for what they are.

This is why the interpersonal approach tends so strongly to skepticism in the matter of ultimate ends and preferences and their corrigibility by 'reason'. For the standard method of correcting attitudes by reason has no entry at all in this matter. Only in the matter of *further* extrinsic reasons can people fail to be influenced by them in the first place by not knowing what there is to provide them; and there is scope here for trying to guide them by dispelling this ignorance, hoping that no more than this will be needed to correct their attitudes. But if someone has reason for the choice of something on its own account and in preference to something else without being influenced by this reason, this could never be caused by ignorance that could be cured by disclosing just another reason to him. It could be caused only by a failure on his part to appreciate an already known reason for the reason which it is, i.e., a failure to *assess what influencing force the consideration before him would have with him if he used his imagination and cashed the value of his symbols in terms of imaginative experience.* Such apprehensions and assessments are not likely to be imparted to people by the outsider. Hence, when people turn to the outsider with a request to be shown a reason for not causing pain as such, or for preferring a full life to a full purse, confusion is generated. The language of the request is ambiguous. In whatever sense the request is taken it cannot be properly met. If taken as "show me *what* would provide me with such a reason," one can only say: "surely, you must know this for yourself." If taken as "show me *that* I have such a reason," one can only say, "Well, surely you should be the best judge of this yourself"; although, in the absence of an argument, there could still be a conversation. Hence the notorious embarrassment which this request creates and the near vacuity of one's reply when one does try to meet it by saying lamely, "Well, causing pain is causing pain" or "Well, a full life is a full life, and a full purse is a full purse."

But not even these replies are completely trivial. They do the job, in fact two jobs at once: they ward off the vacuous request for being *given* a reason when the procedure is no longer logically applicable, and they challenge the questioner to adopt the appropriate procedure for himself, making the claim at the same time that, if he were to look, he would find. For the outsider is here faced either with a question that cannot be asked or with a question *he* cannot properly answer. Because this is overlooked, the erroneous conclusion is drawn that because no reason can be *given* for the correction of ultimate attitudes, there can *be* no such reasons, since what one cannot be taught, one cannot know. The error here would be avoided if rational guidance were approached in the first place from the *agent's* point of view. One's own problem in self-guidance is to know whether or not there is a case for or against doing things. This problem is not solved for oneself when one merely gets acquainted with likely reasons. It is solved only when one is acquainted with them *and* is satisfied that these are reasons and how much so they are. One does not solve this problem just by making oneself come upon information which, if relevant, will take one by surprise by motivating one into action. Self-guidance is not self-propulsion induced by self-instruction in the facts. It is a little like this, perhaps, but not entirely so.

VIII

It remains to make some concluding remarks which will lead back to the beginning of this essay. I referred there to the disputed place of 'ought-language' in action guidance and to the view that, if one agreed that guidance by reason really was by *reasons*, the case for any fact-supervening step in the language of action guidance would finally collapse. This is not the conclusion to which we have been led. One may say that all the knowing that rational guidance requires is of reasons. But one is not then saying anything simple and unassuming. On the contrary, if pressed, the old complexities reappear within reason-language itself. The same logical framework comes to light whether one says that rational guidance requires knowing the facts and knowing what one ought to do on account of them, or that it requires knowing the facts and knowing how much reason one has in them for or against an action. There seems formally little to choose between saying that action guidance requires knowing that there is a *case* for accepting or rejecting something as an end, that it is something *to be* sought or *to be* avoided, that one *ought* to seek or to avoid it, or that there is *reason* for seeking or avoiding it in virtue of its own nature or what it would involve. A stumbling block for the understanding of ought-language has always been to understand how 'and so I ought to' or 'and so you ought to' could be said to 'follow' from the facts in the case. But if this is a problem, it also is one for reason-language. Here, too, one has the transition from the facts in the case to the 'conclusion' that because of them one has a reason. How a reason is 'in' the facts, and how an obligation 'results' from them are similar puzzles. One way or another, one cannot ignore what seems to be a fundamental feature of action guidance by reason: that it requires, in addition to an adequate acquaintance with the facts in the case, some supervening cognitive step, one which is in aid of completing, if need be, persuasion by the facts by bringing home to people their inherent persuasive relevance.

[4]

Action-Guiding Reasons

I

One speaks of action guidance by reason. Doctors try it with pa-
tients, public authorities with motorists. One may 'consult reason',
'listen to reason'. Actions may be judged reasonable or not by the
yardstick of what, had they been directed by reason, they would have
been. Such language assumes capacities of thought, judgment, deliberation, from the exercise of which a rational person can get guidance
for his choices and actions. It also assumes that this job can be done
well or badly: a completely reason-guided choice would be one no
further corrigible by rational methods. There are few, short of the
existentialist fringe, who question that one may speak in these ways.
But there is the problem of how one may do so and make sense.

There is most agreement on one thing. The guidance that reason
can give to our actions must be looked for in the first place in what
judgment can teach us about them. One reasons with the motorist by
telling him about injury on the road; one consults reason for oneself
by exploring the ramifications of what one would be doing; one listens
to reason by taking notice of what one knows. A choice is the more
reason-guided the better it is factually informed. The same applies if
one says that rational guidance is found in *reasons*. The reasons for
(or against) doing anything are in the facts of the case. They are
reasons in proportion as the knowledge of them is choice-supporting.
A rational person can find guidance in knowledge that is of reasons.

Reprinted with permission of the publishers from *The Journal of Philosophy* 60
(1963):702–18.

Accomplished actions may be called reasonable in proportion as they are what they would have been had they been well informed by the reasons in the case.

It is common, since Stevenson's *Ethics and Language,* to describe guidance by reason as by reasons. But not all who echo this description agree on its interpretation. The new controversial question is how guidance by reasons is to be understood: how reasons can supply guidance, how they are contained and found in facts, what makes them good and sufficient reasons, what qualities of mind are required to get guidance from them. Stevenson's answers to these questions recall Hume's view that knowledge cannot be choice-guiding except by being choice-influencing. Knowledge that is of reasons is of matters in which such power of influence can be met, which, as known or believed, will tend to alter, direct, or redirect 'attitudes'. But many today are critical of precisely this view. They repudiate the 'Humean model' and all its works. The concept of a reason that guides through being a kind of choice-determining mental cause is another ghost in the machine, to be exorcised root and branch.

I shall be concerned with this concept of a reason and shall join the critics, but only part of the way. Stevenson's, and Hume's, views of the choice-guiding role of reasons and information ask for revision, but not, I think, on the ground that reasons and causes have no affinity and that never the twain shall meet.

II

The trouble, as so often, is that Stevenson, and Hume offer a package deal, as hard to reject as to accept. There is a primary thesis in agreement with common sense. There are inferences from this thesis in conflict with it.

It seems good sense that what holds as reason should have persuasive force. This is what is looked for in practical deliberation: matters to weigh with one, to correct present action dispositions, to decide one where one had been hesitant. It would be odd to say that one gave someone a reason all right, but nothing that could possibly carry influence with him however well he considered it. Nor is the practical role of reasons easily intelligible otherwise. They are explored and communicated because they are choice-supporting. To take them to be choice-supporting by means of being choice-influencing accounts for their practical role by assimilating it to a familiar pattern of experience. That reasons can influence seems a fact. That they should be choice-guiding by being choice-influencing is intelligible as just another case of a common principle at work. Any objector might fairly be asked: how *could* reasons be choice-guiding if it were not of their essence to be choice-influencing?

The frank presupposition here is that what a person knows (or believes) about what he would be doing can function as a variable in determining his readiness to do it. That this is to endow reasons with causal properties is not necessarily an objection. Any possible affinity between reasons and causes cannot be ruled out a priori, much as *determination* by reasons may differ from determination by *natural* causes. That knowing the injurious consequences of speeding could check one's readiness to speed does not make one a plaything of natural forces. Things known (or believed) do not influence one behind one's back. They are available for influence only to a person who is able and willing to think ahead. That they can influence need not imply that they automatically will do so. But, although reasons and natural causes differ in their modus operandi, they need not therefore have nothing in common. There can be lawlike connections between seeing a sight or entertaining a thought, on the one hand, and organic, psychological, and behavioral changes on the other. Praise may make one blush, a joke laugh, a sight or thought erotically excited. There is no saying that anticipations about one's actions could not function as variables in changing one's readiness to do them.

The main misgivings with this view arise from another contention typical of Stevenson: namely, that, if reasons are forces, traditional views of the scope and method of rational guidance need pruning by a liberal application of Ockham's razor. And here two familiar points should be recalled.

For one, there can be only one paradigm of a persuasive reason: one finds it always and exclusively in the implications of actions, and in proportion as they are matters of desire or aversion. That speeding will cause injury will be, and can be adduced as, a reason against speeding for someone averse to causing it, but not otherwise, unless a further reason against 'causing injury' can be adduced, say, that causing it will be punished. But this would still be to say that whatever is the concluding term in a chain of reasons must be an actually wanted or unwanted consequence. The implication is that reasons are available to correct the choice only of subordinate, not of ultimate ends. Reasons must be persuasive; and there is nothing in the nature of an end itself that could be found or adduced to correct one's intrinsic attitude toward it. It makes no sense to speak of an ultimate choice as 'against reason', if what is against reason must have been corrigible by a reason and a reason must be something that influences choice.

The second limitation concerns the manner in which reasons supply guidance. Because reasons are in persuasive facts, one must learn about these facts, and such learning is all that can be needed for getting guidance from them. To learn or know that drink ruins the liver is *both* necessary and sufficient for getting from such reason-information what guidance it is able to give. It is not only that this *may* be so: someone anxious about his health may be deterred from drinking just by learning about what may harm it. But this also *must* be so: one finds guidance in reasons exclusively through gaining acquaintance with facts that hold them. All the teaching and learning involved concern these facts. The only ignorance that needs curing, the only matter that can raise doubt or dispute concerns them; it is only through ignorance of these facts, in proportion as they hold reasons, that one can fail to be guided by them. "The intellectual processes that attend ethical [practical] deliberation are all of them concerned with matters of fact. They do not exhibit the exercise of some *sui generis* faculty of 'practical reason'. . . . Reasons and reasoning processes become 'practical' or 'ethical' depending upon their psychological milieu; when they direct attitudes they are 'practical'."[1]

Here the catch is again in the denials. It seems that one can conceive of a man not lacking in relevant information but whose conduct is still lacking in 'reason': of the drinker or speedster who is impervious to consequences of which he is not ignorant or unafraid. Knowledge of reason-giving fact does not here seem enough to ensure guidance. There seems point in saying that reasons must be not only known but also 'taken to heart'. Nor do we think that acquaintance with the facts that give reasons is the only significant way in which reasons must be known. There is also the recognizing or making sure *that* some known fact holds a reason, and how much of a reason. Such judgments about the relevance of the known facts in the case are no longer among the judgments about the facts in the case. Stevenson—and Hume—leave no room either for the judgment of relevance or for taking reasons to heart; and this, though paradoxical, is treated as the price to be paid for adhering to the commonsense thesis that whatever can be choice-guiding must be choice-influencing.

III

I shall argue shortly that these consequences are mistakenly ascribed to this thesis, but they follow validly for Stevenson, given his conception of how knowledge (or belief) is persuasive. This conception has

1. Charles L. Stevenson, *Ethics and Language* (New Haven: Yale University Press, 1944), p. 133.

a tradition and underlies many philosophical views of the relation of reason to conduct: the Socratic view that virtue is knowledge, as much as Hume's view that the practical judgment is purely of causes and effects. This conception is not gratuitous. From the logic of the case there is a natural drive toward it. But it does leave behind it a trail of odd consequences.

The question is: what is it to say that reasons are found in persuasive knowledge or belief, or, as Francis Hutchinson put it, "in exciting truths"? The reply seems inescapable that a truth is exciting when knowing it *will* excite. For if it might not excite even when known, there seems no warrant or proof for calling it exciting. Socrates thought it paradoxical for this reason that there could be knowledge with power to master desire that a person might have without having his desire mastered by it. Whatever effect knowing can have must show itself when it is acquired. A like view is found in Hume. "The moment we perceive the falsehood of any supposition ... our passions yield to our reason without any opposition ... I may will the performance of certain actions as a means of obtaining a desired good; but as my willing of these actions is only secondary and founded on the supposition that they are causes of the proposed effect, as soon as I discover the falsehood of this supposition, they *must* become indifferent to me."[2] Likewise, as soon as a relevant belief is acquired it must arouse desire or aversion in proportion to its relevance: "according as our reasoning varies, our actions receive a subsequent variation" (ibid., p. 126). One might call this the "jukebox model" of action guidance by reason. The guidance is automatically provided, for oneself or others, if one presses the right buttons of factual information.

If the proof of persuasive information is that it motivates upon acquisition, then, whatever the appearance to the contrary, the guidance to be derived from it must be simple in manner and limited in scope. Persuasive reasons will be in matters that *will* be persuading in proportion as they are known and are reasons. It must be the mark of a decisive reason that *once known* it must override every contrary reason, desire, or craving in the case. There can be no 'conflict between reason and passions' if, whatever knowledge can contribute, it cannot fail to contribute once one possesses it. There can be no room in rational guidance for any *judgment* except of the facts. To judge of the relevance of the known facts as reasons can amount here only to the recognition that they are motivating one. In fact, it is paradoxical on this view that someone could, with the facts before him, be won-

2. David Hume, *A Treatise of Human Nature*, ed. L. A. Selby-Bigge (London: Clarendon Press, 1967), p. 414. This is a more narrow view than that found in Book III of the *Treatise* and the *Inquiry*. See my "Hume on Practical Reason," p. 155ff. in this volume.

dering which of them held the more decisive reason and be hesitant about what to do for not having settled this question. For if, on the jukebox model, a *known* fact holds a decisive reason, it should ipso facto be decisively motivating and leave no loophole for indecision.

It is also here necessary that persuasive reasons can only be non-intrinsic. Reasons in the implications of an action can fail to be influencing by not being known and come to be influencing by being learned. But there can be no correction of intrinsic attitudes in this way. All that could furnish a reason to correct indifference to 'causing hurt as such' is what 'causing hurt' amounts to as such. And what this is one cannot be taught since one cannot fail to know it already. It is simply that 'causing hurt' is 'causing hurt', and what this is everyone knows who understands the language. There is nothing here to be known that by *being disclosed* could serve to correct a prior intrinsic attitude. All that could so serve is always already in one's possession. If reasons are found in knowledge that is persuading through its possession, intrinsic attitudes must always be as well informed as they could be.

IV

I shall argue that what is at fault is not the force view of reasons but its jukebox interpretation. This is shown most convincingly by its failure to cope with its own paradigm case. There is no doubt that the wanted (or unwanted) implications of actions hold reasons, in fact, as we think, not only as a rule, but necessarily so (i.e., at least *some* reason even if not necessarily always a sufficient one). There is also strong presumption for taking it that such implications hold reasons because the knowledge of them is persuasive. It certainly seems that the knowledge of such implications could not fail to be persuasively relevant if the implications are wanted or unwanted. All the same, the jukebox interpretation of how the interesting implications of actions always furnish persuasive reasons cannot explain how they function as *reasons* any more than why they should *necessarily* do so.

For one thing, it is not believable that knowing such implications will always be proportionately persuading. A doctor's medical knowledge may, but need not, make him immune against habits of over-indulgence with decidedly unwanted consequences. At any rate, no sufficient reason is given why it should *have* to make him so immune. The principle generally invoked here is a psychological mechanism. Knowledge (or belief) tends to act as an 'intermediary' between preexisting attitudes and the formation of new ones (ibid., p. 115). Once an action is known to contribute, through an implication, to a wanted (or unwanted) end, the interest in the end will come to be transferred, through this knowledge, to the action. Now something can be said for this observation. That an action would have a wanted consequence seems, doubtless, to create conditions favorable to our taking an interest in this action and often arouses such an interest. However, it is unexplained why this mechanism of transfer should be invariably at work. We don't think that it is, and even if it were, this would only be so as a matter of *empirical law*. And this would not be enough for the argument. The assumption that persuasive reasons are *persuading* when known would show only that interesting implications furnish reasons *as a general rule*, not why it should seem *inconceivable* that they could fail to.

One may want to meet this difficulty by making it definitive of wanted (or unwanted) consequences that knowing them *will* be persuading: the only evidence for ascribing to people an interest in an end is the interest they show in the means of attaining it. If the overindulgent doctor endangers his health, this can only be proof (since he must know better) that he has no interest in living or, at least, would, seriously, rather be dead soon than not be a glutton while living. Failure to adopt the known means counts here as invariable proof of a corresponding unconcern for the end. It goes with this that 'incontinence' can never be quite what it seems: a case of imperviousness to known consequences that a person has every stake in avoiding. Such imperviousness can show only that the person in question either does not really know or does not really care. It must be logical proof that the facts as known could not have held enough of a contrary reason for him.

On this view, there is never enough logical rope for the incontinent man to hang himself after his own fashion; and if this seems extreme, it is for the good reason that the verificationist assumptions on which this view rests are too tight. The consequences of an action may be 'wanted' or 'unwanted' in more than one sense. 'Unwanted' may refer to what one is anxious to avoid, preoccupied with not incurring; and a test of such overt concern would be one's response to an unwanted consequence when one learned about it. But a consequence is also 'unwanted' (and so as to give one reason for avoiding it) if no more than its final occurrence would prove unwelcome: if, when it happened, one would find it repugnant, suffer under it, feel shaken or remorseful. A carefree driver is without overt concern about causing accidents, but not necessarily therefore a person quite indifferent to causing them, in the sense that he would not be deeply shaken if he did. A hangover would be something 'unwanted' in proportion to the misery of one's condition when one endured it. The misery of this condition would be independent evidence of its being an 'unwanted' consequence, however impervious one kept proving to the prior certainty that one would suffer it. Hence an alcoholic must not (as A. I. Melden suggests) be a person who can wish only he could still mind his condition. He may well be one who, as common sense wants to say, is no longer able to summon his will to avoid a condition that he both knows and minds. That the last should seem an odd description rests on the error of taking anticipatory strivings as the sole test of someone's stake in an end state. It is not therefore a point of logic that knowledge of interesting consequences must be of *persuading* reasons, on the ground that if such knowledge were not persuading, it could manifestly not be of a sufficiently interesting consequence either.

But above all there is no case whatever for saving the view that known and interesting consequences must be correspondingly persuading, either as a matter of empirical law or of logic. For in thinking that such consequences hold reasons, we are simply not implying the jukebox concept of a reason as a *persuading* truth. This should be plain from the grammar of reason-language, provided that the role of reasons in guidance is not confused with that in another context. There are two uses for saying that a person 'has a reason': he may have (1) a reason for wanting or intending to do something, or (2) a reason in favor of doing it, one that 'tells' or 'counts' in its favor, either to some extent or decisively so. These uses differ in the role the reason is thought of as playing. A reason *for* wanting or intending is operating as a motive. One refers to it in order to explain one's action dispositions as they are. But this is not how the role of an action-guiding reason is conceived. One thinks of this as something 'telling' in favor of or against a choice; and, as 'telling', it is thought of as supporting a choice not yet made, rather than as actuating one that has already taken place. That I have, and am aware of having, a reason that 'tells' and 'tells decisively' does not go to show anything yet about my action dispositions or intentions. On the contrary, the grammar of 'tell' leaves it quite open whether or not that which tells will also compel. What 'tells' gives one ground for a change of attitude, and what gives one ground may become one's motive. But there is no contradiction in saying that what gave one every ground, and was known to do so, failed to motivate one in any way. The concept of a ground implies nothing more than that known grounds are *available* to supply guidance to someone willing to *take* guidance from them. All this goes to show that, in learning about a guiding reason, one is not learning a piece of exciting news—as, in learning about a death, one learns a piece of saddening news. One cannot receive the saddening news without being saddened by it; one can learn about a guiding reason and not be guided by it. None of this would make sense if reasons were in matters which, when known, would *be* motivating. If wanted (or unwanted) consequences necessarily furnish grounds in support of the choice or rejection of the action, this cannot be because knowing them will be necessarily persuading.

V

What then do reasons do when, without compelling, they 'tell' and 'tell decisively'? What remains of their persuasiveness if, even when known, they need not be correspondingly persuading? It is tempting here to abandon the force view altogether. It is said that, since reasons can be known without being influencing, it cannot be of their essence to function like motives in any sense. The model of them as serving guidance by being a kind of mental cause imports a misleading mechanistic analogy into the concept of a ground. The logical virtue of a ground is that, since it compels nothing without our concurrence, it need have no power to compel either, and yet not cease to be a valid ground. That reasons must have power to move us, Baier says, "is only a metaphorical way of saying that we have a power to follow them," and this, without any countervailing influence on their part, even "contrary to our strongest desire."[3]

But this is only to go to another extreme. The grammar of a guiding reason is misconceived if it is taken as so *tight* as to make its influence invariable and automatic. It also seems misconceived if taken as so *loose* as to remove all persuasive relevance from it. Although a known reason need not be influencing, it remains hard to conceive how it could be a reason and choice-supporting in default of any capacity to carry influence, how something that 'gives one ground' might have nothing about it to furnish one with a motive. It is certainly not on these terms that interesting consequences are expected to provide reasons. We have no doubt that the knowledge of them is of something persuasively relevant, that the very concern for the end creates a condition for taking a corresponding interest in the means. But we are not thereby implying that just knowing them will always be persuading. And this seems the burden of regarding the knowledge of them as of reasons: namely, that it is of matters in which a power of influence can be met, but a power conceived as in the first place dis-

---

3. Kurt Baier, *The Moral Point of View* (Ithaca: Cornell University Press, 1958), p. 142.

positional. A known reason is not something to straightaway pounce on one; it seems rather something available to pounce, sometimes almost poised to pounce, something that would pounce if only one did what is necessary to let it. A decisive reason need not override contrary desire because it is known, but it would not be a decisive reason if it did not have a latent power to do so. This seems the suggestion of language. What 'gives one cause' need not take effect on one but is there ready to do so. What gives one ground is available to motivate one but need not unless one looks into it. Known reasons are there to carry weight with a 'rational person', one who will 'listen to reason' and not only 'consult' it. The implication is that knowledge of reasons is not necessarily choice-influencing in proportion to its power unless some further condition or conditions are satisfied and, further, that these conditions are such that they may have to be fulfilled by the agent's own concurrence. One may have to *take* guidance from reasons because the guidance they can *give* is there only for the *taking*.

The problem is to understand how and why this should be so. The grammar of reason-language plainly confounds the jukebox assumption that the possession of persuasive information must be sufficient for its taking effect. The very opposite seems to be assumed. Reasons are found in matters the knowledge of which is persuasive, but, in order to be fully influenced by such knowledge, it is precisely not necessarily enough to possess full knowledge. This raises the question of on what more than knowledge itself the possible influence of knowledge on attitudes depends. But this is not here a question in empirical psychology, but one about the assumptions about this matter implicit in the concept of a ground.

Language is permeated with expressions that suggest the persuasive limitations of bare knowing. One may act blindly by acting in ignorance, but also by turning a blind eye to what one knows. One may not face, assimilate what one knows, not let it sink in, ponder, dwell on it. One may know, yet only as 'the drunken man knows the verses of Empedocles'. What would otherwise weigh with one will not then do so. Implicit here is a distinction between 'knowing that' and 'thinking of'. As Aristotle knew, we so use the verb 'to know' that a person may be said 'to know' while not in the least 'exercising' his knowledge. 'To know' is a capacity: one knows what drink does to the liver if one can tell correctly what it does. But to be 'thinking of' what one knows is different. It involves telling oneself the story of what one knows, recalling or rehearsing it; having, bringing, or keeping it before one at the time when it matters; having it before one in a comprehending frame of mind. These are occurrences, things that happen or may be done at will. The bare acquisition or possession of knowledge (or belief) is no guarantee of its influence for this reason. What one knows need not always be before one, or not as well as may be. A doctor's medical knowledge is no guarantee that he will attend to it without let or hindrance when the desire for strong drink is upon him. What he knows, though persuasively relevant for him, will not then be able to be persuading. None of this should be surprising. Only occurrences can have consequences. If any mental antecedents can function as variables in determining action dispositions, these must be objects of 'thinkings of' rather than of bare 'knowings that'.

This is not to say that persuasive information is persuading only if deliberately minded. 'That the house is on fire' will be thought-arresting enough to promote self-protective action without first having to be pondered. There is not time to forget, no occasion for wanting to, no rival interest in repressing the thought that action will save one from burning. But 'that being overweight shortens life' may be different. It is information as persuasively relevant as it is unwelcome. To entertain it threatens contrary desires in possession; to make it efficaciously present will need recall and rehearsal, at the right time, for long enough, without obfuscation. No practical benefit may come from such information without deliberate aid from closing the gap between knowledge and its representation. Persuasive knowledge (or belief) is not persuading unless it is minded and may always fail to be persuading unless deliberately and well minded. Its persuasive essence is in its promise but not necessarily in its performance.

Guiding reasons are conceived as persuasive in precisely this sense. They are judged choice-supporting in proportion to their choice-influencing potential. They are available to become choice-influencing if the appropriate conditions are satisfied and for someone able and willing to satisfy them. And these conditions are conditions of 'minding'. We significantly say that reasons are found not so much in the 'knowledge that' as in the 'consideration that'. We expect the reason-giving fact to afford guidance when known and 'duly considered' or 'duly taken into account'. To 'consider' a matter, or 'take account' of it, is to give thought to it, to rehearse or review it for what it is known to be. To take 'due' account is to give thought to it as well as may be, in all its known ramifications, for long enough, without any let or hindrance. What makes reasons choice-influencing is not, therefore, solely and primarily *knowing* the reason-giving fact but giving appropriate *attention* to it as something known. A wanted consequence holds a reason because *acknowledgment*—not *knowledge*—of the means-ends relation would dispose one in favor of adopting the means. A matter holds an overriding reason not because *knowing* it will override contrary reasons or desires, but because the single-minded *rehearsal* of this matter alongside the opposing objects of striving in the case would neutralize and, if persisted in, continue to neutralize what power of influence they would otherwise have in isolation. We can 'follow' such reasons in opposition 'to our strongest desire' precisely because of the countervailing influence which, as properly reflective persons, we can derive, if we are so willing, from the knowledge of them.

It is also precisely because reasons give guidance not primarily through the knowing, but through appropriate thought being given to what is known, that not all guiding reasons need be nonintrinsic. It was shown before that what is known of the very nature of 'causing hurt' could not serve persuasively as a reason against causing it, if reasons were in matters that became persuading solely through the acquisition or possession of knowledge of them. What causing hurt is cannot become exciting news for anyone who understands the language. But, then, although one *knows* what it is to cause hurt, it may still be that what one knows it is is not *comprehendingly before one*. One may fail to spell it out to oneself by making the thought of it concrete in rehearsing familiar instances and the intrinsic ramifications of the very thing known. This is why the intrinsic nature of what causing hurt amounts to may well give one reason against causing it: namely, if this is to mean that the concrete confrontation of its known nature in thought would have it in it to correct one's de facto indifference to causing it. It remains true that one cannot find or be given a dissuasive reason against causing hurt as such, since what could hold such a reason one cannot fail to know. But one may well find *that* one has such a reason, in finding that what could hold such a reason does in fact provide one.

It is noteworthy that the jukebox concept of a persuasive reason is here modified in two directions at once. On the one hand, that a known matter is not persuading is not here enough to show that it does not hold a reason. On the other hand, that it is persuading, even if the facts were all known, need not here be enough to show that it holds a reason without qualification. That 'causing you hurt will revenge me' may prove a strongly persuasive consideration, although I am not ignorant of the nature and consequences of causing hurt. But, all the same, this need still not be more than a 'bad' or 'insufficient' reason for doing what this consideration is tempting me to do. For it may still be that, if I made way in my thoughts for a more faithful and less passion-distorted review of the act in its entirety, of all its known consequences alongside each other, and of the intrinsic nature of these consequences apart from their special symbolic meaning for me, I would cease to find it choice-influencing altogether. The consideration would be a 'bad' reason and an inferior guide for lack of a 'true' power of influence, i.e., one that could meet the full test of representational adequacy implied in the concept. That reasons must be persuasive in order to be reasons does not here entail that everything sufficiently known, and persuasive, must hold a good and sufficient reason. For a choice to be backed by good and sufficient reasons it would, on this showing, have to be no further corrigible by the discovery of new matters of fact as well as by any more realistically faithful and unreserved representation of them in thought.

VI

I shall give some further consideration to nonintrinsic reasons. The jukebox interpretation could not explain their special feature: that it should seem inconceivable that the fact that an X is a means to a wanted (or unwanted) Y could fail to give some ground (even if not necessarily a sufficiently good ground) for (or against) the action. While this cannot mean that knowledge of the means-ends relations must be always persuading, it should on our showing mean that it must always be (in some measure) persuasively relevant. Kant made a like point in taking it as demonstrably true that he who wills the end and knows the means would will the means likewise "if reason fully determined his will." Common sense holds the same. Indifference to known implications that are of interest is a species of irrationality. Kant takes it that the full use of 'reason' must cure such indifference. The question is how to conceive of the use of 'reason' as having this effect. I have argued that the characteristically practical contribution of reason comes to the appropriate minding of what is known. If this is correct, nonintrinsic reasons should serve as a test case. There would have to be some manner of taking appropriate account of the known relation of means to ends, which could not fail to result in an extension of interest from the end to the means.

Someone who (without good contrary reasons) will not see the doctor while lamenting his health can be charged with inconsistency. The inconsistency is between attitudes, one of favoring an end, the other of lack of favor for what, in effect, would come to the very reaching of this end. Such inconsistency is ascribed only to the *knowing* disregard of the means. The assumption seems to be that in someone who knows there should be no room for these contrary attitudes to coexist; indifference to what, in effect, would be part of achieving the end should give way to interest in achieving it. Contrary attitudes toward practically identical objects cannot here be maintained, or at least could not be maintained by someone who both knew and was in his right mind. For there can *be* inconsistency between attitudes, much as the concept of inconsistency implies that there are conditions, of 'right-minding', which would preclude them from coexisting. What must be at issue here is a 'minding' that appropriately represents the equivalence between reaching what is wanted and the choice of the means toward it. The problem is to understand what this minding would amount to and why it should be credited with necessarily having an effect.

The equivalence is one of description. To want an end (like happiness or health) is to want an achievement, some process by which a certain end state would be reached. And whatever action would lead to such an end may be described (apart from its description as this particular action, like 'seeing the doctor') as tantamount, in the circumstances, to the process, or part of the process, of reaching this very end. 'Seeing the doctor', if this leads to health and if health is wanted, may be viewed as, in effect, an identical part of the very achievement that is wanted. What becomes equivalent in description is the process of which 'seeing the doctor' can be represented as a part and the very process of reaching the end itself. Hume thought that this equivalence should have the effect of extending the interest in the end to the means whenever the means-ends relation was *known*. But such knowledge alone, though necessary, is for various reasons not necessarily sufficient for this effect.

One reason is that the knowledge that seeing the doctor will come to protecting one's health may be insufficiently exercised. Whenever it comes to making an appointment, it is repressed or quickly dismissed. To know the relation of means to end can have no effect unless what is known is recalled at the right time and for long enough. The other reason is that, while the means–ends relation is recalled, the very interest in reaching the end, though it 'exists', is ignored. I am aware that seeing the doctor comes to protecting my health, but not, at the same time, of my health as the very thing desired. Here my interest in the end will not be sufficiently available to extend itself to the choice of the known means. This last point is as significant as it is easily misunderstood. To say one is 'unaware' of one's want for an end is not to say that what is repressed or has slipped one's mind is *the fact that* the end is wanted. One bears one's own wantings in mind not by entertaining the *proposition* that one wants a thing but by entertaining a *thought-object* (the reaching of health as the *terminus ad quem* of a process of change) wantingly or desirously: as a matter that, on being entertained, arouses one's interest. It is easily overlooked here that the fact that a person wants an end does not entail that he will be thinking of it wantingly all the time. One may say, "Of course I want success, but not now; now I want to go to sleep." Of the last I am desirous; I am dwelling on the end as a possible achievement, and in dwelling on it I am under its spell. Of the first, the wanted success, I am not desirous here and now; that all the same I desire it is to say that I am disposed to be desirous of it, will desire it when I dwell on it, and, perhaps, not infrequently, dwell on it desirously. To recall my want for an end is not, therefore, to recall the fact that I want it, but to recall its object as wanted, i.e., to revive and make available to myself a live want for it. There can be no extension of interest from the end to the known means unless the interest in the end is thus available and, if need be, recalled.

The solution of our problem is now at hand. The interest in the end need not come to extend itself to the means unless (1) the act of adopting the means is viewed as part of the very process of reaching the end, (2) the reaching of the end is before one as actually wanted, and (3) the equivalence in description between the action (as a means) and the very thing thought of as wanted is reviewed and kept steadily before one. The identification in thought between choosing the means and the very reaching of the end is here complete; and this is the condition of 'right-minding' in which indifference to the known means can no longer coexist with the want for the end. It is inconceivable how there could be *one* attitude toward reaching the end and *another* toward adopting the means (except for the countervention of further considerations) *as long as* adopting the means is viewed as part of an achievement precisely identical in its description with the description of the achievement that is being viewed with interest.

That identification of the adopting of the means with the very achieving of the end has a necessary consequence must not be misunderstood. It is sometimes supposed that the identifying thinking involved here is one that results in the recognition that the adoption of the means is only a case of doing something of the very kind wanted, with the implication that adopting the means must be the very thing that implicitly had been wanted all along. But this would be a non sequitur. 'Something of an A kind is wanted' and 'X is of an A kind' in no way entail that 'X is wanted' or 'has been wanted all along'. The particular X has no doubt not been wanted before it was *known* to be of an A kind; it is not bound to come to be wanted even when known, unless it is thought of as included in the very thought object of an actual want. The point is that the identifying thinking involved here is practical and not theoretical. It is not concerned with the inclusion of one propositional function in another, but of one thought object in another. What it yields is not a conclusion, but a change in practical attitude. The only necessary proposition involved is the proposition that this is the change it would have to yield.

To assert that the ends-means relation necessarily holds reasons is, therefore, to say that knowledge of it must be (in some measure) choice-influencing if consistently minded and that it may always fail to be so except for a sufficiently 'rational' person. Such a person will here be one who with the knowledge of wanted (or unwanted) consequences in his possession will, if need be, derive choice-guiding influence from such knowledge—and this by confronting at the right time, for long enough, and without mental reservations, the very equivalence of his actions to achievements effectively recalled as wanted (or unwanted). The hard part of finding guidance in reasons is not in getting hold of the facts. It is in allowing these facts to become influencing by making appropriate way for them in one's thoughts. And what is often hardest in the case of means-ends reasons is not the timely recollection of the known consequence, but the recall of the stake one has in it. It is easily ignored how frequently one's stake in a consequence is not available to one except dispositionally. We noted earlier that a consequence would be 'unwanted' if only it were repugnant or a source of suffering when it took place. What is unwanted in this sense is quite often not the object of an actual anticipatory aversion, much as it would become one if dwelt upon. The problem of imperviousness in practice connects frequently with a blocked capacity to view with overt desire or aversion, at the very time when it would matter, what one has a disposition so to view on other occasions, and would so view in the final event. The impervious man cannot summon his *will*, since the desires, fears, or cravings that have possession of him incapacitate him in the matter of collecting his *thoughts* on the very things he knows but would rather not hear of. The intellectualist fallacy is not in Hume's principle that guidance by reason comes from knowing, through the possible effect on the knower of the thing known. It is in the failure to acknowledge the complementary principle that knowing is not all to having the known in one's possession, and that no practical benefit can come from knowing that is left untended.

VII

I have argued in defense of the view that reasons are forces. This view draws its strength from its power to make the choice-guiding role of reasons intelligible. It can be held in a form that avoids the paradoxical consequences into which it has often led its advocates.

But there is one limiting implication, it must be allowed, that is inseparable from it. If reasons are choice-guiding because they are forces, then a circumstance that holds a reason for one need not hold a reason—or a reason of the same weight—for everyone. What, upon being as well minded as can be, can qualify as a choice-determining consideration is in essence an empirical matter. This is not to say that there are not many facts that may be treated as standard reasons among human beings. The suggestion that 'this is poisonous' or 'this will cause hurt' could fail, for some, to hold any dissuasive reason at all may well be treated as incredible. But, except for some logically marginal cases (like 'X will cause you pain'), it cannot on this view be treated as inconceivable. The corrigibility of human choices by reason does not here entail their corrigibility for all in precisely the same way. And, if we treat the corrigibility of a choice by reason as the measure of its reasonableness or unreasonableness, then, in this sense, no kind of choice can be called reasonable or unreasonable per se, but always only relative to some agent. Even if there were another sense in which the onlooker might want to call the agent's choice unreasonable, it might still have to be granted that this choice was not one any further corrigible by reason for the agent. If there is a case for questioning the force view of reasons, the incentive will come from this relativistic implication. The language of 'reasonable' and 'unreasonable', of what would count as 'duly' considered, of what reasons are 'good' or 'sufficient', is also used with normative or conventionalist implications. What is 'reasonable', 'due', 'good', or 'sufficient' may here be treated as being the same for all. These uses create problems, and account must be taken of them. But I doubt that our understanding of the action-guiding role of reason and reasons can be adequately founded on them.

[5]

Fact, Value, and Nonnatural Predication

I

Twentieth-century views on value are broadly divided between non-naturalism and noncognitivism. The choice is between saying that 'x is good' ('is good as such', 'good to experience', 'have', 'behold', 'ought to be', 'ought to be done') asserts some fact or truth, but one which is knowable only in some extraordinary and unique way; and saying that 'x is good', and so forth, does not primarily assert anything at all, but is a way of speaking commendingly or directively. These are opposed views, but they share a common bond. They agree that if 'x is good', and so on, stated any fact or truth, it could *only* be one ascertainable by some nonsensuous apprehension. What is taken to be ruled out, as involving the patent error of committing the naturalistic fallacy, is that 'x is good' could be making a truth-claim which, for confirmation, turned in any way on the testimony of sense, or feeling, or of a reviewer's responses of favor or disfavor. Intuitionism and noncognitivism, of one sort or other, are thus presented as the only serious alternatives.

This situation may seem disconcerting. One does not part readily with the commonsense conviction that 'x is good' is used to make some testable claim, that both 'this claret is good' and 'this claret is mild' have enough in common to be regarded as cases of predication. One may have bought the claret because it was mild and because it was good. One may take trouble to make sure whether this claret really is mild and be rash or careful in judging whether it is good. One may ask to have the mild claret brought to one, or the good claret, adding each time, "Just try and see for yourself which one I mean"; and both times one's instructions may lead to the right object's being picked out. So far, then, 'x is mild' and 'x is good' seem to do the same job, that of ascribing to x some ascertainable mark by which x may be picked out from among other things. And hence one hankers after some account of 'x is good' as expressing a propositional truth. One may equally feel, however, that such an account is too dearly bought if it has to commit one to the notion of goodness as the object of a nonsensuous intuition sui generis. Rather than let oneself be driven to accept this notion, one may accept, even with qualms, the alternative view that 'x is good', whether addressed to others or to oneself, is not primarily truth-claiming at all. The situation may be thought to have the makings of a dilemma, which raises the question, "Is this dilemma really necessary?"

II

The crux of the matter lies in two convictions which it has become common to treat as one. The one is that if 'x is good' is, *like* 'x is mild', a truth-claiming statement, it is also *patently unlike* 'x is mild' or 'x is sweet' or 'x is digestible' or 'x is pleasant' or any statement of the latter sort, by being a statement of quite a *different sort*. The other is that what makes 'x is mild' and the like all statements of one type is that their truth is known in some ordinary empirical way and that, by contrast, if 'x is good' were truth-claiming as well, this could be only as its truth was known in some extraordinary nonempirical way.

There are some striking features of value-language which make one insist on the first. 'X is mild', 'sweet', 'digestible', or 'pleasant' are statements by which one enumerates the facts about x. But 'x is good', one feels, does not state just another fact about x along with the rest. One cannot say that this claret is mild and smooth *and* good into the bargain; its goodness is not another feather in its cap in addition to its mildness and its smoothness. One says that things are good because of the facts about them, but their goodness does not count as just another fact about them. On the contrary, one learns that in answer to "Just give me the facts," one does not say, "x is good." In some sense 'x is good' is no longer a statement of fact just by being a judgment of value. And if, nonetheless, 'x is good' did affirm some fact or truth, this would have to be one manifestly different in type from 'x is mild', 'x is sweet', and so on, in the sense in which the latter count as ordinary statements of fact about x. The puzzle is that on the propositional view one seems to be forced to say *that the goodness of x is a fact which is not among the facts about x.* And this was G. E. Moore's point in insisting that the goodness or value of a thing must not be identified with any one of its 'natural' properties.

It has become almost axiomatic that, in acknowledging the difference in type between 'x is mild' and so on and 'x is good', one is also committed to holding that 'x is good', if propositional, must be the assertion of some nonsensuously intuitable, and in this sense 'nonnatural', fact or truth. This is held on the understanding that what makes mildness and the like members of the class of natural properties or facts is an epistemological criterion: what counts as a 'natural property' or 'fact about a thing' is anything that is known in some sensibly testable way. And from this it would follow that if goodness is by contrast not among the natural properties or facts about a thing, it must be something knowable in some epistemologically nonsensuous way and so must constitute some extraordinary, nonnatural matter of fact. This conclusion is inevitable if what is common and peculiar to anything that counts as a 'natural' property is that it is known in an ordinary empirical way and that it is because of the difference between goodness and the 'natural properties' or 'facts' about things *in this respect* that 'x is good' must be treated as a statement of another type.

But that any of this really is so may be questioned. One might hold that what is common and peculiar to anything that will count as a fact in the case is not that it relates to something empirically known and that what forces the exclusion of the goodness or value of a thing from the 'facts' about it is not that it is known in some extraordinary way. Value judgments may be in some important sense 'fact-supervenient' and no longer contributive to a clarification of the 'facts in the case'. But the sense in which one is made to say this may be such that it does not directly bear one way or another on the question of how goodness or value would be *known* if it were a 'fact'.

III

It is usual to cite Moore as the father of the view I wish to query. Moore insisted that 'x is good' must be recognized as a statement different in type from 'x is mild', 'x is sweet', and the like. Although the latter are statements about the natural properties of x, 'x is good' is no longer such a statement. Moreover, by a statement about a natural property, Moore is taken to mean a statement about some empirically known matter of fact; and by a statement which is no longer about a natural property he is taken to mean one about some matter no longer testable in the way natural properties are, but in some other way. The distinction between goodness and the class of 'natural' properties, of which mildness or sweetness or pleasantness are members, is thus taken to turn on the very difference in the way goodness, as distinct from any member of the class of natural properties, is *known*; and it is in virtue of this epistemological difference that one is driven to speak of a difference in *type*.

It is noteworthy, however, that this is a misrepresentation of what Moore himself had to say. Admittedly there are difficulties in disentangling what Moore actually did want to say. These difficulties exist on his own admission. He avows in the "Reply to My Critics"[1] that in *Principia*[2] "I did not give any tenable explanation of what I meant by saying that 'good' was not a natural property." For an authentic account of his meaning he refers to *Philosophical Studies*[3] and to his comments on this account in the "Reply" itself. There is no doubt that a reading of *Principia* alone, without the light thrown on it by *Philosophical Studies* and the "Reply," may create confusion. Even so, not even *Principia*, especially if read in the light of Moore's later views, makes it *definitive* of the distinction between goodness and the class of natural properties that the latter are properties known in a way in which goodness is not. Still less can such a view be extracted from Moore's later statements. Nor again does the principle of distinction between properties which are natural and those which are not, which Moore primarily employs in *Principia* and unreservedly in his later statements, entail that goodness as a 'fact' *must* be the object of a nonsensuous intuition. It is true that in *Principia* Moore at least seems to suggest that he thought it *was*, though even here it is doubtful how much he wished to commit himself to this position. For he also says that when he calls propositions about goodness "intuitions" he means "*merely* to assert that they are incapable of proof" and that he is implying "nothing whatsoever as to the manner or origin of our cognition of them."[4] But in any case, whether or not Moore wanted to say that goodness was in fact the object of a nonempirical intuition is not the point at issue. The issue is whether his distinction between goodness and the class of natural properties necessarily implied such a view.

IV

Moore says in the "Reply" that the way he tried to characterize the distinction between goodness and the natural properties of a thing in

1. P. A. Schlipp, ed., *The Philosophy of G. E. Moore* (New York: Tudor, 1952).
2. G. E. Moore, *Principia Ethica* (Cambridge: Cambridge University Press, 1922).
3. G. E. Moore, *Philosophical Studies* (London: Kegan Paul, 1922).
4. Moore, *Principia*, p. x.

Principia seems to him "now to be utterly silly and preposterous."[5] But he also says that what he had in mind was "the very same distinction" which he described in *Philosophical Studies* as between goodness and the natural intrinsic properties of a thing. And in spite of the odd formulations which he employs in *Principia*, there is a plain continuity between the two accounts.

According to *Principia*, goodness differs from the natural properties in two ways.[6] (1) Goodness is a property which cannot "*exist by itself in time.*" It depends on the object to which it is ascribed in a way in which natural properties do not. (2) Goodness, unlike the natural properties of objects, is not *among the parts of which the object is made up.* Natural properties "are in themselves substantial and give to the object all the substance that it has." And "this is not so with good." Moreover, Moore treats these two features not as separate but as if entailed by each other. Because natural properties can exist by themselves in a way in which goodness cannot they are also 'substantial'. And goodness is no longer 'substantial' for the *same reason* for which it can also not exist 'by itself'.

Obscure as this was, one can see what Moore was trying to express. There is a sense in which the goodness of this claret could not be conceived to 'exist by itself' in the way its mildness or smoothness can, for one cannot conceive how the claret could be good except through its mildness or smoothness or some other already given property. Nor can one easily conceive how its goodness could be perceived except by way of the perception of what else it is like. But the same does not apply to mildness or smoothness. One can conceive of them as features of the wine which could exist in it independent of what other properties it has, whereas there is something essentially parasitic about the way the value of a thing is always dependent on its other properties. At the same time there is also a sense in which the value of a thing seems unlike its other properties in being no longer among, as it were, its 'body-building' characteristics. Moore expresses this notion misleadingly by saying of natural properties that "if they were all taken away, no object would be left, not even a bare substance: for they are in themselves substantial and give to the object all the substance that it has," and "this is not so with good" (ibid.). But he plainly means that, while ordinary properties are constitutive of the particular nature or specifications of a thing as the object of experience or discourse in question, the same is no longer true of its value.

In *Philosophical Studies*, Moore makes much the same points in dif-

---

5. Schlipp, ed., *Philosophy of G. E. Moore*, "Reply," p. 582.
6. Moore, *Principia*, p. 41.

ferent language. He no longer says that goodness, unlike ordinary properties, "cannot exist by itself in time," but he emphasizes once more that it is typical of goodness to be a *dependent* characteristic.[7] This idea is now expressed by saying that the intrinsic (noninstrumental) goodness or value of a thing 'inheres' in its nature in the sense that what goodness or value a thing has is conditioned by that thing's intrinsic properties. He means by the 'intrinsic properties' of a thing any and all which one would enumerate in answer to the question "What exactly is or would x be like?" (ibid., p. 263); "What exactly are or would be its characteristics as the object of experience or discourse in question?" And he takes the dependence of value on intrinsic properties to entail that for any change in a thing's value there must be some change in its properties otherwise (ibid., p. 265). Moore also no longer says that goodness, unlike ordinary properties, is no longer among the "parts of which the object is made up," or that, unlike them, it is not "in itself substantial"; but he says that goodness no longer counts as another intrinsic characteristic of that to which it is ascribed (ibid., p. 273). The intrinsic properties of a thing are its 'natural' properties: those which between them serve to specify its nature. But goodness, which depends on the intrinsic properties, is such that it cannot itself count as still another one.

This last is the feature of goodness which Moore now takes as the most crucial and distinguishing: 'x is good' is *not an ordinary case of predication*, in the way in which 'x is mild', 'x is sweet', and so on are, so much so that one does not know whether to call goodness a '*property*' or not. One takes properties to belong to a thing, to be its very own, its very specifications as 'this' sort of thing. But goodness, although it is *ascribed* to things, turns out not to function in the ordinary way properties do. It does not add to the distinguishing marks of the thing as the object in question. This is why, in *Philosophical Studies*, Moore distinguishes between the intrinsic properties of a thing and its goodness, which, though an attribute that depends on its intrinsic properties, is not itself another intrinsic property, but rather a 'predicate' to which the word 'property' does not properly apply (ibid.). In the "Reply" he distinguishes the *natural intrinsic properties* of a thing from goodness as a *nonnatural intrinsic property*, while suggesting that by 'nonnatural intrinsic property' he means one which, when it is ascribed to an object, is "not describing that object to any extent at all."[8] The puzzle about goodness to which Moore was trying to draw attention is not unlike the puzzle concerning whether existence is a 'real' pred-

---

7. Moore, *Philosophical Studies*, p. 260.
8. "Reply," pp. 590–91.

icate or not. In both cases one seems confronted with a case of predication such that the ascription of the predicate to an object no longer adds to that object's description.

It seems plain that the distinction in type between natural properties and goodness as a 'property' which is no longer natural is not made to rest on a difference in the way natural properties, as distinct from goodness, are *known*. Admittedly, in *Principia*, Moore calls ethical theories 'naturalistic' which take goodness to be known by "empirical observation and induction."[9] He also warns that "our knowledge is not confined to the things which we can touch and see and feel" (ibid., p. 110), and hints that the knowledge of what is good is not knowledge of this sort, not of an 'object of perception'. But even in *Principia* these scant remarks seem designed to say something further about nonnatural properties rather than to *define* the distinction. In *Philosophical Studies* and in the "Reply," the distinction between 'natural' and 'nonnatural' is drawn exclusively on logical rather than on epistemological grounds. It does not turn on the manner in which these different types of property are known but on a difference in their roles as qualifying characteristics.

It is illuminating in this connection to recall Moore's answer to Broad in the "Reply." Broad, being dissatisfied with Moore's attempts to distinguish between natural and nonnatural properties, offers a distinction in terms of what is sensibly, as opposed to what is nonsensibly, knowable. Moore, in reply, reiterates his own account as given above and adds in conclusion:

> Having failed to find either in *Principia* or in *Philosophical Studies* any account of the distinction between "natural" and "non-natural" intrinsic properties which he considers to be tenable, Mr. Broad goes on (p. 62) to offer an account of the distinction which he does consider to be tenable. And on the account which he gives I have no criticism to offer: it seems to me quite possible that it may be true. He insists that, in giving this account, he is only *describing* natural characteristics, not *defining* "natural"; and it is quite possible that the description which he thus gives of natural intrinsic characteristics, and the description which I suggested in *Philosophical Studies* when I suggested that natural intrinsic properties *describe* what possesses them in a sense in which non-natural ones don't, could, though different, *both* of them be true: it may be that both of these descriptions (and others as well) do apply to all *natural* intrinsic characteristics, and to none that are not natural.[10]

9. Moore, *Principia*, p. 39.
10. Moore, "Reply," p. 592.

This reply deserves further comment. Here we have it from Moore himself that what defines the difference in type between value and the natural properties of a thing is that the latter are constitutive of the 'nature' of the thing but its value is not. Only after having stressed this point does Moore allow, what he takes to be quite another point, that it *might* also be correct to say that properties which are natural in *his* sense are coextensive with those that are epistemologically 'natural' in Broad's sense, and that value, which is first and foremost nonnatural in his sense, may also be epistemologically nonnatural in Broad's sense. It is plain that Moore does not wish to make epistemological nonnaturalness the foundation of the distinction here in question. For in saying that 'natural' and 'nonnatural' *might* be coextensive with 'empirical' and 'nonempirical' he is allowing it to be conceivable that this might not be so, i.e., that there would still be as much reason as before for distinguishing the value of a thing from its natural properties even if it turned out that not all of the latter were known 'by observation and induction' or that goodness were not known by some 'nonsensuous intuition'.

On Moore's own showing, however, there are some residual problems. One of them is that he is baffled by his own main conclusion. It is odd that value, as dependent on intrinsic properties, should not be just another intrinsic property. Ordinarily, when one fact about a thing depends on another, the consequent will count as a further fact about this thing, as being another specification of its prior specifications. And if this seemed to be not so with value, it was counterintuitive enough to need an explanation. Moore felt that there ought to be something to show why value properties are not, and cannot be, intrinsic to the nature of their object; there should be "some characteristic of intrinsic properties which predicates of value never possess." Moore, however, can only add: "And it seems to me quite obvious that there is; only I cannot see what it is."[11]

There is another, and related, problem. Finding it impossible to explain *why* value properties should be nonintrinsic, Moore claims that he can at least 'describe' *what it comes to saying that they are.* But with this project, too, he is only partially successful.

His device here was to say that intrinsic properties differ from value in that their ascription to an object always adds to its description, whereas the ascription of value to it never does; and this might be read as meaning that value ascriptions are in no way whatever descriptively contributive. But this is not Moore's view. His formula in

11. Moore, *Philosophical Studies*, p. 274.

Philosophical Studies is to say that intrinsic properties "describe their object *in a sense in which predicates of value never do*" (ibid., p. 274), which suggests that value ascriptions, rather than being in no way descriptively contributive, are not so only *in a sense* in which intrinsic property ascriptions are. And this notion is confirmed in the "Reply." There is, he says there, "a sense of the word 'describe'," "*one* of the senses in which the word is ordinarily used," in which the ascription of an intrinsic property to a thing always adds to its description, whereas the ascription of value to it never adds to its description "*in that same sense*."[12] The implication is plain: value ascriptions are not different because they have no descriptive role but because they have no such role in *one* ordinary sense of 'describe'.

It is plain why Moore has to draw the distinction with this qualification. His object is to describe what is special about value as a property; and a property is nothing if it is not a mark that characterizes its object. Hence if the difference between value and ordinary properties were to turn on their role in characterizing their object, it could turn only on some difference in the sense in which either performs this role.

In fact, some such distinction as Moore here draws is implicit in ordinary thought. If, say, of two clarets, one is judged good to drink and the other not, one is characterizing them in some way; one ascribes to them a feature by which, at a pinch, they could be identified and distinguished from each other. This is why one may think of their 'being good' or 'poor' as a property. All the same, if asked to 'describe' them, using the term in its ordinary sense, one will not reply that they are good or poor, but that they are mild, or fruity, or acid, or other such terms. One will take these features of the wines and not their degrees of goodness to be constitutive of their ordinary description.

Moore is therefore pointing to a distinction of which ordinary usage has an intuitive comprehension and which is convincing to that extent. But the sense of this intuition is still unexplained. One wants the description spelled out in its ordinary sense: by what principle properties like 'being mild', or 'fruity', or an indefinite host of others are part of it, and how, by the same token, value ascriptions are excluded. Short of such an explanation, whatever rational grounds there are for distinguishing ordinary properties from value will still be unresolved. But here, once again, Moore stops short of an answer. His position in the "Reply" is summed up by saying that the account he has finally been offering is "still vague and not clear." And he adds:

12. "Reply," p. 591.

"To make it clear it would have been necessary to specify the sense of 'describe' in question; and I am no more able to do this now as I was then" (ibid.).

In the end, therefore, Moore can no more explain how exactly value properties are not 'ordinarily descriptive' than he can explain what precludes them from being so. And this problem raises new questions.

V

We saw that Moore resisted Broad's suggestion that 'natural' and 'nonnatural' should be identified with 'empirical' and 'nonempirical'. But Moore's difficulties in explaining his own view may make it appear that Broad had been right after all. The difference between ordinary description and what is not ordinary is explained by the difference between description in empirical and nonempirical terms.

Such a view is not infrequently thought to be entailed by the common meaning of terms such as 'descriptive' or 'factual'. What makes 'x is good' nondescriptive must be the absence of the very same feature that makes natural properties descriptive, or ordinary 'facts in the case'; and what makes a property, in the ordinary sense, descriptive of a thing, or makes it count as a 'fact' about it, is precisely that it is known in an ordinary empirical way. 'Descriptive' or 'factual' are here taken in a way in which 'being fattening' would be part of the description of, or among the facts about, eating pork, whereas 'being counter to the will of God' would not. The reason why 'x is good' may not count as an ordinary descriptive characteristic is that only empirical characteristics count as such.

But such a view could not resolve Moore's problem. Possibly, one may mean an 'ordinary description' to be one in empirical terms, or 'a matter of fact' to be a 'matter of empirical fact'. But this would not be conclusive. 'Descriptive' and 'factual' may also be used in other ways, according to the contrast to which one is drawing attention. 'Describing' may be contrasted with 'explaining'; 'stating a fact' with 'conjecturing' or 'predicting'; a 'point of fact' with a 'point of law'; a 'matter of fact' with a 'matter of opinion' or 'of religious belief'. Each time, what will count as 'descriptive' or 'factual' will vary with the context.

Nor does any of this correspond to the sense in which what is part of the ordinary description of a thing, or what counts as the 'facts' about it, is contrasted with its goodness or value. For Moore, the value of a thing contrasts with its 'intrinsic nature', which is with all that goes to make it what it is as the object for evaluation in question. And it is in the sense in which all these features are part of the ordinary object description that the value no longer is.

Now, quite evidently, what in this context counts as ordinarily descriptive, or as fact in the case, is not confined to what can be empirically known. True, such matters will bulk large among value-determining characteristics. Whether this wine is good to drink will depend in part on whether it is mild or acid; whether I ought to eat pork will depend on whether pork is digestible. What here counts as 'fact' is either what is actually the case and directly verifiable by experience or, as is typical in the case of actions, what can be conjectured with reasonable certainty.

But judgments of another sort may bear on the complexion of the case as well. 'To put this in writing would be to enter into a contract' would add to the 'facts' although making a point of law rather than a point of fact; 'because you would die in the attempt, the consequences would not be for you to face' would make a logical point rather than a factual one; 'employing him would cost that much, given the time and rate of pay' would be to state the result of arithmetical calculation. Nor again would it be any less to refer to a fact in the case (in the required sense) whether one said that this picture was painted on canvas, with oils, mainly in blues and reds, or that the colors were intricately balanced, the design firm and harmonious, the shapes expressive and symbolic. The list, though not scientifically descriptive, would contain the very 'facts' on which the aesthetic value of the picture would largely depend. Likewise, it would be no less to refer to the facts in the case whether one said that this action would destroy the vegetation or the beauty of the countryside or that eating pork leads to indigestion or will be punished by God. All these would be contributions toward the description of the case in the sense in which evaluation is founded on the facts about it, though the specifying claims may express facts or conjectures, empirical or logical truths, symbolic interpretations, or supposedly revealed truths.

All this shows that if 'x is good' is, by contrast with 'x is mild', 'x is sweet', and so on, no longer ordinarily descriptive of x, or a fact about it, in the way these are, this is not because only what is empirically verifiable counts as descriptive or as properly a fact about x. 'Eating pork will be punished by God' is no longer part of a 'factual' (here empirical) description of eating pork. Yet it *is* part of a description of the action on which one could base the claim that it would be bad or ought not to be done. 'Will be punished by God' still counts as another *fact in the case* even though it details a 'fact' in some nonempirical order of discourse. But 'eating pork is bad' or 'ought not to be done' is debarred from counting as *still another* fact about eating pork, in the sense in which even 'will be punished by God' is not. What prevents the value of x from straightforwardly counting as another fact about it cannot therefore be that value is a fact in some nonempirical order of discourse. The crucial ground of the contrast between value and ordinary fact must still lie in something else; and what this is, provided that 'x is good' is not merely prescriptive but affirms some fact or truth, remains to be explained.

VI

It is well to note here that prescriptivists can deal more successfully with this problem than cognitivists. Given that their view is otherwise acceptable, they can explain why 'x is good' is felt not to state another fact about x even in the tenuous sense in which 'x is willed by God' would. The characteristic function of value judgments is to be choice-guiding, to direct affective or conative attitudes; and value judgments perform this job by way of making commendations to others and of making choices for oneself. 'This wine is good' supervenes on 'this wine is mild', 'you ought not to eat pork' on 'pork is fattening' not by way of making a further truth-claim but by way of making an exhortative or otherwise direction-giving noise; and, if so, it is plain that these are utterances which are over and above the facts in the case. The least that all descriptive statements have in common is that they make some truth-claim: 'x is good' is no longer descriptive by being unlike any descriptive statement in no longer doing this. If the non-cognitivist premise is correct, it would explain why 'good' is a misfit as a predicate term. But it is well to note that this explanation implies that the original form of the problem had been misconceived. The question was why 'good' is not an ordinary descriptive term, but that is not really the question. 'Good' is not an *ordinary* descriptive term only because it is not a *descriptive term* at all. Noncognitivism preserves the logical gap between value and fact by reinterpreting it as a hiatus. On the other hand, if there are or seem to be reasons for thinking that 'good' is used in asserting some fact or truth, then the puzzle remains as to what makes it not an 'ordinarily descriptive' fact or truth. If no answer can be found consistent with the assumption that 'x is good' is propositional, this would heavily count in favor of prescriptivism.

VII

I believe, however, that such an answer can be found and that Moore failed to grasp it, though it was before him all along. He was always aware that value predication had two salient features: that value is, on the one hand, essentially resultant, depending on the prior existence of other properties of its object; and that, on the other, it is nonconstitutive, no longer directly adding to the object another qualifying property. *What he failed to see was that the special manner in which value results from the other properties of a thing also makes it nonconstitutive.*

The last was certainly not Moore's view. In the "Reply," he says, in answer to an objection of Broad's, that he would never have suggested that 'good was nonnatural' if he had not supposed it to be 'derivative', but that he did not think that it was nonnatural for that reason. That goodness is 'derivative' is to say "if a thing is good, then, that it is so, *follows from the fact that* it possesses certain natural intrinsic properties"; and there are properties other than goodness which are also derivative but are not nonnatural (ibid., p. 588). The assumption here is that the property dependence of value is not as such different from that of other resultant properties. Moore is aware that goodness does not depend on what a thing is like in any ordinary sense 'of depending on'; that 'this claret is good' does not follow from the fact that it is mild by ordinary material, or formal, implication. The connection, he thought, was, somewhat mysteriously, synthetic and necessary. Nevertheless, he takes it that the fact that this claret is good is as directly a consequence of the fact that it is mild as the fact that it is intoxicating is directly a consequence of the fact that it is alcoholic. Hence the reason why value was not among the natural properties could not be that it was property-dependent.

There is difficulty in presenting the dependence relation in this way. For Moore the dependence of value on the object is on its 'intrinsic nature', and this means on *all* that makes it what it is like as the object in question. But it seems impossible to say that anything *further* follows from the fact that a thing has *all* the properties it has. It is possible to say only that something further follows from the fact that a thing has *all the other* properties it has. And it is plain why. One cannot count the specifications of a thing as *complete* and also say that something further *follows from the fact that* it has these specifications, for in affirming the last one would be denying the first. And yet this is what Moore finds himself committed to saying about goodness. It therefore seems that the crucial point about the fact-dependence of goodness cannot be made by saying that the goodness of a thing is a consequence of *the fact that* the thing has *all* the properties it has. And if one has to say, as one does, that the value of a thing turns on *all* its properties (and not only on all its *other* properties), then there must be something very special about the dependence of value on fact, such that it would allow one even as much as to state this relation without contradiction.

I think that Moore went wrong, however, in not seeing that value, though essentially a resultant characteristic, is not a resultant characteristic in the ordinary way. The goodness of the wine does not depend on its mildness in the way the indigestibility of pork depends on its fat content. The indigestibility of pork depends directly on the *fact that* pork is fat, but the goodness of a wine does not depend directly on the *fact that* the wine is mild. This point is crucial, and, although language may conceal it, it can also illuminate it. One may say that pork is indigestible *because* it is fat, as one may say that this wine is good *because* it is mild. So it may seem that both times one is saying the same sort of thing: the indigestibility of pork is a consequence of the fact that pork is fat, and the goodness of the wine a consequence of the fact that it is mild. Language also suggests a difference, however. One may say that the wine is good both *because* it is mild and *on account of* its mildness, *on the strength* or *on the score* of it; one may also say that one ought not to do this both *because* it would cause hurt and *on account of*, or *in view of* the fact that it would. This language is not applicable to the indigestibility of pork. One may indeed *judge* or *claim* that pork is indigestible on account of the evidence, as one may also judge or claim on account of the evidence that this wine is good. But the difference is that the wine not only is *judged* good but also *is* good on account of its mildness; pork, however, may be judged to be indigestible only on account of its fatness but *is* indigestible because and not on account of it. One may likewise say that it is its fatness that *causes* pork to be indigestible, while one will refer to the mildness of the wine not as the cause of its goodness, but as a *reason* why it is good and to the facts about an action as the reasons or grounds that render it obligatory. 'Reason' figures here like 'reason' for a judgment or belief, as something of which one is cognizant and on which something further depends. But what depends on the reason is not a conclusion or belief but the goodness of a thing or the obligation to do an action. Value is such that things *have* it for reasons, and they are judged to have value by reason of the reasons that confer value on them.

The difference between saying that the wine is good on account of its mildness and that it is intoxicating because it is alcoholic is radical. 'On account of', 'on the score of' suggest 'on taking account', 'on a computation of', 'on a reckoning with'. For something to be good on account of what it is like is thus to say that it is good through what it is like, by way of being correctly accounted for, computed, or reckoned with. Its value is conceived to depend on its properties, but on them as disclosed in experience or beheld in contemplation or anticipation.

What makes the wine good is that, as experienced, it would be experienced as mild and so on, on a truly discriminating perception of its properties. What makes a novel good are its content and form as they would disclose themselves to a perceptive reader. What makes the death penalty bad is what is involved in inflicting it as correctly understood and contemplated by someone. What makes it that one ought not to inflict it is what would be involved in inflicting it as correctly and imaginatively anticipated. Every time the goodness or the obligation is conceived to arise from the properties of the thing or action as the object of a true perception, computation, or anticipation.

The dependence of value on fact is therefore unlike the ordinary dependence of one fact about a thing on another. If the wine is intoxicating because it is alcoholic, then that it is intoxicating will be the *direct* consequence of its being alcoholic. But if it is good because it is mild, its goodness will not result directly from its being mild but only *mediately* so, by way of the effect of its recognition. Of course, if the wine were not mild, it could not be experienced as mild, in a discriminating perception. What a thing is like entails what having a true comprehension of what it is like would be. Hence one may say that the goodness of the wine follows from what it is like, from the existence of certain properties in the wine, but still not directly so but only mediately so, by way of the mildness being correctly appraised. This is why things are good both *because* and on *account* of what they are like.

The difference in the dependence shows up clearly *in how the consequent comes to be known*. If the wine is intoxicating because it is alcoholic, the consequent will be the case whenever the antecedent is the case, and it will be *perceptible all by itself, whether the* antecedent *is known or thought of or not*. But if the wine is good because it is mild, the consequent will be *perceptible only* when the antecedent is not only the case but is *also known and attended to*. It is a basic truth about the judgment of value that value cannot be judged of except when the facts from which it results are before one. Only then will the value that belongs to an object *come to be in evidence*. The cognitive object-dependence of value entails that it is discerned only by some cognitively object-dependent perception. Moore did not notice this point, but it was stressed by later intuitionists such as W. D. Ross. Whatever it is, he says, that causes a noise to be loud, "I can perceive it to be loud without knowing anything of the causes which account for this"; but "it is only by knowing or thinking my act to have a particular character . . . that I know, or think, it to be right."[13]

13. W. D. Ross, *The Foundations of Ethics* (Oxford: Clarendon Press, 1939), p. 168.

Moore should therefore have allowed that the dependence of value on fact is as distinctive a feature as its noninclusion among the facts. For such dependence is uniquely different from the ordinary dependence of one fact about a thing on another. Actually, Moore was groping for this point in *Principia*, when he said of goodness that it could not be '*imagined*' otherwise than property-dependent. The natural properties of things may or may not depend on the prior existence of other properties of them. But the value of a thing could not be conceived at all except as depending on the features it otherwise possessed; and this follows from its cognitive dependence. As resulting by way of the comprehension of its object, value cannot be conceived to exist without dependence on what is featured in such a comprehension. This is why nothing *can* be good without something further about its object to make it so.

Here is also the reason why the value of a thing can be said to depend on *all* the facts about it. If value depended directly *on the facts*, it could not depend on *all* of them but only on all the *others*; for anything that depends on the fact that a thing has a certain characteristic will add to it a further characteristic. But value can depend on *all* the facts since it does not directly, but only mediately, depend on *any* of them.

Here also is the reason why the value of things should be a fact which is not among the ordinary facts about them. This is implied by the very dependence of value on these facts. In counting the properties of a thing one will count any feature that would qualify it as the object of discourse in question, including any feature it would have as a direct consequence of its having certain other features. Let us call these the object's *first-order properties*: the ones which between them constitute the nature of the object as the object in question and, through its nature, as the possible bearer of its value. It will then be a truism that its value will not be among them. That a thing has value *presupposes* that it has a constituted nature already; and it has value by virtue of its nature, as a property that supervenes on what it is like, instead of being part of what it is like. In relation to the object properties on which it depends, value is a *second-order property*, one which emerges only when its antecedent first-order properties are correctly and fully taken into account.

It is only as depending on first-order properties, however, that value will be a second-order property. It may also be a third-order property depending on a second-order property. Thus one may say that these oak trees ought to be preserved because they are beautiful. That they are beautiful may here be represented as a second-order feature, one depending on account being taken of other features which are first-order features; and 'ought to be preserved' would thus be a third-order feature depending on account being taken of a second-order feature. The general point is simply that value, on whatever grounds it is ascribed, is never on the same level of discourse with these grounds themselves. That the trees ought to be preserved is no longer part of their nature as aesthetic objects for the same reason for which that they have aesthetic value is no longer part of their nature as 'natural' objects. That they have aesthetic value depends on their nature as 'natural' objects; that they ought to be preserved on their aesthetic value as comprehended. Both times what *depends* on some prior nature or description of the object *as comprehended* cannot be part of the comprehension of that very nature or description on which it depends. It can add nothing to the first-order nature of the trees that, if their first-order nature is taken note of, they are something good to see; and it adds nothing to their second-order nature as something good to see that on taking this into account they ought to be preserved.

Here, then, is the principal reason for speaking of value as a 'nonnatural' property, as a 'fact' that is no longer an 'ordinary' fact, as a predicate that can be ascribed to things without further specifying their distinctive character as the sort of things they are. It is part of the ordinary description of this wine as a beverage that it is mild, alcoholic, and so on, but no longer that it is good; and part of the ordinary description of eating pork that it is fattening and, maybe, frowned upon by God, but no longer that it ought not to be eaten. That the former are properties which are part of the ordinary description of the wine or of eating pork is to say that they are part of their description in the first instance; and to say that '*x* is good' and '*x* ought to be done' is no longer ordinarily descriptive of *x* is to say that they are no longer part of the description of *x* or of its description in the first instance.

The reason why one speaks like this is patent. That anything can be good or ought to be done presupposes that it can be conceived as possessing a distinctive nature in the first place, fully accountable in itself and distinct from anything that would follow from it only as taken account of. This is what forces the apartheid of value from ordinary fact. Value, which as fact or truth turns on correctly beholding the nature of things, cannot be a fact or truth in the same order of discourse as is the nature of these things themselves. As a 'fact' that is not among 'the facts in the case' it is not necessarily esoteric but essentially supervenient.

As mentioned, Moore sometimes hesitated whether value may strictly be called a 'property'. The role of property terms is to ascribe to things a mark by which they can be identified and distinguished from others;

and value performs this role, but not in the standard way. It is not that 'x is good' in no way characterizes x. 'Bring the good wine' is no less a workable instruction than 'bring the mild wine'. It also characterizes the wine, not in terms of its first-order nature but of an implication of beholding it in this nature. Though their value properties can make objects distinguishable, however, that is not their most characteristic role. This remains reserved for the first-order properties on which value supervenes. The reason is partly that things of different natures can share the same value properties, so that 'bring the wine which is mild and dry' will distinguish the object more unambiguously than 'bring the good one'. But, more essentially, characterization in value terms is logically secondary to it in first-order terms. To recognize the object as good, one must first recognize it in the character which would be the ground of its goodness; and, for purposes of identification, instruction in terms of this character would suffice, without need for also drawing the evaluative conclusion. Value therefore plays the part of a property term, but not all the way. It *can* serve as an identification mark, but broadly it is *supernumerary* in this role.

VIII

It is well here to note the implications of these reflections for the notion of the naturalistic fallacy. When Moore uses this term in its specific sense (rather than in the generic sense of the patent miselucidation of any term, whether a value term or not) he means by it the patent error of trying to elucidate the meaning of 'good' in terms of some 'natural' characteristic, whether complex or simple. 'X is good' cannot mean the same as 'x is desired', or 'pleasant', or 'conducive to survival', because these are not properties which, like goodness, are distinct in being both object-dependent and nonintrinsic. By this standard all such attempted elucidations would be ruled out on a point of principle.

But all that this standard implies, on Moore's own showing, is that any elucidation of 'good' would have to satisfy these formal requirements; and there is nothing *in them* to justify the wider claims often made for the naturalistic fallacy argument. As far as Moore's own characterization of these requirements goes, there is nothing in them to entail that goodness must be a simple quality and could not be defined in more complex terms; or that, if a property, it could only be one apprehended by some nonsensuous intuition and not possibly one apprehended by the testimony of feeling or a reviewer's responses. All of this may or may not be so; but none of it, one way or the other, follows directly from Moore's attempts to clarify the logical role of value as a property term.

IX

How this conclusion may offer release from the deadlock between intuitionism and prescriptivism I shall briefly indicate in the rest of this essay. It has been noted that for 'x is good' one may substitute 'x is such that it would be rightly desired', 'x would be the fitting object of a pro-attitude'; and there are other substitutions: 'x deserves favor', 'x would justify favor', and 'there is a case for favoring x'. One may interpret these sentences as expressing the claim that x has the power to evoke favor by way of a true comprehension of what it is like; that it would justify favor in the sense that it would sustain, on a true comprehension of its properties, the favor of those who are for it already; or would deserve favor, in the sense that it would command, on a true comprehension of its properties, the favor of those who are not yet for it. It is presupposed here that certain properties of things, like mildness in wines, contrasts or harmonies in pictures or music, will evoke favor in those who experience them or will come to evoke it once they have become familiar with them; or that certain properties or states of affairs, for example concerning the contribution they would make to the life or well-being of sentient beings, would evoke approval in those who contemplate them, or would come to evoke it if those beings used their imagination on them. It would follow that what favor is *actually* bestowed on things or states of affairs is corrigible by what may be broadly termed 'rational methods'. One may learn to bestow on things greater favor than before by becoming more discerning or discriminating about their properties, and one may conceive of this process of learning as approximating or as reaching an ideal limit. This limit would have been reached when the favor bestowed on something would no longer be corrigible by any more discriminating and sustained experience of its properties or by any more knowledgeable and imaginative assessment of them. One may speak of such favor as well founded and distinguish it from other value attitudes which, by contrast, might be described as misplaced, cockeyed, capricious, biased, compulsive, or plain stupid; and one might speak of things or states of affairs as being such that they have it 'in' them to evoke such well-founded favor. That something is good, that it would be rightly or fittingly favored, would here be taken as entailing precisely these points. 'Rightness' and 'fittingness' are relational terms commonly used to express that one thing is in agreement or in line with another in a certain respect. That an object would be rightly or fittingly favored would here entail that an attitude of favor toward it would be in line with *all* its favor-evoking capacities, that it would be supported by a true and sustained appraisal of the properties of the object.

Goodness or value on this showing would be a *dispositional property* of things as truly comprehended, and it would be defined in terms partly psychological and partly not: in terms of a power to evoke responses, but responses as they ultimately would be in the ideal case of a *perfect*, no-further-corrigible, comprehension of the things in question. Value judgments would therefore be only weakly verifiable and in principle all corrigible, for the ideal limit of a perfect comprehension may always turn out to have not yet been reached.

The support for the claim that something is good or has value would, on such a view, be empirical. Judiciously conducted experiment would be the method of settling questions of value for oneself. It would be the method for others to use in verifying one's claims about the value of things. In trying to settle such questions for oneself one would seek to determine what favor something would evoke in one on a sincere attempt to comprehend it perceptively and patiently; and in trying to convince others, one would invite them to engage in such experimentation, while aiding them as far as possible in acquiring the necessary discrimination or information. Judgments of value require one to seek *acquaintance as a responding being* with what can be tasted in foods or wines, seen in pictures, read in novels, heard in music, experienced in love or friendship, in exercise or cogitation, in a free or dependent form of life. In trying to judge what is good in this way one will come to learn how to favor things in accordance with the favor they have it 'in' them to evoke. But there need never be anything finite about learning well-founded appreciation. There may always be more to be learned about things through greater discrimination and familiarity that may still modify what favor one has toward them at any point prior to the ideal case of perfect comprehension.

This view has its antecedents jointly in Hume and Kant and differs from emotivist views, as well as from Moore's, while incorporating features from each. Emotivists view 'x is good', 'x deserves favor', and the like as utterances whose primary use is to express commendations, not involving any testable objective claim. They also allow that such commendations may be supported by 'rational methods', or indeed that it is a feature of commendations using 'good' or 'ought' to make the *implicit* claim that they are so supportable. But once this last is admitted, there seems little point in persisting with the emotivist approach. This approach had been devised on the assumption that no cognitive meaning could be given to 'x is good', 'x deserves favor', 'x is commendable'. But the very assumption that favor for x can be supported by rational means implies that one may also *say* and *judge* that favor for x is so supportable; and, if taken as affirming this, 'x is commendable' and 'x is deserving of favor' turn again into statements that make some objectively testable claim. It thus becomes possible to reverse the emotivist approach by saying that it is the primary and explicit function of 'x is good' to stake out the claim *that* favor for x would be supportable by appropriate rational procedures in a broad sense. And this could be held without prejudice to the point that in using 'x is good' in speaking to others, one uses it with characteristic emotive or prescriptive overtones. 'This wine is good', when said to another, is typically said commendingly, with a view to promoting his 'agreement in attitude'. But in thus *speaking* commendingly, one seeks to achieve one's aim by way of gaining assent to the claim one is making, namely, that what is commended is also commendable, that a case for favoring the thing in question will be found by those who will look for it. At the same time one can now treat the commendatory use of value language as the special case it really is. Emotivists must say that someone who is judging or thinking to himself that something is good is engaged in commending it to himself, or exhorting himself to be for it, or resolving to be for it in the future, all of which is decidedly odd. On our showing one would be free to say that he was simply engaged in judging or thinking, for example, that the wine before him has got what it takes.

That 'x is good' makes an objective claim brings this point of view into line with Moore's in that on both accounts the value of things is essentially dependent on what they are like. At the same time it becomes clear why their value depends only *indirectly* on their properties; for it is only by way of being comprehended, and not simply through being existent, that the properties of things can arouse responses of favor or disfavor. Moore also insisted, however, that if value depends on what things are like, it must be conceived as depending on this *solely*.[14] The dependence is such as to entail that if two things are exactly alike, and one is good, then the other *must* also be good *in every conceivable universe*. There is therefore mutual exclusiveness between the view that the value of things depends on their nature and the view that it depends on their being an object of interest. If the value of things depends to any extent on the last, one could no longer say of two things exactly alike that if one is good the other *must* be

14. Moore, *Philosophical Studies*, p. 260.

good *in every conceivable universe*, but only that it *must* be good among members, as it were, of the *same psychological universe*.

The view suggested departs from Moore on this point. That something has the power to evoke favor on a true comprehension of what it is like would depend partly on what it is like and partly on the affectivity of those who experience it or contemplate it for what it is like. The value of things, on our showing, would always hold in relation to beings or to a class of beings with a nature receptive to what is disclosed in experience or contemplation. Nothing could conceivably have value except for those who can love or hate. Nor is there anything necessarily noxious in such a view. That the value of things depends on the facts about them does not entail that it depends *solely* on them. This would be entailed only by a further assumption which Moore in fact makes, namely, that when A says that *x* is good and B denies this, A and B must *always* be contradicting each other. True enough, this assumption is supported by the fact that in ordinary discourses we tend to act on it. One takes disagreements about value between human beings as primarily a result of differences in comprehension. One's approach is regulated by the initial assumption that if one is right in thinking that there really is a case for favoring *x*, others too could be brought to favor *x* if only they came to be as comprehending about it as one is oneself. But one is also prepared reluctantly to treat this assumption as defeasible. If one were to contend that taking exercise was good on its own account, and someone else denied this, one would first inquire when he had last taken it. Only when he had assured us that he had been taking it every day and been loathing it all the time would one feel forced to fall back on saying, "Well, then, it really isn't good as far as you are concerned." Many cases are such that, unlike this one, there is no reasonably sure way of deciding whether or not the difference in value judgments might still be caused by a difference in comprehension. In such cases, one is neither inclined nor compelled to treat the general working assumption as defeated.

One should not therefore be misled by the fact that in ordinary speech one claims that things are good or have value without adding the qualifying clause "at least as far as I or all or most humans are concerned." For that such a qualifying clause is not normally *mentioned* does not imply that it is not *logically presupposed* or that it may not sometimes be in place to bring it into the open. The situation here is not so different from that which applies to the logic of dispositional properties otherwise. When A says '*x* is digestible' and B denies this, they will normally be taken to be contradicting each other; nor will one expect them to add each time, "I mean, of course, only as far as

I or all or most humans, and not necessarily as far as Martians or koala bears or anteaters are concerned." Nevertheless, these are qualifications which are presupposed and so '*x* is not digestible' is sometimes not the contradictory of '*x* is digestible'. '*X* is good', '*x* would command favor on a true comprehension of what it is like', are similar. That one here means that it is the favor of *humans* that *x* would command goes without saying; and that one can speak of humans per se rests on a working assumption in which, more often than not, it makes sense to persist.

My principal contention in this essay is that a view of this sort cannot be ruled out as just another instance of committing the naturalistic fallacy. One may call such a view a naturalistic, as distinct from a metaempirical, account of value on the ground that it makes value a natural fact or characteristic: there is nothing epistemologically or ontologically 'nonnatural' about the fact that some things are, in virtue of their nature, more fitted than others to command the favor of human beings. But to *call* a view naturalistic is not yet to *brand* it, unless its 'naturalism' involves some patent error; and the patent error of 'naturalism' in any account of goodness or value lies in another dimension. It relates to the confusion of goodness or value with anything that could still count as part of the nature or description of the thing evaluated. And this error cannot be imputed to the view that the value of things consists of their power to justify or to command favor on a true comprehension of what they are like. On the contrary, the necessary apartheid of 'fact' from 'value' would, on such a view, be patently clear. To conceive of human responses to a world of objects or states of affairs as these responses would be on a true comprehension of these things, one has to conceive of such objects or states of affairs as already fully describable in themselves. Value predication must be in a separate order of discourse because it relates to *noetic* responses, that is, to responses *to* things *on account of* the character which is conceived to *be* theirs whether taken account of or not. There is thus a logical bar to including the world of value in the world of fact, if 'the world of fact' means anything that in turn can become an object of evaluation.

That value is no part of fact in this sense does not mean, however, that it cannot be fact in any sense, or only some odd 'nonnatural' fact. It simply means that the logic of discourse requires a distinction between the world of things comprehended in the character they have or would have and a world of human responses in full face of the character of things so comprehended. That value affirmations relating to such responses are also in a characteristic way normative or direction-giving is implied rather than contradicted by this account. The

enterprise of judging the power of a thing to evoke favor on a true
comprehension is in the service of learning to appreciate that thing
with the aid of such judgments and in accordance with the ideal canon
of sufficiency implied in them.

[6]

Hume on Is and Ought

I

Unlike old soldiers, the rhetoric of the great neither dies nor fades away. And so Hume's celebrated 'is-ought' passage still provokes debate.

Hume was worried about the relation between ought statements and those supporting them: between 'tolerance brings peace' or 'is God's will', and 'so one ought to be tolerant'. He denies the deducibility of the latter from the former, as the 'ought' expresses 'a new relation or affirmation', 'entirely different from the others'. And this is commonly taken as saying that the ought statement is 'different' and nondeducible because it is no longer a 'purely factual statement', to wit one that makes another ordinarily testable truth claim.

However, recent criticism, by W. D. Hudson[1] and others, points out that Hume says other things seemingly inconsistent with this. In the passage, he mentions 'ought' and 'virtue' interchangeably, and 'tolerance is virtuous' as in the same boat as 'one ought to be tolerant'. But, also, he treats the virtue of an action as sensibly discernible by the approbation which it evokes, and takes us to mean by a virtuous action that we will approve of it on contemplation. That tolerance is virtuous seems here as ordinarily 'factual' as 'tolerance brings peace', and this would contradict what he is saying about the 'entire difference' in kind between the two statements.

How is one to understand Hume here so as to save him from incoherence? It is said by Antony Flew that Hume really meant that

Reprinted with permission of the publisher from *Canadian Journal of Philosophy* 6 (1976):359–78.
    1. W. D. Hudson, ed., *The Is/Ought Question* (New York: Macmillan, 1969).

moral statements, rather than being about attitudes, serve to express them. The real Hume was the ancestor of noncognitivism and the 'is-ought' passage its early charter. By contrast, it is said by Alasdair MacIntyre that really Hume did not mean to deny deducibility. When he said that it 'seemed inconceivable', he meant that it only seemed so without really being so. Hume anticipated John Searle: 'ought' is used to state an institutional fact, and so can be entailed by other matters of fact. Instead of arguing with these views, I shall offer a counterthesis. Hume meant every word of what he said; that 'is' is entirely different from 'ought', that 'ought' is not deducible from 'is', and that ought-statements are about a kind of sensibly testable fact. Moreover, he was entirely consistent, if not right as well.

Before I start, one preliminary observation. I shall not discuss the problem specifically by reference to ought-statements. Nothing is gained by focusing on some alleged special features of Hume's use of 'ought' (e.g., as the term for being prescribed by a commonly accepted rule). Hume's concern is with moral and evaluative language generally, and 'ought' is only one, and the least common, term in his moral vocabulary. 'Moral distinctions' are made in calling things good or bad, praiseworthy or blameworthy, virtuous or vicious, laudable or contemptible, amiable or odious, entitled or not entitled to our regard, approbation, esteem. One makes them when ascribing merit or demerit to actions on specifically 'moral' grounds, but also, more broadly, in any ascription of merit or demerit. In this broad sense, one makes 'moral distinctions' in ascribing merit to foods, wines, works of art, or any other 'species of natural beauty'; praiseworthiness to wit or humor, odiousness to uncleanliness or to being a bore. All such judgments, for the same reason, belong to a class of their own by not being about 'matters of fact' or deducible from them.

II

I think that problems arise out of an insufficiently careful and sympathetic reading of what Hume is trying to say about ascriptions of merit. The 'is-ought' passage becomes intelligible and consistent on what I take to be Hume's overall view, one expressed quite un-ambiguously in the *Inquiry* as well as in places in the *Treatise*. But there are passages in the *Treatise* which, though not necessarily inconsistent with his definitive views in the *Inquiry*, are sufficiently open-ended to allow other interpretations; and some note will have to be taken of them.

I don't see good enough reason for taking Hume to say that merit statements are nonfactual by having no truth value, and for taking the nondeducibility thesis to be the expression of this. At most some Hume passages could be taken as implying that 'x has merit' expresses rather than states approbation of x. But there is nothing in Hume to suggest that 'x has merit' derives its meaning from its prescriptive force as an utterance, much as Hume stresses that it is not among the 'calm and indolent judgments of the understanding'. If it is in the nature of merit judgments to 'beget passions', it is not because of their illocutionary force. Quite on the contrary, the persistent evidence is that Hume takes merit judgments to have a propositional meaning like others and like them, to make some kind of testable truth-claim. He opens the *Inquiry* saying that only the "disingenuous disputant" can deny "the reality of moral distinctions" and pretend that "all characters and actions are alike *entitled* to the regard of everyone."[2] The question is not whether 'knowledge of them can be attained', but how it can, and what it is of. In both *Treatise* and *Inquiry*, Hume debates how merit is 'distinguished', 'discovered', 'discerned': whether "by means of our ideas or impressions," "by demonstrative reasoning," or "by means of some sentiment," "by sentiment alone,"[3] or "by reason with the concurrence of sentiment". There are "judgments by which we distinguish moral good and evil,"[4] and there is testimony by which to make the distinction.

Hume also quite plainly claims that this testimony, although not of a kind to support 'matters of fact', is not nonempirical either. At the very opening of Book Three he recalls his logical-positivist program. "We must preserve to the end the evidence of our first propositions": "nothing is ever present to the mind but its perceptions" (ibid.). The question is "whether we distinguish betwixt vice and virtue by means of our ideas, or impressions"; and he decides that, as "they are not discoverable merely by the comparison of ideas," they must be "discoverable by means of some impression or sentiment." In Book II of the *Treatise* (p. 276) he says programmatically that they are discernible by "a calm impression of reflection," an impression of "affection or disgust, approbation or blame." Things have merit or demerit if, on a calm reflection, they command such responses, or, more generally, are to our "taste"; and taste, aided by understanding and reflection, shows what merit they have.

It seems strange to contemporary ears that Hume will say this, while

2. David Hume, *An Inquiry Concerning the Principles of Morals*, ed. Charles W. Hendel (New York: Liberal Arts Press, 1957), pp. 5–6.
3. David Hume, *A Treatise of Human Nature*, ed. L. A. Selby-Bigge (London: Clarendon Press, 1967), pp. 456ff.
4. Hume, *Treatise*, p. 456.

evidently sensitive to the distinction between statements of merit and of fact and the unique status of the former. He is emphatic that the merit of things is not found among the facts about them. The primary role of merit judgments is not to make us better informed about things; it is to correct our practical, rather than our propositional, attitudes. But Hume's grounds for distinguishing between statements of merit and of fact cannot have been ours. He could not have meant that 'x has merit' was 'different' by having no truth value, or one not testable in familiarly intelligible ways. He does allow, in fact he insists, that merit discernment is different from ordinary cognition. Merit is not proved demonstratively, or 'perceived by reason'; it is known by a 'concurrence of reason and sentiment'. But the merit judgment does not need any unfamiliar cognitive skills: what enters into it (as the *Inquiry* shows) are reasoning from premises, inference, object understanding, contemplation, and a species of perception ('internal feeling'), all in a special mix. If the merit judgment is 'different', this is not therefore because it is epistemologically 'nonnatural'.

What Hume says is that 'tolerance is good' differs from 'tolerance brings peace' by not belonging, like the latter, to the 'disquisitions of the understanding'. And this is a distinction not about cognitive method but cognitive orientation. Understanding and 'taste' (by which merit is judged) address themselves to different issues. The one is the 'discovery of truth or falsehood', the other the importance of things to us, their 'tastiness', as it were, their relevance for us as things to be responded to with favor or disfavor. The researches of the understanding seek truth purely and simply; their sole object is to make our beliefs and expectations conform to how things are. The discernments of 'taste' are in aid of acquiring a *practical sense* of the importance of things, an effective appreciation of their weight for us, rather than just, or even primarily, of getting to know that they are important. The quest for importance, though for some kind of fact or truth, is no part of the 'calm and indolent' quest for natural fact or truth.[5]

III

I said earlier that problems of Hume interpretation arise from a faulty reading of what Hume is trying to say about ascriptions of merit, and I shall have to give further consideration to what he takes judgments of merit to be about. I have so far attributed to him the

5. Hume, *Inquiry*, p. 105.

view that things have merit or demerit if, on a calm reflection, they command responses of favor or disfavor; and that merit is discerned by the responses evoked, on the view of them, on this condition. What has merit on this view will be an object of favor, but not everything that is favored will have merit, nor will everything that has merit be favored. That things have merit will be to imply that the truth about them will direct us to favor them, rather than only that we are favoring them. Only if some such view is attributable to Hume have his views on value and fact a chance of being viable and consistent.

But Hume is not commonly read as if this was his view or if, to the extent that it was, this was important. And this may be as much Hume's fault as it is his reader's. It is only in the *Inquiry* that Hume succeeds in making his position unambiguously clear, whereas the *Treatise* allows, though it doesn't compel, a different interpretation.

Hume introduces the Book on the Passions in the *Treatise* with a division of the impressions into 'original' and 'secondary'. Original impressions "arise in the soul without antecedent perception," secondary or reflective impressions by interposition of some "preceding thought or perception." The latter are the passions, which in turn may be calm or violent. And it is, from a calm passion, "a calm impression of reflection," that, he says here, "the sense of beauty and deformity in action, composition, and external objects"[6] is derived. There is also no doubt that this same view is elaborated and refined in the *Inquiry*, where beauty or deformity, merit or demerit are said to be shown by a sentiment founded "on a proper discernment of the object." The principle recalls Butler's view of moral perception as resting on a 'sentiment of the understanding'. However, Hume's way of speaking in the rest of the *Treatise* is less well-defined. He speaks of merit being shown by a sentiment which "the reflecting on actions naturally occasions," by a sentiment of blame or approbation "which you have from the contemplation of an action," or one which an action "gives us by the mere view or survey" (ibid., p. 475). The omission here is the qualification of 'contemplation' or 'reflection' by reference to its 'calmness', with its implications of dispassionateness and object-adequacy. The omission may not have been intended, the 'calmness' of reflection or contemplation being taken for granted. But at best Hume in the *Treatise* must have been less aware of the need for being definite on this point than he was in the final statement of his position in the *Inquiry*.

In any case the omission permits another interpretation. What is approved of, on a bare contemplation or view, may be approved of

6. Hume, *Treatise*, p. 276.

at the bare thought of the thing, whether adequate to the truth about it or not. What has merit will then become anything that is so approved of. The merit of things will be decided by the de facto favor that we extend to them, and statements of merit will be *reports about what we favor or not*. Hume is frequently taken as saying just this, and had he meant this, he would be liable to every stricture that has been laid on views of this kind.

In fact, there is no good reason for thinking that he ever did, for this would make him incomprehensibly inconsistent with himself. The passage most frequently quoted against him comes directly before the 'is-ought' passage which was meant to sum up the preceding argument. And plainly if merit judgments merely reported de facto approval, the very question of their relation to supporting fact would not arise. De facto approval, being de facto, stands in no need of being backed by the facts in the case whether demonstratively or otherwise.

But, in any case, and however one reads the *Treatise*, that merit judgments are reports of de facto approval is no part of Hume's final summary in the *Inquiry*. Merit, he says there, is discerned by sentiment, but only by a "proper sentiment," and not by a "false relish," one which can still be "corrected by argument and reflection"; and a 'proper sentiment' is one antecedently founded on a "proper discernment of the object."[7] The discernment of merit depends on the concurrence of reason and sentiment.

The judgment of merit here becomes complex. It relies on object responses as they would be had the object been thoroughly understood and presented to view. The sentiment that testifies to the merit is not in one's immediate response: that for a time needs "suspending." It must be elicited: object exploration is the first step—"if any material circumstance be left unknown or doubtful, we must first employ our inquiry or intellectual faculties to assure us of it": "it is often necessary that much reasoning should precede, nice distinctions be made, just conclusions drawn, distant comparisons formed, complicated relations examined, and general facts fixed and ascertained." In addition, object exploration must be sufficiently complete—"everything must be known and ascertained on the side of the object or action": "all the circumstances of the case" (ibid., p. 108), "all the objects and their relation to each other." And, after thus "paving the way," evaluation can take place, once again with the mind's aid. The facts, complete as ascertained, must be received in "review" or "contemplation." The "proper sentiment" is elicited by testing out our responses against such a view. Evaluation may be vitiated not only by a mistake "of *fact*," but also by

7. Hume, *Inquiry*, p. 6.

one "of *right*." This latter results from a lack of evaluative probity, a failure to review whole what one full well knows. This knowledge is thus prevented from taking effect. Oedipus killed his father innocently and in ignorance. On the other hand, when Nero killed his mother he knew "all the circumstances of the fact." If we can see Nero's deed as detestable, as he did not, this is a consequence of "the rectitude of our dispositions" (ibid., p. 109), a rectitude Nero was without—a rectitude which stems from not closing one's mind to any part of known fact.

Hume's account here misleads in suggesting that all of this must be gone through in actually making an evaluative judgment. Had all the facts to be ascertained first, one might have to wait forever for one's right to pronounce on merit. Rather, Hume was laying down the conditions which would make the judgment of merit itself right or warranted. The object's worth would be conclusively indicated only by a response that, if put to the test, could survive every relevant object-scrutiny.

The *Inquiry* says that things have merit when they "give to a spectator the pleasing sentiment of approbation." Hume's account of the merit judgment is not, however, quite captured by this definition. One must interpret the 'spectator' as the diligent reviewer; the 'sentiment of approbation' as the one that has first run the gauntlet of critical testing. Hume might have underlined the fact that one discerns merit by way of assessing it; and that what we assess, by testing out our responses to things, is their power, through what they are like, to engage and support our favor by way of a correct appraisal of what they are like. Such things are not merely held in regard. They are 'entitled' to our regard. This is because, to a diligent human reviewer, they give license, as well as cause, to bestow his regard on them.

IV

We can now return to Hume's logical motivation in dividing merit from fact, 'taste' from 'reason'. The critical assessment view of the merit judgment is the pivotal point. Merit is known with 'the concurrence of reason'; precisely because of this it cannot be 'derived from reason'. Because of the way it depends on ordinary fact, it cannot be part of ordinary fact.

It was said earlier that Hume's right to this distinction can be questioned. Merit, he claimed, is a sensibly discernible fact, but it "consists not of any matter of fact, which can be discovered by the understanding."[8] The judgment of merit expresses an entirely "new relation or affirmation"; the "vice entirely escapes you as long as you consider the object" (ibid., p. 469). The objection is that Hume cannot have his cake and eat it: insist that merit is not within the category of ordinary fact and define it as another epistemologically 'natural' fact. But Hume's position is not due to an oversight. His idea, in both *Treatise* and *Inquiry*, is that it is precisely his naturalist interpretation which entails the dichotomy between merit and fact. Because merit is discerned by critical taste it is not and cannot be among the matters addressed by the understanding.

The question is on what grounds, if not epistemological, merit can be a fact which is not among the facts discovered by the understanding. Hume's answer is at first odd. The role of reason (or understanding) is "the discovery of truth and falsehood" (ibid., p. 458). The matters discovered by reason comprise every matter of truth or fact about an object. But one wonders what is left then of the cognitive role of taste. Hume seems committed to saying that the merit of x is a fact which is not among the facts about x; and this seems incoherent. But it need not be so. He could mean that the merit of an object, though a matter of some fact, was not, in the ordinary way, a matter of fact *about the object*. While also a fact, it was not another fact in the case. He could then contrast the discernment of object-merit by critical taste with that of object-truth by the understanding.

In describing "the boundaries between reason and taste,"[9] Hume implies just this. Each has a cognitive role, but they relate to formally different issues. Reason, in "conveying the knowledge of truth and falsehood," "discovers objects as they really stand in nature, without addition or diminution"; without the "gilding or staining" of "natural objects with the colors borrowed from internal sentiment" (ibid.). Reason here covers everything true of objects, considered in the character in which they can be met in experience, and indifferently to what they are to us, to any 'impression of reflection' (any affective response) which the perception or thought of them might arouse. Taste, by contrast, in discerning merit from a calm impression of reflection, addresses itself to what things, given what they are, are to us. It is exercised in raising the question of object-relevance which, in exercising reason, we suppress. And, in doing so, it addresses an issue which is formally different from the issue for the understanding. The reflective importance of things to us is not, and cannot be, in the same

8. Hume, *Treatise*, p. 468.
9. Hume, *Inquiry*, p. 112.

category of fact about them as the facts about them 'as they stand in nature'.

The reasoning is not quite so clear in the *Treatise*. Hume says, in at least one place, that merit is not a matter of fact about the *object* because it is one about *ourselves*. That a thing has merit "means nothing but" that a person has a sentiment of approval from the contemplation of it. This is why the merit escapes one as long as one "considers the object," and is found only in turning one's reflection into one's own breast, to a sentiment occasioned by "the reflecting" on the object. "Here is a fact; but it is an object of feeling, not of reason."[10] The fact is about our response to the object, not in any way about the object itself. However, if a person has a sentiment of approval from the contemplation of an object, then, likewise, the object will command his approval on such contemplation. The relation is the same, one way or the other; and Hume states it normally (and more naturally) in the second way: what is good "*gives* a certain satisfaction upon the general view or survey" (ibid., p. 475); it "*gives* to a spectator the pleasing sentiment of approbation." This formulation keeps merit ascribed to the object as a kind of dispositional, and sensibly discernible, property. The question therefore remains why it should not count as just an additional fact about the object.

Hume's general view implies that it cannot be a dispositional property like others. Objects have the power to evoke a response only by way of the perception or thought of them in some character or other: one discerns their power from an "internal feeling" which is an "impression of reflection." This power is not among the properties of the object "as it stands in nature," those which are directly disclosed by the "original impressions" to be had from it, and which give it the character in which it can be perceived or thought of. It is rather a property which belongs to the object indirectly, and once removed; one reflexively conferred on it by our mental representations and the effect of them on our responses to what they represent. This is why taste, in eliciting this power with the aid of reflection, "has a productive faculty"; it "raises, in a manner a new creation."[11]

However, Hume's case cannot rest only on this feature. That merit is a reflexively conferred, rather than a "natural," property of objects makes it a different, but not necessarily "entirely" different, fact about them. Some reflexively dependent properties are readily counted among the matters of fact about their objects. Tigers are both striped and

10. Hume, *Treatise*, p. 469.
11. Hume, *Inquiry*, p. 112.

terrifying; and much as these properties differ in how they relate to their object, they are counted side by side among the matters of fact about tigers. The same book may have a chapter on their appearance, and another on their impact, through the sight or thought of them, on the hunter, while being throughout a factual study about tigers. This applies generally to the ascription of de facto value to things. There is no 'entire' difference between saying that a beer is light and a favorite, an athlete successful and much admired. Only the judgment that the beer is good and the athlete admirable seems entirely apart from the antecedent judgment of fact. This is why it is important that Hume can distinguish between the good and the approved. Reflexive dependence cannot be all that sets merit off from the category of ordinary fact. What matters also is how it is so dependent.

It needs Hume's final account of the judgment of merit in the *Inquiry* to show the logical strength of his case. Merit here is discerned by *critical* taste: it consists of the reflective power of things to evoke regard for them, through what they are like, and by way of a true, rather than some random, view of what they are like. It is here built into the concept of merit that it cannot be within the same category of 'fact' as the facts explored by 'reason'. A thing has merit only if it will arouse a favorable sentiment by way of a correct understanding of it; and this entails the concept of an object with a nature, or character, in which it can be identified and known *in extenso* in the first place, and in which it has to be known before the question of its merit may be raised.

This primary character of the object, 'as it stands in nature without addition or diminution', is the domain of the 'understanding', and coincides with that of the sum of the value-neutral facts about it: with everything true of it, short of its affective meaning for us. These are the 'circumstances', 'relations', 'general facts', first to be 'known and ascertained on the side of the object'. And what makes them 'the matters of fact in the case', is not that they are the *hard* facts, the ones empirically or scientifically ascertainable, but that they are the *cold* facts, the ones characterizing the object short of any affective significance. It could equally be a matter of fact in the case that this action will destroy the vegetation, or the beauty of the countryside; that eating pork will cause indigestion, or be illegal, or against the will of God. The facts may be scientific, institutional, theological, aesthetic. They will all count as 'facts in the case', in a sense in which the merit, as reflexively grounded in these facts, cannot just be another one.

This must be so because of the manner of the dependence of merit on fact. Being conceived as reflectively dependent on the facts as known, it cannot be a member of the class of facts on the knowledge of which it reflectively depends. One could not without hitch include *in* the description of the object for evaluation in question a feature defined as only emerging from the effect on a reviewer of sufficient cognitive contact *with* this description. To do so would be to destroy the identity of the object-description before and after evaluation which the logic of merit ascription requires.

There is no reason for not predicating merit of things. But the merit will have to be a feature which supervenes on, rather than further qualifies, the character of the thing of which it is predicated. 'That tolerance brings peace' adds to the factual specifications of tolerance; but 'that it is good' expresses, as Hume has it, a 'new relation or affirmation' 'entirely different' from the other. It *assumes* what tolerance is like; and it *affirms*, which is an entirely other and supervening matter, that by way of a correct view of what it is like, it will occasion a favorable response to it in a human reviewer.

This is how, for Hume, the judgment of merit is necessarily no longer one of 'fact'. The reason is not that there is no fact for it to judge, or only some esoteric nonempirical 'fact'. Merit too is an experientially testable fact; 'taste' or feeling, by which it is judged, is a species of sensible perception. But 'taste', unlike sense-observation, is no longer among the 'perceptions of reason', because as a mode of perception it is directed to a categorially different issue. 'Reason', by sense-observation and reasoning, addresses itself to what things are, and adds to our knowledge of the world, of objects, states of affairs, characters, actions. But the perceptions of 'taste' are not among those of 'reason' precisely because they are no longer knowledge-yielding in this way. Critical taste shows how objects, on being confronted as what they are, will make us respond to them; necessarily, therefore, what objects are is here taken as known, and no further in question. The new issue is about the dynamics between things as they are and ourselves: their affective relevance for us, given what they are, as objects of approach or avoidance, acceptance or rejection. This is why Hume can say that merit is discernible, but not so that, in ascribing it to things, we are any further contributing to an understanding of the facts about them. Merit is a logically fact-supervening, though otherwise sensibly testable, fact, reflexively leaning on the sum of first-order object truths, and so no further part of them.

I may say in passing that the peculiar dependence of merit on fact entails not only that the merit cannot be ascribed to the object as another *part* of its primary character, but also that it cannot be ascribed to it as just another fact about it *alongside* with this character. Here is the difference between 'tigers are terrifying' and 'tigers are odious'. One may say they are treacherous as well as terrifying, where one would hesitate to say they were treacherous as well as odious. The reflexive dependence of their being odious on their being treacherous (where there is such a dependence) would be a bar to using the two descriptions alongside each other in the same characterization. Their being odious, rather than being just another fact, would be a super-venient, and descriptively supernumerary, conclusion from the first fact in another order of discourse.

I can't forbear pointing to the parallels in the distinction between merit and fact implicit in Hume's cognitive naturalism and the same distinction in Moore. Moore says of goodness that it differs from the natural properties by being, on the one hand, a non-self-subsistent or nature-dependent property and by being, on the other hand, such that it cannot be included in or added to the ordinary description or 'intrinsic nature' of that to which it is ascribed. Both of these are the features which, in Hume's system, mark off merit from fact. The main difference is that Moore found both, the dependence of merit on the nature of the object and its noninclusiveness in this nature, to be something just to be recognized, but strangely incapable of being understood or explained. And, with his view of goodness as a simple and unanalyzable quality, this can well be expected: there is nothing, in the concept of goodness, that Moore could distinguish to account for either its fact-dependence or its fact-supervenience, let alone the logical interdependence of the two. Hume's concept of merit explains all of this while still succeeding in allowing to merit a testable proposi-tional meaning. But for this Hume had to differ from Moore in one respect. Moore says that goodness is solely dependent on the intrinsic nature of the object. Hume can show why it necessarily depends on it, but he must deny that it depends on it solely. Merit rests on two variables: on what the object is like on its own, and on the natural responsiveness of humans to a view of what it is like. Overall, Hume's cognitive naturalism is far from being a bar to marking the distinctive difference between merit and fact on which Moore's antinaturalism was based.

V

With Hume's position understood, as I have been attempting to, the nondeducibility of 'ought' from 'is', of 'merit' from 'fact', will now fall easily into place. But before I say how, some comment is needed on Hume's overall intent in the 'is-ought' passage. Hume's nonde-ducibility thesis is often taken as the claim that merit is not entailed by the description of any state of affairs. There are no definable truth-conditions for the ascription of merit, either because merit is simple and unanalyzable, or because there is nothing to be asserted in ascribing it. But as far as Hume is concerned, this is sheer fabrication. He does not say this, nor could he have meant it. His own view of merit discernment spells out complex, and transparently intelligible, conditions under which an ascription of merit is formally warranted.

Hume's real concern in the passage is to assert that the possession of merit cannot be proved by argument: it cannot be treated as a demonstrable conclusion from the nonevaluative facts in its support. The move which he questions is precisely the one from 'tolerance is willed by God', or 'tolerance brings peace' to 'so it is good to be tolerant', 'so one ought to be tolerant'. It is clearer again from the *Inquiry* why an understanding of this move had to be central to his position. What he says there echoes the 'is-ought' passage and reads like a comment on it. In merit assessment, he says there, one must work one's passage from first exploring the facts in the case to the final judgment; and there is a notable resemblance between moving from the facts to an evaluative conclusion, and moving from facts to a conclusion which they formally prove. We say "tolerance brings peace" and "therefore it is good"; and we say "a triangle is a figure formed by the intersection of three straight lines" and "therefore the sum of its angles amounts to 180 degrees." In both cases we move to the conclusion by reviewing our premises, so in both cases the conclusion seems logically derived from them. However, the formal resemblances here are misleading. Merit has to be cognitively derived from the facts in the case; but the suggestion that this derivation amounts to a formal proof needs warding off. "Notwithstanding the appearing similarity in the two cases, there is at bottom an extreme difference between them" (ibid., p. 108). Hume's point in the *Inquiry*, and in the 'is-ought' passage, if read in the light of his comments in the *Inquiry*, is not to deny that merit is cognitively derived from fact but to make sure that this derivation is not mistaken for deduction.

The difference in the passage from premise to conclusion in the two cases turns, for Hume, on what the review of the premises is in aid of. One reviews the nature of the triangle, he says, with a view to examining the "relation which its several parts bear to each other," and from "thence infers some unknown relation which is dependent on the former." But in evaluation one reviews the nature of the case not in order to clarify further either its logical or empirical properties; but to extract, from all that one knows it to be, one's response to a proper view of it. One passes from the facts to the merit by obtaining perceptual evidence for the merit from the effect on one of reviewing them.

Given what the merit judgment is about, this is as it must be. It is an illusion from the form of speech that merit, because it holds by *reason* of the facts, must be *provable* from them. Anything entailed by the description of what a thing is would only specify further what it is, and this could bring us no further in discerning its merit. The move from fact to merit faces one with a new issue, the affective relevance of the facts to us on a true view of them. And what this relevance is, or would be, only the test of assessing it can reveal.

The *Inquiry*, more so than the *Treatise*, shows Hume's concern in this matter to be two-edged: to ward off the entrenched confusion of evaluative inference with demonstrative proof; and to show what cognitive procedure it is instead. Merit is known by cognitive derivation from the facts on which it depends. The question is how the passage from the facts to the merit conclusion is effected. Hume's point is that the facts as known are the basis, not of a formal, but rather of an experimental, proof of the merit. Merit is perceived by critical taste, by a reviewer who is in sufficient possession of the facts and who will intelligently and patiently let himself respond to them. One cannot prove merit to others but only take them to the facts and hopefully invite them to sample and digest them. Merit learning is more like wine-tasting than like doing detective work. In merit discourse we explore and exchange points rather than clues. This is not to say that demonstrative reasoning may not play a part. Tolerance may be good because it brings peace, and peace protects life; and if the latter is good, then by implication tolerance will be good. Still, that the last link in the chain is good has no formal proof; it must be perceived to be good from the effect on us of its nature as calmly reviewed.

VI

Once again, it is remarkable how Hume's account here is in form like that of the intuitionists. They said that merit cannot be proved but must be perceived, or intuited, from the nature of the case as thought of. They stressed the two odd features of merit cognition: that, in a way, it rests on premises which do not supply a proof, and on a perception which needs premises. On both views, merit is known from a reflexively object-dependent perception: of a property so dependent on the primary character of the object as to come into evidence only with its character knowledgeably before one.

There are the obvious differences. For the intuitionists, merit is a nonempirical, not further describable, quality, perceptible by 'a purely intellectual apprehension', and found to emerge, as the immediate object of a nonsensuous perception, from the nature of the case as reviewed. (Like a nonsensuous halo, I dare say, rather than a warm glow.) For Hume, merit consists of a sensibly testable and describable power, or aptitude, which things have, through their primary nature, in relation to human respondents and which is discerned indirectly from the perceptual evidence for this power in our responses to the nature of the case as reviewed.

Hume's rationalist opponents, like Samuel Clarke, much admired by Sir David Ross, were the intuitionists of his day, and it is well to recall his objections to them. The rationalists made merit epistemically mystifying, while being unable, at the same time, to explain its most telling feature; and this last is, for Hume, the crucial point. Ordinary thought takes it that whatever is good is also lovable and liable to be approved or prized and this necessarily and not just contingently so. But the abstract and indefinable goodness of the rationalists has no evident connection with affect: the connection could at most be contingent, or would have to be inexplicably a priori. There is no showing, Hume says, that the eternal 'measures of right and wrong' of the rationalists must have an 'influence on every well disposed mind'. But Hume has no problem here. 'Good' does not denote another property which may, or may not, make a thing loved. It is the term used in assessing its lovability itself, its true potential as a thing to be loved. This is why whatever is good must be lovable: only what can be loved can be good, and only what has got what it takes to be loved is good. Moreover, with this understood, merit will cease to be epistemically mystifying. The potential of things to be loved is a natural fact, comprehensible in part psychological, part rational terms, and testable by the exercise of critical taste. Recognition of the essential affect-relatedness of goodness is the cure against intellectualizing it.

There is the official doctrine, with us since Moore, that any such view as Hume's is vitiated by its naturalism. If merit is known by an empirical test, it is reduced to just another natural fact, known by ordinary observation or induction; and no such view can account for the difference in type between goodness and other ordinary properties. I am not especially concerned here with this view, except for one thing. The example of Hume should make one wonder how well founded it has ever been. The doctrine takes it as proved that a naturalist epistemology of value must involve its conceptual misrepresentation. True, quite a few naturalists are guilty of this, but it is less clear whether this follows from the principle of naturalism itself.

What seems so striking about Hume is that his epistemological naturalism does not have the effect of conceptually reducing merit to just another 'natural property'. It is Hume who insists that merit is no part of the facts in the case and that its discernment is not the work of scientific reason. It is he who uncovers its odd fact-dependence and supervenience and the peculiarities of its cognitive derivation. In fact, it seems that Hume's critical naturalism is just what is needed to make sense of these much vaunted features. The intuitionists, with their idea of goodness as nonsensuous and indefinable, were at a loss to explain them to themselves or others. They could not tell what made goodness a property-parasitic property; or how it should be so dependent on the primary properties of the object as to come into evidence only upon a review of them. But for Hume these thing fall into place. Merit, as the tested aptitude of things to dispose us toward them, is the kind of property which must reflexively depend (though not exclusively so) on their primary nature and which can be in evidence only, in our responses to them, upon the review of their nature.

Did Hume, then, commit the fallacy of perceiving clearly what the intuitionists perceived obscurely and confusedly?

VII

Well, if Hume was right, he committed no fallacy. But there are other ways of giving offense. A doctrine may be resisted, not because it is false but because of its threatening implications if true; and this does raise a question to which some concluding reference must be made.

The problem is in the nature of Hume's project. In demythologizing value, he humanizes it and makes it party to human frailty. Merit is placed in the natural relevance of things for human respondents. It is merit always relatively to someone, which raises the question of whether there can still be merit which is so relatively to everyone. The threat is that Hume's scheme jeopardizes the intersubjective ascribability of merit. One might no longer be allowed to ask whether tolerance *is* good, only whether it is good with me or with you; or, worse still, with me or you *now*, never mind tomorrow. Such consequences would imply that naturalism is less a clarification than the skeptical disproof of the possibility of merit ascription as we are used to it. Hume himself draws no such drastic conclusions, but the fear is that this is where he must be headed.

Moore complained that on any view like Hume's goodness becomes 'a purely subjective predicate'. The merit of the Ninth Symphony would be made to depend on the listener's reactions, and not on what

Beethoven put into the music. But this misses the point. Merit is as necessarily object-dependent for Hume as for Moore; but not, as for Moore, exclusively so. Things have merit through their nature, but not absolutely, only relatively to respondents capable of attachment to things of this nature. Hence Hume could not have followed Moore in saying that whatever is of the same nature must be perceptible as equally good anywhere, anytime, in every conceivable universe. All that he could have said was that whatever is of the same nature must be perceptible as equally good by all members of the same psychological universe; by humans, say, but not necessarily by Martians.

This brings out certain logical limitations which, for the naturalist, must hold of merit ascription. Merit does not belong to things through their nature absolutely, but relatively to someone. Hence, conceivably, the contending parties in a dispute may only appear to, but not really be contradicting each other. Each may be right, as an object, for precisely the same reason (the nature of the case), may have merit in relation to one respondent and not another. It is here, as Hume observes, that the good divides from the true. The standard for the latter is "eternal and inflexible" in being founded on "the nature of things"; while that for the former is variable, in depending on "the internal frame and constitution of animals" (ibid., p. 112). When it comes to the good, there is no longer the usual connection between the rational and the intersubjective. What, on the evidence, is rational to believe for one must be rational to believe for everyone. But what, with the concurrence of reason, has value for one is not necessarily what, with the concurrence of reason, will have value for another. And this is a vexing thing to have to allow.

These are necessary implications, but their effect is not to be judged from them alone. In fact, if Hume is right, they bear more on the philosophical understanding than on the actual practice of merit ascription. The latter will still not be notably relativistic. The reason is that *human* merit ascription is all that is at issue; and humans may broadly be taken as members of the same psychological species. Hence, while our merit ascriptions are valid only for us (and not necessarily for some other creatures), they are, for us, valid and broadly shareable. In our merit judgments we may address ourselves to what is 'entitled to *our* regard', or just good (relatively to human sensibilities); we may take differences in evaluation to be due to differences in comprehension, rather than basic sensibilities, to be resolved mutually 'by argument and reflection'. Hume also thinks it undeniable that some things are entitled strictly "to the regard of everyone." This applies especially to characters or actions contributive to public utility, as one may assume "a universal sentiment," "common to the human species" (ibid., p. 6) in favor of the generally beneficial. What is called 'morally good' is what is favored on this ground; hence the morally good will necessarily commend itself to every reflective human reviewer.

On the other hand, not all our merit assessments have the same degree of interpersonal ascribability. On some matters we differ in our basic 'leanings', on some more so than on others. The differences in evaluation cannot here be resolved "by argument or reflection" (ibid.), especially so in the matter of some 'species of natural beauty', as of the merit of spinach or rice pudding or lying in the sun (but already not in the case of wines, let alone works of art); that is, cases where there is a lack of logical room for still deploying the distinction between uncritical and critically sophisticated appreciation. In fact, in the limiting case here, the distinction between the liked and the good would shrink to zero. In all such cases one will have to grant that one's own merit assessment is no more than defeasibly valid for others; and one would have to speak of what was good in relation to oneself, and maybe others, but not in relation to everyone.

It looks then that Hume can argue that his naturalism is without serious counterintuitive consequences. The merit judgments made by each of us express our own personal merit assessment in the first place; but they also do, and may, express the conviction that our own assessment is not idiosyncratic, but shareable with others even if, to a varying degree, only defeasibly so. There is a conservative relativism here which should be welcome rather than threatening to common sense.

VIII

But this will, of course, depend on whether Hume has proved his point. And this raises one more question, at which, though, I can glance only briefly now. In my view, Hume's substantive thesis is right: that naturalist merit assessments need not all be speaker relative and idiosyncratic; but that speakers do, and may, claim an, if variable, measure of interpersonal validity for them. The flexible pattern of merit ascription which Hume delineates corresponds far more closely to actual practice than that of the absolutists. But I also believe that Hume's strategy in reaching this conclusion was not the best. He tries to justify the shareability of our own personal merit assessments by what he takes can be known about our common psychological nature: as if, if such knowledge, regarding universal sentiments or such like, were not first obtained, we would have no right of escape from the solipsism of our own personal value assessments. But if assured psychological information were a condition of this escape, we could hardly begin. For such information, concerning the uniformity of our basic sensibilities or otherwise, is not systematically and with any certainty available.

But then is such prior information necessary in order to initiate, or justify, the practice of treating our personal merit assessments as in some measure shareable? The answer seems no. One finds that, prior to any assurance of success, this is our practice already. We are deeply, and almost ineradicably, addicted to a policy of assuming that unless there be positive proof to the contrary, our value disagreements with others are rooted in differences of comprehension rather than basic sensibilities. In finding one's own assessment contradicted, one will, except in the limiting case, invariably respond with a 'but'; this 'but' being the overture to an argument, signifying one's initial presumption in favor of the shareability with others of our own merit ascriptions. The presumption is that they are innocent of the lack of interpersonal validity unless proven guilty. It is also striking how unwilling we are to concede the defeat of this presumption. In fact, language only barely allows us to do so unequivocally. It is not a natural way of speaking to concede by saying: "Well, what is good with me need not be so with you." One will rather say: "Well, the same things need not be 'found', 'considered', 'thought' to be good by everyone." And this is equivocal, compatible with suggesting that the difference is either a matter of the merit which things have for us or of our judgment about it. Our language leaves open whether the gap between you and me might not still be bridged some time by more discrimination, reflective insight, experience. Also, one may be adamant about not conceding defeat at all. One would not even consider Nero's plea that he, with his exceptional sensibilities, could not be expected to find matricide bad. And, in order not to disregard this plea, one would not have to know that the universal sentiment of humanity must be part of Nero's endowment too. It might be enough that one had no way of deciding whether he was so endowed or not but was resolved not to exempt him from responsibility for the reflective integrity of his social attitudes where one had only his word that such attitudes could not be imputed to him. One's judgment that inhumanity was just bad would here, by one's own justifiable stipulation, be made to hold indefeasibly for everyone.

All this suggests a transcendental argument for the view that, in a world of value naturalists, the merit assessments of each will converge toward intersubjectivity, tempered by a reluctant readiness to grant exemptions in the face of brute fact. This convergence will result from a practice of inquiry and discourse which would seek out interpersonal value agreement, or be protective of not stifling its emergence in the future, always in advance of an empirical proof of its real possibility. It would be a practice carried out with a backing of successful experience but without its prior justification. But rather than elaborate this further I stop. It is enough that, as usual, having got to the limits of Hume, one has passed into the territory of the pragmatists and of Kant.

[7]

Hume on Practical Reason

I

Hume says of moral and evaluative judgments in general that they "do not belong to the calm and indolent judgments of the understanding." The office of judging things to be good or bad, praiseworthy or blameworthy, amiable or odious, of merit or demerit, is "to excite passions," and "to produce or prevent actions."[1] Any viable account of the judgment of merit must show how it differs from ordinary judgments in playing this role.

Hume's observations have a contemporary ring, but less so what conclusions he draws from them. Some contemporaries deny this, and see him as the ancestral noncognitivist, though with some lapses into cognitivist heresy. But Hume is no modern style prescriptivist. He nowhere suggests that 'x has merit' derives its meaning, and practical import, from its commendatory force as an utterance. The judgment of merit serves to 'beget passions', and it does so by way of the thought or 'opinion' expressed by it. Much as Hume rejects all "the vulgar systems" of the past, he still rather modifies, than completely breaks with, the Aristotelian-classical view of a practical judgment which derives its regulative import from its propositional content.

Hume is usually read as wavering between a covert noncognitivism and some crude psychological naturalism, and this has reasons. Being the first in the modern period to stage a full-length critique of stan-

Reprinted from *Philosophical Studies* 27 (1975):1-18. All rights reserved © 1975 by D. Reidel Publishing Co., Dordrecht, Holland.
1. David Hume, *A Treatise of Human Nature*, ed. L. A. Selby-Bigge (London: Clarendon Press, 1967), p. 457.

dard rhetoric about 'reason' and 'practice', he wavers in getting a grip on his own final position. There are differences between parts of the *Treatise* and the *Treatise* and the *Inquiry*. This essay will be based on the final summary of his position in the *Inquiry* and a reading of the *Treatise* in the light of it. This reading is not the only possible, but if Hume may be read as an abortive noncognitivist, or as a crude naturalist, he may as well be read, and perhaps with more profit, as an updated Aristotelian.

II

For Hume, the practical role of judgments of merit is not their only distinctive feature. When he says that evaluative judgments are not "calm and indolent" like those of "the understanding," he is assuming that the judgments of the understanding are distinguishable as a class from those of merit on grounds other than merely the 'indifference' of the former and the practical import of the latter. Much as Moore later, Hume insists that there is a sense in which matters of value are distinct from matters of fact. 'That tolerance is good' is not found among the facts about tolerance in the way in which 'tolerance brings peace', or 'is willed by God' is. "The vice entirely escapes you, as long as you consider the object." The judgment of merit or demerit expresses "a new relation or affirmation," 'entirely different' from an affirmation of fact, or judgment of the understanding (ibid., p. 469).

Hume's underlying assumption is that the same reasons which generate a difference in kind between judgments of merit and of fact also explain the differences in practical role between the one and the other. But Hume's meaning here presents problems. In distinguishing merit from fact, he does not adopt either of the strategies familiar to us since Moore. Judgments of merit are not 'nonfactual' by being about some nonempirical 'fact' or truth, nor by not asserting any fact or truth at all. Judgments of merit and of fact both have a cognitive sense, which in its own way is sensibly testable. They differ by being about logically distinct cognitive issues. This is a confusing thesis to contemporary ears. Moreover, as Hume presents it, it is elusive and not so readily understood.

Hume claims that judgments of merit are not among "the disquisitions of the understanding," or are "not derived from reason." The office of the understanding, or "reason," is to 'convey the knowledge of truth or falsehood'; to discover, by sense observation and reasoning, "how things really stand in nature."[2] By contrast, the judgment of merit is not derived from "reason," but from "taste" or sentiment. Instead of contributing to the discovery of truth, it "gives a sentiment of beauty or deformity, merit or demerit." The logical divide is between judgments which add to our knowledge of what things are and judgments which give us a sense of their importance for us, given what they are. The first is achieved by the exercise of 'reason', the other by that of 'taste'. The dependence on the one or the other faculty yields judgments of logically distinct types. On examination, this turns out to be a viable view, but it needs exploring.

Contemporary readers want to understand the principle of division here as simply Stevensonian. Hume says that reason "discovers truth" in a way in which taste does not. Merit "is more properly felt than judged of"; "it is certain that it is derived from feeling and not from reason."[3] This suggests that the role of merit judgments is to express 'attitudes' rather than 'beliefs'. But this is not Hume's view, or if it were, it would clash with much else he says. It could not account for the practical role of the merit judgment. The expression of one's feelings toward things would not "give one a sentiment," "beget passions," or "regulate" them. Moreover, Hume clearly says that merit judgments make truth-claims, based only on "taste" rather than "reason."

Hume opens the *Inquiry*, saying that only "the disingenuous disputant" can "deny the reality of moral distinctions" and pretend that "all characters and actions are alike entitled to the regard of everyone."[4] The question is not whether knowledge of them can be attained, but how it can: how merit is "distinguished" or "discerned," whether "by our ideas or impressions," "by demonstrative reasoning," or "by some sentiment."[5] There are "judgments by which we distinguish moral good and evil," and there is testimony, in our sentiments, by which to make the distinction. The ascription of merit rests on taste, or sentiment, because they testify to what merit is ascribable to things.

It is a standard charge against Hume that, on this cognitive view, he cannot maintain any significant difference between judgments of merit and fact, 'taste' or 'reason'. Both make empirically testable truth-claims, with the only difference that those of taste are based on psychological evidence. Critics take this objection as conclusive, but the problem which Hume presents is more complex. The objection is

---

2. David Hume, *An Inquiry Concerning the Principles of Morals*, ed. Charles W. Hendel (New York: Liberal Arts Press, 1957), p. 112.
3. Hume, *Treatise*, p. 470.
4. Hume, *Inquiry*, p. 3.
5. Hume, *Treatise*, pp. 456ff.

conclusive only if one understands Hume's substantive view of the merit judgment in the usual, and least perspicuous, way.

The critic takes his clue from passages in the *Treatise* which say that to call things good is to say that one has a sentiment of approbation from the contemplation of them, or that they give one such a sentiment on a 'mere view' of them. The natural inference is that, for Hume, to judge things good is to report one's de facto approval of them; and that all that it takes to 'distinguish' their goodness is to consult one's feelings on the bare thought or view of them. Evidently, there are no cogent reasons here for distinguishing the judgment of merit from other judgments of 'fact' or 'reason'. 'That this wine is intoxicating' and 'that it gives a pleasing sentiment of approbation on tasting it' are both empirically testable judgments; and that their truth is discerned by sense-observation and sentiment, respectively, seems no reason why both should not count equally as being about some 'matter of fact' about the wine.

But this does not dispose of the issue. It is not clearly Hume's view in the *Treatise* that the 'good' is the 'approved'; and this is quite clearly not his view in the *Inquiry*. There is no confusion there between what is held in regard and what is 'entitled' to it; no implicit commitment to the fallacy that whatever arouses favor has merit, and that nothing has merit which is not arousing favor. Hume's views on the special logical properties of the merit judgment fall into place only against this background.

Hume's view is not that merit, because it is judged by taste, is judged by taste alone. He introduces Book II of the *Treatise* with a division of the impressions into original and secondary; original impressions "arise in the soul without antecedent perception"; secondary, or reflective, impressions "by the interposition of some precedent thought or perception." The latter are the passions, which in turn may be calm or violent. And it is from a calm passion, "a calm impression of reflection," that "the sense of beauty and deformity in action, composition, and external objects" is derived (ibid., pp. 275–76). The same view is treated at length in the *Inquiry*. Merit is discerned by sentiment, but only by a "proper sentiment" and not a "false relish," one which can still be "corrected by argument and reflection"; and a 'proper sentiment' is one first founded on a "proper discernment of the object." The discernment of merit depends on "the concurrence of reason with sentiment."[6]

Plainly, merit judgments are not here reports on de facto approval or disapproval. Not any sentiment evoked by some view of the object

6. Hume, *Inquiry*, p. 6.

decides its merit, but only one informed by a 'proper' view of it. In 'pronouncing' an object 'good' one may well *express* approval; but this will go with the claim that the object is such that, on being properly viewed, it will evoke such approval in the future, and in anyone of the same sensibilities.

Hume is so concerned to stress the proven capacity of things to command our favor as the final arbiter of merit that he underemphasizes in the *Treatise* the distinction between a critically unqualified and a critically qualified judgment of 'taste' and the prominent part played by 'the assistance of our intellectual faculties' in the latter. But there is no mistaking his view in the *Inquiry*.

Here the judgment of merit has become a complex affair. It relies on object-responses, but only as they would be had the object been thoroughly understood and presented to view. The sentiment that testifies to the merit is not in one's immediate response which, for a time, needs 'suspending'. It must be elicited, with object-exploration for a first step. "If any material circumstance be left unknown or doubtful, we must first employ our enquiry, or intellectual faculties, to assure us of it." "It is often necessary that much reasoning should precede, nice distinctions be made, just conclusions drawn, distinct comparisons formed, complicated relations examined, and general facts fixed and ascertained." Also, object-exploration must be sufficiently complete. "*Everything* must be known and ascertained on the side of the object or action," "*all* the circumstances of the case" (ibid.).

And this still is only 'paving the way'. The evaluative judgment takes place on the strength of these explorations, and, once again, with the mind's aid. "In moral deliberations we must be acquainted, beforehand, with all the objects and all their relations to one another; and *from a comparison of the whole* fix our choice or approbation" (ibid., p. 108). The facts, complete as ascertained, must be received in 'review', or in 'contemplation'; and the 'proper sentiment' is elicited by testing out our responses against such a view.

This is also why evaluation may be vitiated by a 'mistake of right', and not only one of 'fact'. The former is due to a lack of deliberative rectitude, a failure to review whole what one full well knows, thus preventing it from taking effect. Oedipus killed his father, innocently and in ignorance; but when Nero killed his mother, he knew "all the circumstances of fact." If we can see Nero's deed as detestable, as he did not, this results from a "rectitude in our dispositions" which he was without, a rectitude which stems from not closing one's mind to any part of the known fact (ibid., p. 109).

Hume's account here is misleading in suggesting that all of this must be gone through in actually making an evaluative judgment. If all the facts had to be ascertained first, one might have to wait for one's right to pronounce on merit forever. Rather, what Hume was doing was to lay down the conditions which would make the judgment of merit itself right or warranted. Only a response that, if put to the test, could survive every relevant object-scrutiny, would be conclusively indicative of what the object was worth.

The *Inquiry* says that things have merit when they "give to a spectator the pleasing sentiment of approbation"(ibid., p.107). But Hume's account of the merit judgment is not quite captured by this definition. The 'spectator' must be seen as the diligent reviewer; the 'sentiment of approbation' as the one that has first run the gauntlet of critical testing. Hume might have emphasized that one discerns merit by way of *assessing* it; and that what we assess, by testing out our responses to things, is their power, through what they are like, to engage our favor, by way of a correct appraisal of what they are like. Such things are 'entitled' to our regard, rather than are just held in regard, because, to a diligent human reviewer, they give license, as well as cause, to bestow his regard on them.

III

We can now return to Hume's logical motivation in dividing merit from fact, 'taste' from 'reason' (ibid., p. 112). The key is in the critical assessment view of the merit judgment. Merit cannot be 'derived from reason' precisely because it is known with 'the concurrence of reason'.

For Hume, 'reason' discovers the truth about things, "how they really stand in nature, without addition or diminution" (ibid.). This covers everything that is true of objects, as far forth as they are considered on their own, indifferently to their importance to us; and, whatever operations of the mind (sense-observation, inference, logical reasoning) are involved in this, belong to 'reason'. 'Taste', on the other hand, discerns merit, which is the importance of things for us, given what they are. And the claim is that between these two enterprises there is a logical divide. The truth about merit cannot be within the same category of 'fact' as the facts about things explored by 'reason'. The concept of object merit presupposes that of objects with a character of their own in which they can first be known and described *in extenso* and with a *view* to which merit becomes ascribable to them.

This is why Hume quite naturally separates the merit of things from *all* that is matter of fact about them. There is no other way of expressing the reflexive dependence of merit on what the object is otherwise like. An object's ability to impress us by way of the knowledge of what it is like cannot count as part of what it is like and confers this ability on it. One could not without hitch include among the specifications of a thing a feature which is defined as emerging only from the effect on a reviewer of sufficient cognitive contact with these specifications. To do so would be to destroy the identity of the object-description before and after evaluation, which the logic of merit-ascription requires.

There is no reason for not predicating merit of things. But the merit would have to be a feature which supervenes on, rather than further qualifies, the antecedent character of the thing of which merit is predicated and on which it reflexively depends. 'That tolerance brings peace' adds to the specifications of tolerance; but 'that it is good' expresses, as Hume has it, 'a new relation or affirmation', 'entirely different' from the other. It *presupposes* and *assumes* what tolerance is and *affirms*, what is quite another and supervening matter, that, by way of a correct view of what it is, it will occasion a certain response in a human reviewer.

This is how, for Hume, the judgment of merit is necessarily no longer one of 'fact'. The reason is not that there is no fact for it to judge, or only some esoteric nonempirical 'fact'. Merit too is an experientially testable fact; 'taste' or feeling, by which it is judged, is a species of sensible perception. But 'taste', unlike sense-observation, is no longer among the 'perceptions of reason', because as a mode of perception it is directed to a categorially different issue. 'Reason', by sense-observation and reasoning, addresses itself to what things are and adds to our knowledge of the world, of objects, states of affairs, characters, actions. But the perceptions of 'taste' are not among those of 'reason' precisely because they are no longer knowledge-yielding in this way. Critical taste shows how objects, on being confronted as what they are, will make us respond to them; necessarily, therefore, what objects are is here taken as known and no further in question. The new issue is about the dynamics between things as they are and ourselves: their affective relevance for us, given what they are, as objects of approach or avoidance, acceptance or rejection. This is why Hume can say that merit is discernible, but not so that, in ascribing it to things, we are any further contributing to an understanding of the facts about them. Merit is a logically fact-supervening, though otherwise sensibly testable, fact, reflexively leaning on the sum of first-order object truths, and so no further part of them.

However, it is not just the cognitive issue which divides the two judgments. It is also their role, what the enterprise of making them, is primarily in aid of. Hume says that the office of reason is "to discover truth," whereas taste "gives a sentiment"; and while this may seem like denying that taste too has a cognitive role, this is not Hume's point. He says clearly enough that both "reason" and "taste" yield their own kind of truth. But he implies that the acquisition of truth is not equally their office. The understanding is exercised "to gratify a speculative curiosity," to add to our store of knowledge about things and the world. But the inquiry into good and bad is "a practical study." It does more than inform us that things are good or bad; it also contributes to shape our practical attitudes toward them, to "give" us a sentiment or taste for the good and a distaste for the bad (ibid., p. 5). This is what the enterprise of merit assessment and judgment, and the inculcation of merit opinions in others, is primarily in aid of. The discernments of taste are therefore doubly distinct from those of the understanding. Their truth does not add to the truth about the world, and its acquisition is not the primary objective in seeking it.

IV

Hume's contention is that the difference in practical role connects necessarily with that in cognitive orientation which divides the two types of judgment. Those of the understanding are in their nature "indifferent," "cold," "inactive"; those of merit are "of themselves" active, apt to "excite passions," to "regulate our lives and actions." They differ in this way for the same reason that makes the ones fact-stating and the others fact-supervening. There is a contemporary ring about this, but Hume's interpretation is notably different. 'Tolerance is good' is active and regulative, while 'tolerance brings peace' is not; but the former is not fact-supervening and regulative because, instead of being truth-claiming, it voices a commendation. The practical import of the judgment is not a function of its illocutionary prescriptive force as an utterance. For Hume, there are factual truths, and merit truths supervening on them. They are inactive and active, respectively, by being the kind of truths they are.

Hume insists that judgments of fact are literally "inert" and "can beget no desire or aversion." And he means this without denying that 'tolerance brings peace' or 'these toadstools are poisonous' could have practical effects. His point is that, if they do, this will be due to the context, but still not strictly to the nature of the judgment. What is 'inert', 'indifferent', and unable 'to have hold of the affections' is the judgment of fact 'of itself'; and the reason is that matters of fact are, by definition, matters of cold fact. Judgments of fact address themselves to whatever things are, exclusive of whatever they may be to us, of any feeling engendered by the perception or thought of them.

One judges them under the logical constraint of *disengaging* one's responses to them; of discounting any 'secondary', or 'reflective impressions', to which the view of what they are may give rise. One reaches conclusions which are in themselves as value-neutral as the considerations which lead to them, and which represent strictly what the object is, while keeping the *issue of its affective relevance* unraised and in abeyance. This is how "reason is cool and disengaged," and how, among its findings, there "is no motive to action."

The findings of reason may, of course, contribute to motivation. 'That tolerance brings peace', considered as a means to a desired end, may arouse interest in tolerance and cause it to be adopted. But, while the judgment of fact is here active, by furnishing a reason for a choice, its contribution will still turn on circumstances quite outside itself. No fact is necessarily and of itself relevant as a reason, but only in proportion as it connects with some interest. No judgment of fact is therefore necessarily and of itself a practically relevant judgment. 'These toadstools are poisonous' does not have to be practically relevant, nor will it have the same relevance for a gourmand or a suicide.

Furthermore, even if a judgment of fact is of something practically relevant, it is not thereby of itself motivating. At the least, the relation of the fact to a matter of interest must be *attended* to; and often the relevance of the fact as a reason, and as one of sufficient moment, must first be *recognized*. But neither of these is part of the judgment of fact itself. The facts may be judged correctly; that they hold reasons, and how much so, may pass unnoticed, and is altogether another matter. Much therefore as judgments of fact can contribute to practice, and frequently do, no judgment of fact is of itself practically relevant, let alone efficacious.

By contrast, Hume takes the practical import of judgments of merit to be necessary. They are judgments which of themselves "take possession of the heart"; which "tend to beget passions" and by which we can "regulate our lives and actions." The reason is that the judgment of merit touches on the very issue to which that of fact is indifferent. Instead of addressing itself to what tolerance is, it addresses itself to the supervening question whether, given what it is, a reflective view of it will engage our favor. And, to Hume, the practical import of such a judgment is necessary. There can be no question that 'tolerance is good' expresses a truth relevant to extending favor to it, with an inbuilt potential to make us do so.

This may not seem obvious. Why should 'tolerance brings peace' be a *cold* fact and 'it is good' ('such as to commend itself to one's favor') be *exciting* news? The former is a normal consideration to arouse interest in tolerance; the latter hardly another such consideration at all. But Hume's angle is different. 'That tolerance brings peace' is not necessarily and of itself a reason in its favor: that it brings peace could be true, and that there is reason, and reason enough, for favoring it false. On the other hand, 'tolerance is good' does not itself proffer any reason for favoring it: but, if true, it will be true that there *is* such a reason. For this is what '*x* is good' certifies: that an *x* is such that, in the facts about it, there is reason for viewing it with favor. In this sense, the practical relevance of '*x* is good' is necessary, and not just contingent: precisely because, instead of proffering any reason, it settles the issue of the relevance of the facts in the case as providers of reasons.

But Hume also claims practical efficacy for the merit judgment, and one may object that it need not have this any more than any other conclusion of fact. One may know that some *x* gives one every reason for favoring it and still view this with indolence. Hume says himself that our passions do not always "readily follow the determinations of our judgment."[7] How then can he say that merit judgments of themselves have "a hold of the affections" and "set in motion the active powers of men"? The answer to this is that the active force of the merit judgment is not, for Hume, in its conclusion, but in the judgmental process that leads to it. Merit truth may well be *known* with indifference; but one cannot *judge* it, confirm or reconfirm it for oneself, while remaining cool, and without effect on one's sentiments.

This follows from the nature of the judgment. Merit is gauged from the effect on one's sensibilities in meeting an object in a knowledgeable review or discriminating perception. One cannot therefore explore and settle a question of merit and not 'beget passion'. Here the object must be viewed with feeling, just as in judging of fact it must be viewed coldly. The problem is to engage one's responses in an encounter with object-truth, elicit them, test them out, persist in correcting a "false relish" by further "argument and reflection," fact-finding, deliberation, and review, in order to arrive at a "proper sentiment," the one that the object is liable to make one feel from a "proper discernment." This sentiment is "a new impression of affection or disgust, approbation or blame," acquired by way of critical object review; and in this novel, and reflectively self-engendered, sentiment is one's warrant for ascribing merit. The liability of the object to evoke one's approbation or blame on a critical view is discerned in the feeling which one has for it as one critically views it.

This is why merit is not judged indifferently, without making one sensible of a taste for the good and a distaste for the bad. The very

7. Hume, *Treatise*, p. 583.

judgment relies for evidence on an *affect* to be engendered by the exercise of object-presentational practical thinking. But there is a question whether Hume does not claim too much. In assessing merit, one invokes one's reflective responses experimentally, simply with a view to judging the liability of the object to evoke a like response on a reflective view in the future. And this process does not ensure that the affect engendered in making the judgment will survive the making of it. Of *known* merit one need not be sensible as one must be of the same merit in the process of *judging* it. But Hume does at times express himself more strongly. The truth about merit, he seems to say, "takes hold of the affections" and "sets in motion the active powers of men" as surely as the truth about fact is "inert." The knowledge of what is laudable, honorable, fair "takes possession of the heart, and animates us to embrace and maintain it."[8]

But Hume does not hold that to *know* the good must be to *love* it. All that he insists on is that one cannot judge, or 'pronounce', things to be good without affect. At the time of giving one's 'verdict', one must be sensible of the merit which one ascribes to the object. One cannot perceive it as good, and not view it with favor. But whether this favorable sentiment will survive the judgment is another matter. Hume's considered view here is that it well may, and, frequently and typically, does. Merit truth, being judged from the heart, with the concurrence of the head, has at least "a tendency to regulate our lives and actions." "Men are often deterred from some actions by the opinion of injustice, and impelled to others, by that of obligation."[9] The reflective sense of approbation or disapprobation, uppermost in arriving at the judgment, remains here with them to "regulate their conduct." One may gain a novel and lasting appreciation of things by simply once having discerned their merit. One finds merit in a work of art, or realizes the shamefulness of some action, and henceforth favors the one and refrains from the other.

But, equally, this need not be so. Our passions may not "follow the determination of our judgment"; and this applies to volitions and actions particularly. One may be "fully convinced" that one's good health a year hence "excells" in value some pleasurable indulgence today and be indifferent to this conviction. The affect which warranted one's original judgment is not here preserved in the knowledge it yielded, and the reason is plain. In *judging* one's good health to be preferable, one finds oneself to give preference to it on "a distant view of reflection," with the facts known, compared, and dispassionately

8. Hume, *Inquiry*, p. 5.
9. Hume, *Treatise*, p. 457.

reviewed for what they are. But in *knowing* it to be preferable, one only knows, or is entertaining the thought, that such preference would be due to one's health upon such a distant view. This unfulfilled conditional is not of itself a motive to action, let alone a counterweight to a "violent passion" for what is "near," nourished by partial and imaginatively distorted representations.

All the same, a merit judgment which fails to regulate our actions still leaves us in possession of a "practically relevant" truth. This is a truth by which we necessarily can regulate them, though in practice Hume is skeptical, in hard cases, of our psychological ability to do so. The principle is that, just as one cannot judge of the merit, or "tastiness," of anything without coming to feel some taste for it, so one cannot fail to recover and develop one's taste for it if one confirms or reconfirms to oneself on what grounds one first judged that it had it. Given it is true that one would give preference to an object on a distant view or reflection, one can always cause oneself to give preference to it by making oneself realize that one does so on adopting a distantly reflective view. One then "counteracts a violent passion" by reinstating a "calm determination of the passions founded on some distant view or reflection" (ibid., p. 583).

In the *Inquiry*, Hume says that such practical self-regulation by the judgment of merit or demerit is the final end "of all moral speculations."[10] Their end is "to teach us our duty, and by proper representations of the deformity of vice and beauty of virtue, beget corresponding habits, and engage us to avoid the one, and embrace the other." This is flowery language but makes the previous point. One does, and can, seek knowledge of good or bad for its practical relevance, because, as practical intelligences, we can make ourselves seek the one and avoid the other by 'proper representations' to ourselves of the grounds on which our judgment of their goodness or badness was based.

Hume's reference here to "the end of all moral speculations" shows how he considers morals as "a practical study," by contrast with the pursuits of the understanding which "gratify a speculative curiosity." The two undertakings not only differ in being about logically separate issues, and in being motivationally 'inactive' and 'active' respectively, but also in their very role as truth-finding enterprises. The one, in exploring what things are, has as its primary objective to regulate our beliefs and judgments, to enlarge our intellectual horizons. The other, in judging of the affective relevance of things for us, serves to regulate our interactions with things, our responses to them as objects to be approached or avoided. We engage in the one to learn what things

10. Hume, *Inquiry*, p. 5.

are, in the other to learn to respond to them as they are. Both are learning problems in need of our 'intellectual faculties' for their solution. But the one is a matter of learning what is the case, of shaping our cognitive attitudes toward things; the other is a matter of learning how to relate to things, of shaping our practical attitudes to them.

This is not to say that the judgment of merit is not truth-yielding; it is rather that the acquisition of merit truth, instead of being a final end, is an integral part of an undertaking which is practical rather than cognitive in its aim. The judgment of merit is geared to this job. In projecting to ourselves the liability of things to engage our favor upon knowledgeably reviewing them it mobilizes our responses to them as they are, tends to settle them, or enables us to regulate them accordingly. And this, rather than gather idle truths, is what merit assessment and judgment is primarily about. "If morality had naturally no influence on human actions and passions, it were in vain to take such pains to inculcate it; and nothing would be more fruitless than that multitude of rules and precepts with which all moralists abound." But, then, it is noteworthy that, for Hume, this practical thrust of the merit judgment is neither in the *knowing* that things have merit, nor in the *saying*. It comes from the *affect* engendered if and when anyone renders himself account of what makes this *judgment* true; an affect mobilized when he views the object, as a reflective intelligence, in the process of confirming, or reconfirming, the judgment. It is idle to disseminate merit truths to others unless they will appreciate their force by exercising their own practical intelligence and judgment; or to accept them from others, authoritative as their judgment may be, without critically endorsing them for oneself. Merit truths are not practical unless their validity is recognized and taken to heart, and their possession is idle unless it is made practical. This is how I take Hume to mean that the discernment of merit, though of some kind of fact or truth, is no part of the 'calm and indolent' quest for object-fact or truth, and not primarily part of the quest for the truth at all.

V

This reading of Hume leaves one more question. It says that, for Hume, merit judgments are practical because of their integral part in regulating our practical attitudes "with the concurrence of reason." But there is also Hume's skepticism of "reason as an influencing motive of the will"; his contempt of the traditional rhetoric which enjoins "every rational creature to regulate his actions by reason"; his claim that there is a "fallacy" in the "supposed pre-eminence of reason over passion." How is this compatible with his evident reliance on "the concurrence of reason" in the regulation of passions and volitions?

The answer is that Hume's real intent is to rectify rather than subvert the traditional teaching on the relation of reason to practice. Our "intellectual faculties" have a place in the settlement of practical attitudes; there are "calm passions" which, "when corroborated by reflection and seconded by resolution" can oppose, and be made to counteract, the "violent ones."[11] But this practical contribution of the mind is not "strictly and philosophically speaking" one of 'reason'. A calm passion is founded on "reflection" or "a proper discernment of the object," but it is "improperly" described as founded on 'reason'; the opposition between "calm and violent passions" is not strictly one "between reason and the passions." What is at issue is a philosophical distinction. For Hume, 'reason' is naturally and primarily associated with the exercise of the understanding in the discovery of truth, the regulation of our cognitive attitudes, judgments, beliefs. The mind's contribution to practice is not properly one of 'reason' in the sense and manner in which 'reason' belongs to judgment.

Basic here is the observation that passions or volitions cannot agree or disagree with reason, and be directed by it, as judgments or beliefs. Cognitive attitudes picture or 'represent' things: they 'agree with reason' when what they picture conforms to truth, 'to *real* relations of ideas, or to *real* existence or matter of fact'; they are based on 'reason' when they are informed by its exercise as it attends to, or 'regards' logical relations and observable facts.

But no such agreement with 'truth and reason' applies to practical attitudes. They are dispositions to approach or avoid, accept or reject things upon some view of them; and, although they presuppose dispositions to view or picture their object, they are not themselves such dispositions. Approaching an object is not the same as picturing or 'representing' what it is; and only an object-representation, and not an object-approach, can be 'rational' by conforming to truth on the showing of reason. The exercise of reason, as it regulates our judgments or beliefs about things, has no direct bearing on regulating our approaches to them.

Hume allows that the exercise of 'reason' or 'understanding' can have some practical relevance. But this admission is guarded with qualifications.

The first is that, where this relevance applies, it is indirect, and not direct. One approves or disapproves, seeks or avoids things with a

11. Hume, *Treatise*, p. 437.

view to them, and reason can modify this view. It can discover implications and consequences, and if they can arouse our sensibilities, the discovery can change our attitudes. An attitude based on a true judgment will then 'agree with reason', one based on error be contrary to it. But this is direction of practical attitudes by 'reason' in only an *indirect* and *attenuated* sense. The attitude is modified not by an act of mind directly, but indirectly by a discovery resulting from it; and not by this discovery alone, but insofar as it connects with some interest. Strictly, all that agrees here with reason, or not, is not the practical attitude, but the belief attending it. The exercise of error-free judgment is the sole agency in the regulation of passion by reason.

Hume's other qualification is that direction by 'reason', if it amounts to this, does not justify traditional expectations about its scope. His skepticism of reason as practical has its place here. A passion agrees, or disagrees, with 'reason' as it is 'accompanied' by a true or false judgment; and, by this token, there is no manifest rational defect in what is frequently condemned as 'contrary to reason' and taken as corrigible by it. A man may know that saving will protect his good in the future and not save; he may know that revenge will bring ruin on himself, or the world at large, and still seek it, even willfully. His attitude is not due to a faulty judgment about the action: it is not therefore 'contrary to reason', and further corrigible by it. There is no logical room here for his passion to be in 'combat' with reason: for whatever passion is attended by a true judgment is necessarily the one which agrees with reason.

Hume's view here of the limits of reason as practical is consistent. But it must be understood as delimiting the practical scope of the theoretical understanding and not of the mind altogether. Error-free judgment is all there is to the exercise of 'reason'. But there is also *"that reason which is able to oppose our passions"* but is *"falsely supposed to proceed from the same faculty with that which judges of truth or falsehood."* If a man seeks revenge while knowing its ruinous consequences he is possessed by a "violent passion"; and a violent passion, though not *against reason* in not being attended "by a false supposition," is still *wrongheaded* in some way. The mark of a violent passion is that it proceeds "independently of all consideration" of what "reason" tells about its object. One is not ignorant of the consequences, but avoids to regard the act in its relation to them; or, while aware of their nature, one thinks of it in the abstract, without forming a determinately particularized idea of it; while, at the same time, one is moved by a distorted imaginative representation of one's immediate objective. The violent passion fails to be steadied by a true representation of its object as it would be on "a calm reflection," "on deliberation," on "taking a distant view." It can be opposed, and corrected, not indeed by "reason" but by "a calm passion": "a general calm determination of the passions founded on a distant view or reflection" (ibid., p. 583).

Hume's point then is not to deny the corrigibility of practical attitudes by the mind but to oppose the traditional description of this as one, principally and essentially, by 'reason'. And this is not trivial, but in aid of accenting the radical difference between the theoretical and the practical roles of the mind. The intelligence which regulates our responses to things is only remotely connected with that which regulates our beliefs about them. It presupposes object-understanding, but it is of itself different from and additional to it. Practical intelligence is the exercise not of judgmental but of presentational thinking; a species of 'thinking of', not of 'judging that'. *Its role is to bridge the gap between understanding and sensibility by making object-knowledge available to impinge on our sensibilities.* Theoretical thinking is ratiocination which terminates in a conclusion. Practical thinking is deliberation which terminates, as it did for Aristotle, in "moving the soul." The exercise of practical thinking is not of itself that of practical judgment. The practical judgment, or judgment of merit, is about the liability of things to arouse an affect *upon* the exercise of practical thinking. It rests for evidence on a presentational thinking, and its outcome, which is causative, and not judgmental.

Implicit in this is Hume's deepest motivation for withholding the word 'reason' from the practical intelligence and its works. A calm passion, though formed "with the concurrence of reason," cannot rival the 'rationality' of a judgment or belief. Their rationality stems from ratiocination and conformity to truth; and there can be only one outcome of proper ratiocination. But a passion cannot be 'rational' with this implication. Its formation by 'reason' would be by deliberation, and not ratiocination; the product would not be a rational insight, but an effect. Its outcome, therefore, would not have to be the same for every properly thinking mind alike. (There is an exception to this in the outcome of syllogistic practical thinking which presents the choice of the means under the description of pursuing the end.) As Hume keeps stressing, the 'standard' of theoretical rationality is 'eternal and inflexible' by being founded 'on the nature of things'; whereas that of practical rationality, of what can commend itself to the favor of a reflective intelligence, depends on our human sensibility, "the internal frame and constitution of animals." There is practical intelligence, but no "eternal and inflexible" reason, to regulate our object-responses.[12]

12. Hume, *Inquiry*, p. 112.

The final implication is that the merit of things, although consisting of the liability of things to commend themselves to men who are exercising their practical intelligence, need not be the same for everyone alike. But this relativistic implication does not lead Hume, and I think rightly so, to extravagant conclusions. In judging things good on the evidence of our own critical taste, we make and are justified in making, interpersonal truth-claims. We are doing so on the general presumption that differences in evaluation may be taken, in the first place, as due to differences in comprehension, rather than in basic sensibilities. Hume assumes this presumption to be indefeasible where the merit of public utility is concerned, assuming "a universal sentiment," common to the human species, in favor of the generally beneficial. In the case of other merit judgments, especially about the arts and other 'species of natural beauty', he is more flexible. They may be taken as making presumptively, but to a varying degree, defeasibly interpersonal truth-claims. In this Hume sees no harm. The role of theoretical rationality is necessarily to homogenize our judgments or beliefs. That of practical intelligence is to steady and objectify our object-responses, but not necessarily to make them all the same.

PART TWO

MORALITY

[8]

Morals without Faith

You have invited me to speak about morals without faith. Briefly, I
take it, this question means: is there any moral law for agnostics? But
it might be more interesting to put it rather differently: to ask, not
simply whether there is a moral law for those who do not believe in
God, but whether there is any such law even for those who do *independent* of their belief? We are then asking: Does being under a moral
law mean nothing more than being commanded by God? Is the only
incentive for obeying it in our love or fear of Him, the only criterion
by which to judge the morality of actions in their conformity to a
revealed standard? Or would it be more true to say that the law which
God wishes us to obey is that law to which we ought to conform because
it corresponds to our nature and conditions in this world, a law which,
apart from being God's will, we can understand as being indispensable
to the kind of beings we are?

Much depends on which of these alternatives is in fact the case. If
the first were true, then, indeed, there would be no morals for agnostics, and for believers none, except those particular laws to which
their religion commits them. Hence, if only people could rid themselves of the belief in God's watchful presence they could with a sigh
of relief turn to being as grasping, as aggressive, and as self-indulgent
as they liked. But if the second were true, then, even if they disregarded the revealed will of God, they would still have only exchanged
one authority for another. Something in their own nature would give

Reprinted with permission of the publisher, Cambridge University Press, from *Philosophy* 19 (1944): 3-18.

them the sense of a categorical *must* keeping their desires and ambitions in check.

In this essay, I shall state the case for this second view. It is the view implicit in the classical tradition, and revived—with passionate emphasis—by the great moralists of the seventeenth and eighteenth centuries, by Grotius, Spinoza, Bishop Butler, Hume, and Kant. What prompted this revival was the desire to emancipate morals from religion; and the reasons which made success in this undertaking an issue of vital importance are worth recalling. The moralists of that time were faced with forces which tended to disrupt moral life altogether, and they thought these could be matched only if the foundations of morality were natural and independent of creed or faith.

There were three main forces of disruption: the advance of science, the Reformation, and the birth of the nation-state. With the advance of science metaphysical speculation about nature was superseded by mathematical demonstration and observation; and men steeped in these methods began to distrust restrictions based on nothing more than supernatural inspiration. Moreover, the Reformation—with the many sects to which it gave birth—multiplied the interpretations of the scriptures: there were many conflicting precepts for each of which someone claimed that it was rightly derived from the same revealed text. For a Lutheran, the Bible taught that man owed unconditional subservience to established political authority, for a Leveller that all men were equal before God and that no man had a right to make himself the master of another. Each view was held with religious fervor, and hence all became discredited for the more sober-minded. They observed that the law of God is known only through man's fallible interpretation and through texts which may have been corrupted in their transmission. Was there then any code that could be regarded as authentic, or was for lack of certainty one way of behaving as good as another? Hence, for many, sectarianism combined with the new scientific outlook terminated in moral skepticism. This conclusion appealed above all to the politicians. If divine law and divine sanctions were as uncertain as they appeared, the state at least, having no soul to lose, might disregard them. Why not agree with Machiavelli that the state's right went as far as its might, and that politics was out of the bound of morality? Hence, Grotius wrote of his times: "I saw prevailing throughout the Christian world a licence in making war of which even barbarous nations would have been ashamed; recourse being had to arms for slight reasons or for no reasons; and when arms were once taken up, all reverence for divine or human law was thrown away, just as if men were henceforth authorized to commit all crimes without restraint."

The remedy, it was thought, lay in the *emancipation of morals from religion*. As long as morals rest on nothing but the love and fear of God, then, as Lord Shaftesbury observed, "the stress being laid wholly here, if this foundation came to fail, there is no further prop or security to man's morals." And, with men who had ceased to believe in a personal God, and others perplexed about what rules God expected them to keep, this foundation had come to fail. Hence it was vitally important to find another foundation for morals: to show that men as men are under a law, necessitated by their nature and accessible to their understanding. This law was found in the *Law of Nature*, a conception familiar to medieval thinkers, but now reexamined and given first place. The Law of Nature commands men to respect the life and interests of others, to keep agreements, to refrain from war except in the defense of rights, and to conduct war without pillage and cruelty. This law has authority because men must be ready to follow it if they want to act consistently with their social nature and long-term well-being. It can be discovered by anybody with the power and will to reflect; it applies to all men since their natures and conditions are uniform, and it substantially coincides with the main tenets of Christian revelation. Where it differs, it was thought, the supposed revelation must give way. God would not have enabled us to discern natural laws of conduct if he had not meant us to do so. He has given us *revelation* so that the uninstructed may know what they ought to do before they can discern it for themselves; but He has given us *understanding* so that we may discover the need for moral conduct for ourselves and may be able to correct our corrupted or fanciful interpretations of His word by reference to the Law of Nature. Hence, though Divine Law has priority in the *historical* order, natural law has priority in the *logical* order. Christian revelation, as Bishop Butler put it, is a "re-publication of the Law of Nature"; it is binding only when it prescribes what is reasonable for men to do. "Reason," he said, "is indeed, the only faculty we have wherewith to judge concerning anything, even revelation itself. . . . For revelation may contain clear immoralities or contradictions and either of these would prove it false."

Not all of this seems to me defensible. The age of reason, for all its admirable sobriety, was too prone to believe in easy shortcuts from the worst to the best of all possible worlds. I think it is true that we are naturally bound to live by *some* rules or laws. Yet I don't think that our understanding can disclose a system of rules which is final, and not in need of further scrutiny and revision. Nor is it certain that the dictates of natural reason must be the same for all men at all times, or that they must always agree with all aspects of Christian revelation. Moreover, some Christian duties essentially presuppose religious belief. The duty to confess our sins to God presupposes belief in God's word, and it cannot be justified independently of this belief. The agnostic is not bound to it. Nor do I think will the religious find the arguments for the complete subordination of revelation to natural reason conclusive. They might well argue that God has given us revelation because of the imperfections of our understanding, and that we would fail in our duty to God if we tried to set our mind against His.

Still, I think, none of this invalidates the vital importance of a *lex naturae*. If there are rules or laws, ascertainable, however imperfectly, by our own understanding, and compelling because they conform to our nature and conditions in this world, then, even heathens and agnostics are under some moral restraints. And also, I think, it is then true of the adherents to any religious creed that as little as they can lightly set the dictates of natural reason against what they think has been revealed, as little can they lightly set revelation against the dictates of natural reason. For as God has given them the one, He has given them the other. And where natural reason and supposed revelation manifestly conflict, where religion appears to demand what natural reason considers wholly uncalled for if not pernicious, the fault *may* equally be either in our corrupt understanding of God's will, or in our corrupt understanding of our natural duties. Hence, if there are dictates of natural reason, they can never lightly be ignored, and they must serve as some corrective to the conclusions which we draw from belief. However, it is not for me to attempt to draw the correct line between reason and faith. All I shall try to show is that for those who seek them there are dictates of natural reason even if there may be rules of faith as well.

What I can say on this topic is, to be sure, very inadequate. The problem has engaged philosophers from Plato to the present day. It is *the* problem of moral philosophy. Most philosophers have regarded it as soluble but their answers differ widely. Obviously, I cannot enter into polemics. All I can do is sketch my own grounds for holding this view.

Now, to begin with, I must grant that the conception of a natural law of conduct is very perplexing. In what sense is it *natural* and in what sense is it a *law*? There are difficulties here which we must try to understand before we can attempt to solve them.

First, it is plain that when we think of a moral *ought* we think of a *command* or *imperative*. Something within me says: I *must* write this letter which I have put off so long, or I *must not* give away this secret although it would make such a good story; and I must do the one however much I should like to avoid it, and must not do the other however much I feel tempted to do so. The point about the moral ought is that it commands without deference to our wishes.

But this is only one aspect of the matter. There is also another. For, on our supposition the moral command is a *natural* one, and hence it must not simply be the expression of some other being's will, but the expression of something within our own will. If the duty to write the letter is a law of our own nature, we must be bidden to write it by some voice within us that is *part of our self*. And, indeed, this is what we commonly have in mind when we think we *ought*. We think we are somehow internally constrained, that we cannot neglect our known duty without disregarding an *impulse* whose influence we had previously felt. Nor could this be otherwise. For we do assume that 'ought implies can', that a man can only have a duty which he can be expected to fulfill. But we cannot be expected to do anything if we feel no impulse whatever to do it. It could not seriously be my duty to write the letter simply because somebody else wanted me to write it, and while the thought of doing so left me totally indifferent. The presence of some natural impluse is constitutive of a natural duty to do anything.

Here is our first difficulty. When we say we have a duty to write the letter we cannot simply mean that we *want* to write it; and, yet, in some sense, we must mean that we *do want* to write it. To be obliged is to be impelled, yet not to feel inclined; it is to feel impelled with some special imperativeness or necessity.

Some popular accounts of the origin of natural morality overlook this difficulty. There are some who say we realize that we have a natural duty simply when we see that an act open to us would be of a certain kind, e.g., that it would be just, or equitable, or would cause more happiness or good all round than any other. But, plainly, merely to realize that I *could* do any of these things is not the same as to realize that I *must* do it. I know I could, but why should I if I did not want to? Clearly, I could only be induced to do it by an impelling motive; and as we have seen, if this motive is to be a sense of duty, it must be a special sense of internal constraint. Hence, what makes equitable or just or good acts duties is not simply that we know that some acts of ours *would* be of this kind *if* we did them, but that we know in addition that we are somehow *necessitated to do* such acts.

There are others who agree that to have a duty is, in some manner, to be impelled, but they think that the moral impulse consists in instinctive dispositions to do actions of a *certain kind*: in an instinctive desire to preserve the species, to be truthful, just, or charitable, to refrain from cruelty or faithlessness. But, once more, this does not explain why we *ought* to do any of these things. To act truthfully or charitably from an instinctive desire, even if it has the best of objects, is to act from *inclination*, not from a sense of *having to act in this way and no other*. This sense sometimes accompanies our natural readiness to act in any of these ways, but by no means always. I may feel inclined to tell the truth, and yet think I ought to withhold it, e.g., from somebody too ill to bear the shock of tragic news. I may feel inclined to support a friend, but think I ought rather to pay my bills; and, yet, in some circumstances, I may think that the support I am inclined to give is also the one I ought to give, even if my creditors have to wait. Consequently, it is not simply my natural readiness to do any of these things which makes me *obliged* to do them. In order to be obliged, I must be ready, but ready in a way which seems peculiarly *inescapable*, and the sense of this inescapability is not permanently attached to *any* particular impulse.

We have then to account for this sense of inescapability, of constraint, of necessary readiness, in some other manner, but there is a further difficulty to be met on the way. If I *ought* to write this letter means "I *must* be ready to write it," I am using the term *must* in a very unusual way. I am not using it as it is used in physics or psychology. If I say, the sun *must* rise tomorrow, or Jones *cannot* resist taking things he does not need because he is a kleptomaniac, I think that this is what, in fact, is bound to happen. These events must occur because they conform to some causal law. But, when I say I must write this letter, meaning not that I am an obsessional letter-writer, but I *must* in the moral sense, then, I don't think that this is what in fact is bound to happen. On the contrary, I may think I must, and yet, knowing myself, expect confidently that I won't. The necessity of the moral law is the very contrary of a bare physical or psychological necessity.

All this makes talking about natural laws of conduct seem very paradoxical. If there are such laws man must be a very curious being, a Jekyll and Hyde, with a dual nature. He must be able to feel ready to do certain things and even to think that he has *no option* but to do them, and, at the same time, he may feel quite unready to do these same things and will in fact not do them. One part of himself tends in a direction from which some other part shrinks away. No wonder that some people feel repelled by such a strange hypothesis: that they think it preferable to suppose that the moral law is not the voice of one part of their natural self divided against another, but that it can only be the voice of another being's will, breaking into their nature from without.

And yet, there is really nothing strange or paradoxical about such a divided nature. The duality between *want* and *must, actual* and *ideal,* is natural to man because of the one faculty which distinguishes him from the animal: the power of reflection and judgment. His will when he is reflective is different from his will when he is unreflective, for his volitions depend in some measure on his understanding of the nature of the things which he wants to do. And since men are forever wavering between states when they are clear-minded and others when their minds are under a cloud, they are forever divided between volitions which correspond to the one and to the other state. This is the principle. How does it work out?

Here is one point which I am very anxious to stress. Moral philosophers, I should say, even moral philosophers, are inclined to regard the moral *must* with a kind of superstitious awe. It is an anomaly. There is nothing like it in the human frame. This, I think, is wrong. The moral *must* originates in reflection and judgment. We are unaware of any duties as long as we don't rise above mere passion and feeling and do some practical thinking. Animals, imbeciles, small children are incapable of having duties. "Lex Naturae est lex Intelligentiae, quam tamen ignorat Pueritia, nescit infantia," the schoolmen said. But practical thinking occurs not only on the moral level and it leads to more practical *must*'s than the moral one. "I *must* ring up the dentist," "I *must* stay at home rather than go to the pictures," "I *cannot* really approve of wasting my time at sherry-parties," are familiar *must*'s, though commonly not yet moral ones. They come to our notice as the result of practical thinking, and the thinking here involved affects and organizes our everyday lives at each step. In my view, the moral *must* is only the most highly evolved product of these same thought processes. Hence, as it is a sound principle in science to study the simple before the complex, the cell before the complex organism, so I think it would be a sound principle in ethics to study the simple functions of practical thinking before its more comprehensive ones, and the *little* practical *must* before the *big* one. If we do this we will no longer regard the moral ought as an anomaly, but rather as the termination of ordinary thought processes carried to their utmost limit.

Now, practical thinking is constantly operative in us in three different ways. It *directs* our desires for one object to others, as when we realize we must desire the means because we desire the end. It *awakens* desires for some objects and *eliminates* desires for others, as when we realize that we must really want to exercise our mind, or cannot really want to be cruel, if we consider adequately what doing the one or the other means. And, finally, it *selects* between different desires, as when we realize that our desire for a life of ease is incompatible with the desire to succeed in our career, and that since we cannot have both, we must devote ourselves to the one rather than the other. These are the *directive*, the *elective*, and the *selective* functions of practical thinking. They are distinct, though in practice they cooperate; and the effect of their operation is that we constantly *project* to ourselves the thought of what we *would have* to be ready to do, or *could not* be ready to do on reflection, and that we feel the thought of this conflicting with the natural drive of our unreflective volitions.

I should like to say something more about these three processes. The first is the most familiar. All the time, there are many things which we don't desire for their own sake, getting out of bed, or out of a warm bath, or making a dentist's appointment; and, yet, we do them, and often only because we think we *have* to. What happens is that we find these actions are also constituents of the process of attaining some other end which we do desire, having breakfast in time, or having our teeth seen to before they hurt. And hence we come to realize that, though not desirable in themselves, yet, when considered as constituents of this other attainment, the thought of these actions must attract us with the same force as the thought of the attainment to which they conduce. Our readiness to do the one is *borrowed* from our readiness to do the other.

Of course, I am not saying that the end always justifies the means. We may dislike getting in touch with our dentist on its own account: we may not have paid last year's bill. Then our considerations will be more complex: we will realize, that on account of our teeth we *must*, but that on account of the unpaid bill we *cannot* want to ring up our dentist; and we will then have to decide whether our end still necessitates the adoption of the means in spite of their intrinsic ineligibility, or whether we will have to abandon the end. But, whatever the conclusion, our considerations will terminate in a *must* judgment: that, in the circumstances, we must or cannot be ready to make the appointment. And the *must* expresses our conviction that this is what we would feel ready to do if we thought about it, and that as far as we can judge, we are *unable to alter* this impression by further consideration.

Clearly, this judgment does not express a mere *physical necessity*. We may think we must make the appointment, and yet not make it. It merely says, we would have to be ready to make it *if we were reflective*, but not also that we *will be reflective*. Of course, while we give undivided attention to the thought of what we would have to do, and the reasons for it, we are also in a state of readiness to do it. But this thought may go out of our mind before we have done it. Or, what is more frequent, it may become dimmed, because our attention reverts partly to our previous unreflective state of mind—the comfort of staying in bed, the unwillingness to make the appointment. And, then, we are only partly influenced by judgment and partly by our feelings as they are without judgment. We are then *divided against ourselves*. We know we must be ready to get up, and yet we are not. Our unreflective volitions are at loggerheads with the thought of what our volitions would be if we reflected. "I must because I want, and yet I resent what I must"; this is no anomaly but the familiar state of mind of being determined completely neither by mere impulse nor by intelligence.

Directive must's are very common. Once we want to attain anything, there is usually a host of other actions which we must or cannot do on account of it, whatever our unreflective likes or dislikes. If only for this reason, our life is invariably hedged in by injunctions and prohibitions. If we want others to consider our interests, we must be ready to consider theirs; if we want them to keep faith with us, we cannot be ready to break faith with them. So all-pervading are these directive necessities that some have thought them to be the very basis of natural morality.

But this would be going too far. The *moral must* commands categorically. It says, *you have absolutely no alternative but to do this.* But the *directive must* does not command categorically, for it merely says you must do one thing *if* you want to do another. You must work hard and be ruthless if you want to get rich. But what about this end? Is it eligible by itself? I may not have to get rich, and, then, it remains uncertain whether I really must work hard and be ruthless.

Now, the questioning of ends is the province of *elective* practical thinking. There are some who deny its possibility. They say, there are no ends which, considered by themselves, the reasonable man *must* or *cannot* desire. Desirable is what is desired and there is no disputing of tastes. As Hume said, "It is not contrary to reason to prefer the destruction of the whole world to the scratching of my finger." There is some truth in this. Ultimately, our desires depend on our dispositions. No one can convert me to the value of mental exertion if I am made to enjoy ease and comfort, or to the value of kindness if I am naturally indifferent to well-doing. Still, this admission is not fatal to the distinction between the *desired* and the *eligible*. Significantly enough, we constantly try to draw it. We feel like going to the pictures, but wonder whether we can really want to go. What do we do when we try to answer this question? We ask ourselves: what would going to the pictures really *mean*? We say: really, going to the pictures means sitting in a stuffy room, watching a poor story, feeling that sense of waste I had last time: and, when I consider all this, I *can no longer* desire what, *before*, had appealed to me.

Here, in brief, is the distinction between the desired and the eligible. The *desired* is what happens to attract us, without an adequate consideration of its nature. The *eligible* is what would attract us if we formed, as Spinoza said, an *adequate idea* of it. The latter is what we *must* desire. For we judge that here is a desire which we don't have by accident, but one which could not be modified by any further consideration, and hence is forced upon us by the nature of the object in relation to our dispositions. Sure enough, no judgment of eligibility is more than probable. Nor need what is eligible for one be eligible for another. But in spite of this there is for everybody a distinction between the actually desired and the eligible as it is for him: between impulses inflated by fancy, or starved by lack of insight and others which he thinks *must* move him or *could no longer* move him if he faced their objects as he thinks they really are.

But even the *elective must* is not the *moral ought*. To get rich may be not only desired, but also eligible. But this alone does not make it categorically necessary for us to devote ourselves to the Stock Exchange. Nothing that considered by itself we must be ready to do is, simply for this reason, what we *ought* to do. Here I must appeal to another familiar experience. There is always a host of things which are intrinsically eligible: to have material security, to keep our body healthy, our mind alert, to care for our friends. But this is not to say that, on reflection, we can be ready to pursue these objects all at once. For, on reflection, we realize that pursuing the one is (wholly or partly) incompatible with pursuing the other. Hence we get another restrictive *must*: that we cannot both be ready to do the one *and* the other, but only the one *or* the other. On what principle then do we select? Here we have the third, the *selective* function of practical thinking. We ask ourselves: would we rather be ready to do *x* without *y*, or *y* without *x*, develop our talents and forego material security, or get material security and forego developing our talents? We try to form adequate ideas of each, and we test our reactions to the thought of the one without the other, and the other without the one. And, when we have carried this process to the point at which we think we cannot modify the result any further, we realize that we *must be ready to do the one rather than the other.* This is choice. In choice, we ask a question and receive an answer, and the answer is a new *must*. This *must* often weighs on us particularly heavily. For since the excluded alternative is intrinsically eligible our attention is only too prone to revert to it: and then we are acutely and painfully aware of being divided against ourselves. Anybody who has once chosen to pursue a long-term end knows the intensity of this conflict between the thought of *what he cannot but prefer on reflection* and the eminently eligible and yet forbidden alternatives which lie in wait for him on the way.

I think I have said enough to illustrate my point. I wanted to impress on you that the dualism between *want* and *must, actual* and *ideal*, pervades our ordinary life intimately and in more ways than merely in the big conflict between natural impulse and moral ought. The elective, the selective, and the directive *must* are essential normative principles. With their help we steady, coordinate and direct our natural impulses. They do not impose upon them an alien norm. They merely *project* to ourselves our impulses as they would be if they were determined by their objects as we think those objects really are, both in themselves and in their relations to one another. These impulses we regard as for us *rationally necessary* because we think that no further mental exertion which we could make would make them any different; and it is against them that our unreflective volitions rebel as soon as we are off our guard. Here is the same conflict between *must* and *want* that is commonly associated with the moral law. And, I think, this strongly suggests that the moral law is not an unaccountable anomaly, but rather the crowning result of the same thought processes which present us with the *little must's* of our ordinary experience.

In my view, the moral law differs from the other forms of practical necessity in one respect only; it is *categorical*. It says, *you must do this and nothing else.* No other imperative goes as far. It is not categorically necessary to go out into a cold and rainy night if I think I must merely because I want to see an ill friend: for I may not *have* to see him; nor to go to see him if I must only because by itself this would be an eligible thing to do: for I may still find it necessary not to do it in view of the *means* to be employed, like walking through the rain and catching a cold, or because of some more eligible *alternative*, for example, working. Nor have I reached a categorical necessity when I think I must pay the visit rather than work: for then I still think only I must do the first *rather than the second,* not I must do the first *rather than anything else.* All these *little must's* bind in view of only some facts considered in isolation from others. They say what we must do from *this or that point of view,* but not what we must do from *every point of view.*

Normally, we inquire no further. We judge of practical matters as we happen to have doubts about the one or the other aspect of the case. We either consider only the requisite means, taking it for granted that the end is eligible, or the end, taking it for granted that the means are eligible and that the end does not conflict with alternative ends. We don't systematically combine all these considerations into one, carrying them to the point at which we can say: *this is what we must do everything considered.* But to do this is within our power, and when we do it we arrive at a judgment of *categorical practical necessity.* We then let a given project run the gauntlet of elective, directive, and selective practical examination, and we regard it as categorically necessary if it survives this test, and as categorically prohibited if it fails to survive it.

The process by which we discover categorical necessities has, I think, three stages. We have first to consider whether what we want or could do is *eligible by itself*, in view of its properties and effects. We ask: what will our visit mean to our friend, to ourselves, how would his landlady take it? Maybe this suffices to rule it out. Our first impulse may have been a sentimental whim. But supposing we think that so far we have to do this act. Then the second step will be to consider the *means*. Here we must make both directive and selective judgments: what must we do in order to pay the visit? And would we still feel we had to pay it if we considered the intrinsic ineligibility of some of the means? Once again, a project may be ruled out at this stage. Charity, normally, must not be carried to the point of forging checks. There is nothing more pernicious than the view that some ends are eligible absolutely, regardless of the eligibility of the means. But supposing we think we must do the act both on its own account and in spite of the means. Then, the third step is to consider *alternatives*. Here we will first consider those already in our mind. We must want to pay the visit, but we cannot do this and go on working. Once more, our project will be ruled out if we decide that in spite of the eligibility of the first we must rather do the second. But let it pass this test as well; then there is still one more step to be taken. For we want to know, not whether to see our friend is necessary for us in spite of *some* eligible alternative, but whether it is necessary *categorically*: and for this we must, last, consider whether it would still be necessary for us in spite of *every other* eligible alternative competing with it at the same time. If it is, then we have reached an inescapable or categorical practical necessity. For then we are faced with an action which we think is *unalterably forced upon us by the thought of its own nature and effects, and despite any sacrifice involved in doing it.* As far as we can see there is no alternative to this action in the circumstances, and hence there is *nothing for it but to do it.*

It is plain that categorical necessity can never pertain to any particular kind of action merely considered as such. It can pertain only to an action *in relation* to given circumstances, that is, if in these circumstances it is not only intrinsically eligible, but also *more* eligible than any other which it excludes. Hence we can never say that to tell the truth or to keep the peace or anything else will *always* be categorically necessary: for it depends on the circumstances whether or not there is something else which *by comparison* has greater eligibility. All we can say is that if we consider any situation as a *whole* we will always find something or other the thought of which, we think, *must* move us on its own account and *must* remain preeminently moving in spite of everything that has to be subordinated to it.

Now, I think that when we are moved in this manner we are moved by a sense of *natural duty*, and hence we have come to the end of our long search. For we can now answer the question from which we set out: in what sense is a natural law *natural*, and in what sense is it a *law* or *duty*?

Plainly, the sense of categorical necessity on which I have tried to focus your attention can be accounted for without reference to anything beyond ourselves. It is rooted in our constitution as human beings, and it issues jointly from the *rational* and the *appetitive* part of our nature. *Materially,* natural duties depend on our natural dispositions, *formally*, they depend on reflection and judgment. There would be no duties for us without the one *and* the other. The duty to care for the sick, to obey the laws of the state, to devote myself to creative work, depends on some natural incentive to do any of these things, whether this incentive be rooted in an innate disposition to be kind, or an acquired disposition to be law-abiding, or in the expectation of good for ourselves. But, equally, no natural incentive alone constitutes a duty. I may be honest, temperate, industrious, I may even endanger my life for the sake of others from a strong inclination to behave in these ways, and yet this is not to act from a sense of natural duty. There can be no duty without an awareness of necessity, and this awareness can be acquired only by reflection and judgment. It is not enough to *feel* ready to give our lives. We must *judge* that this readiness is also inescapably called for of a person of our temperament and upbringing, by the nature of the case; and, moreover, that it is inescapably called for, in the situation, despite the means to be employed and the alternatives to be sacrificed. Only then do we obey a *dictate of conscience*. Conscience is more than feeling. It is inward knowing, con-*scientia*, in-*wit*, Ge-*wissen*. Feeling alone could not give us the sense that *here we stand, we cannot do otherwise*: for the absence of any alternative must be judged of, it cannot be just felt. Moral thinking is discursive; not intuitive.

You may object that this is to overrationalize the moral sense. Do we not know what we ought to do without protracted deliberations? Certainly, sometimes we do, but at others we don't. It depends on the case whether deliberation must be protracted; but protracted or not, there must be deliberation. It is easy to see that we ought to answer a letter but hard to decide whether we ought to visit a sick friend abroad. Here, the nature of the project, the means, the alternatives may keep us in suspense for a long time. I say, for a long time, but there may be no time for delay. Here is a factor which, in a sense, simplifies moral decisions. Conscience must give its verdict before the moment for action has passed. There is no time to lose when I see a child in the water; and then, however complex the decision might be if there were no hurry, I can make it only by reducing it to its simplest terms. But even in this case I have to make it, or else I act from a sense of *panic*, not from a sense of *duty*. For an instant, at least, I must question my impulse: and at that moment I must *judge* that, as far as I can see, and naturally I cannot see far, *this and nothing else is what I must do*. In fact, the time factor always forces us to make decisions before we can be *certain* that the data on which we make them are complete. Perfect insight would require infinite time. In some ways this simplifies the moral calculus; but it entails that no moral decision is ever certain to conform to the ideal standard of perfect insight and that most are likely to fall considerably short of it.

I need hardly repeat that the *morally* necessary is not the same as the *physically* necessary. To think that we *must*—in the moral sense— is not to think that we *will*. It is to think that we would have to be ready to do some action *if* we maintained the effort of being reflective; but this is not also to think that we will maintain it. It is true, while we are informed by the judgment that this is what we must do on reflection, we cannot fail to be under its influence. But we may forget. Or, more commonly, our attention may become divided between the thought of what we must do if we were reflective and what we want to do while we are not; and, then, the force of the moral ought is in-hibited. Once again, we are then divided against ourselves and faced with the conflict between *want* and *must, actual* and *ideal*. I have main-tained throughout this essay that this conflict is a natural consequence of man's power of rational self-determination, and obviously, it must be most pronounced in case of the *moral must*. This *must* projects to ourselves our own will as it would be if it were determined by reason as completely as we think we can make it; and it therefore conflicts most with our uninformed passions, our thoughtless indolence, and all those aversions and desires which, however legitimate in them-selves, must give way so that our predominant impulse may live. No wonder that the law of our nature appears to command without de-ference to our wishes.

And, yet, I think, there is no escaping this law. It is true, we impose it upon ourselves by reflection and judgment. We could be without it if we were prepared never to face the thought of the rationally nec-essary. But this, I think, is the very thing we can never afford to do. For one thing, we would forsake the only means we have for directing and adjusting the outflow of our natural energies: we would be unready to do what is requisite for the attainment of our ends, ready to do what is not worth doing, afraid of doing what is not worth avoiding; we would dissipate our energies in the futile attempt to combine what cannot be made compatible and subordinate the more to the less satisfying. I am not denying that the escapist may not *sometimes* be lucky nor maintaining that the conscientious is *always* rewarded by success. Our insight is fallible and the outward effects of rational self-direction are remote and uncertain; yet this can never be a reason for abandoning the attempt.

For, moreover, rational self-direction has another effect which is near and certain and which has a value for us to which the value of everything else is subordinate. To break into our impulses as they happen to affect us, to make them conform to adequate ideas, to subordinate the conflicting many to the predominant one, is to be mentally alive: it is to *find the identity of our self in the diversity of our states*. Self-identity or unity of consciousness is not a self-subsisting thing: it is constantly in jeopardy, increased or diminished by the extent to which we offer resistance to our impulses and view them before we follow them in relation to the true nature of their objects and to one another. Be engrossed in each impulse separately as it succeeds another, and each time you are no more than this impulse: *you* are your anger, your fear, your sympathy, for you are immersed in it. But attend to it and at the same time to what it would be on reflection, and you become aware of your self as the one perceiving subject of a diversity of feeling-states, distinct from each of them and conscious of them all. From a bundle of successive states you turn into a *person* conscious of and distinct from his states and enduring through them. This achievement is beyond the escapist. He may be lucky in attaining his particular ends, but he cannot be himself. For what essentially contributes to the formation and preservation of a unified consciousness is every single occasion on which we make a moral choice and abide by it. Each time we fail, its cohesion is broken; each time we succeed it becomes more closely knit. Hence if it is worth being the unified, distinct, and enduring subject of our own feeling-states, then we must always be ready to submit to rational self-determination.

But is it? I will venture a brief answer. I think, when we reflect, we will find that we value a unified self precisely as much as we value life itself: that the desire to be *is* a desire for personal identity. We are afraid of death because we are afraid of *losing* our personal identity, and physical existence without it we would not regard as worth having. The life that is valued is essentially the life of the soul, and clearly without it nothing else would be worth having: for we can only possess anything precisely to the extent to which we are mentally alive to having it. Now, it is in moral conduct that we gain a unified consciousness which is distinct from our states and in escapism that we dissolve the unity of our person. And hence the need for submission to the laws of natural morality is rooted in our very desire for life and sanity itself, as Spinoza said in the "conatus in suo esse perseverare." The *wages of sin is death*, even for the agnostic.

It is time to summarize my argument. I have been trying to show— with arguments which lay no claim to novelty—that there is a natural foundation for morality. There will always be some laws which are imposed on us from within, regardless of whether they are also imposed on us from without. We find them if we seek them, and we must seek to find them. Moreover, what we find will not be vastly different from the precepts of revealed morality. There are good enough reasons in our mental and bodily constitution and in the conditions of social life to make it imperative to be temperate rather than self-indulgent, faithful rather than treacherous, modest rather than conceited, sociable rather than grasping and aggressive. Nevertheless, there is at least one fundamental difference between natural morality as I see it and life by a moral code accepted as a matter of faith. Natural morality cannot have the same finality. It does not make any particular duties necessarily binding on all men at all times in all circumstances. All, I think, we can say with confidence—although even this is either an empirical generalization or a matter of definition–is that sane human beings will always be bound to submit themselves to the rule of some law. But beyond this, I think, we cannot go. What people will find when they seek their duties depends on the way they are made, the circumstances in which their actions take place, and the degree of their insight into these circumstances.

This is an inevitable conclusion from our premises. We cannot divorce the moral eligibility of actions from their effects, from the means to be employed and the alternatives to be sacrificed: any of these factors may vary with the circumstances of the case. Nor can we divorce it from the way people are made, since their dispositions may vary, both by nature and by education, and what is good for one need not be good for another. Nor, finally, can we divorce it from people's insight, since we can have no duty of which we are ignorant, and hence what we ought to promote is what *as far as we can see* we must do, and not what we would have to do if we had *perfect insight*. Of some people we can expect no more than that they should be true to the values in which they have been brought up or which prevail in their social environment, and we may even think that, on reflection, they ought often to accept the limits of their own understanding and not to try to evolve new evaluations of their own. Of others we will think that they have not only a right but a duty to question and to reverse preconceived notions of the eligibility of actions in the light of some new insight into their nature and effects. On the basis of natural morality no accepted standard is sacrosanct, and the search for the *ideal* morality, based on *perfect insight*, is a never-ending adventure charged with responsibility and as full of potential perils as rewards. Such, I think, is the law to which we are bound if we disregard faith. It binds the agnostic, and, I think, it cannot be ignored by those who believe.

[9]

Morality and Nature

The history of moral thought, from the Greeks to the present day, shows the recurrence of the view that morality is founded on 'nature' or 'the nature of things'. My object in this essay is to discuss this view.

I

First, I must try to explain it, which has its difficulties. Not only are there different versions, some of which differ radically, but the use of the words 'nature' and 'natural' is notoriously elusive and diverse. How they are used can be determined only from the context and often only by contrast with something to which they are being opposed. Sometimes 'natural' is contrasted with 'supernatural' or 'divine', sometimes with 'artificial' and with 'acquired': in one context it is identified with what has some objective existence, in another with what is given in sensible experience, in another still with what has a 'reason' or 'explanation': sometimes 'nature' is used for the whole of experience; sometimes 'what man meets in nature' is contrasted with 'what he meets in himself'. I must therefore begin by asking: in what contexts, and in opposition to what views, has the doctrine of the naturalness of the moral order been developed?

Most often it has been put forward in opposition to the view that moral laws are commands issued by some divine authority. What is denied here is not that a divine will may desire man to live by moral

Reprinted with permission of the publisher from *Australasian Journal of Philosophy* 28 (1950): 69-92.

rules, but that moral rules *consist in* divine commands. No matter whether or not God has informed man of his duties, these duties have a natural existence *independent* of a divine will, and indeed whether or not such a will exists. Here 'natural' is used in opposition to 'supernatural' or 'divine'. But it is also used here to oppose a further implication of the theological view, an implication the latter shares with another, with the view that morality is founded on immemorial custom or convention and that moral laws are demands issuing from this source. For both imply that morality is somehow the product of artifice; a moral order can be posited at will by divine or human agency. And from this point of view, to insist that morality is founded on nature is to deny *this* implication. Moral laws do not owe their being to willful caprice; they are 'natural' in the sense that they are no less a constituent of the objective world than the laws of nature. Like the latter, they cannot be created or destroyed by any positive enactment. They are not made, they are discovered.

But to insist on the objective existence of moral demands in this sense, and to call this an existence in 'nature', is not yet to settle whereabouts in 'nature' they subsist, or what sort of being they have; and this introduces a new cleavage of opinion. According to some, moral laws exist objectively in the 'universe', or 'the nature of things and situations': and here 'universe' and 'nature' are used roughly in the sense in which we contrast what we meet in 'nature' with what we meet in ourselves, in our own mind or feelings. This view became prominent in the eighteenth century, with such moralists as Samuel Clarke and Richard Price, after it had always been an undercurrent in the doctrine of the naturalness of the moral order since the Stoics; and it is the one which prevails among the 'intuitionists', the once leading school of British moralists. Broadly, this view amounts to saying that moral duties are demands or claims on man residing somehow in his environment, in the 'situation' in which he acts, though how and where, it is said, cannot be further described. In this connection it is noteworthy that, for this school of thought, moral duties, though existing 'in the nature of things', are not 'natural existents' in another familiar use of this term; they are not facts given to sense or constructions out of what is given to sense. They belong to a 'supersensible' nature which is sui generis and is perceptible only by a special faculty of moral intuition. To say that morality is founded on 'nature' is not here to say it rests on empirical foundations.

But the main view of the naturalness of the moral order, from the Stoics to at least the middle of the eighteenth century, was another. Here man's subjection to moral laws is said to be founded on nature not as he finds it without himself, but in himself, on human nature.

A passage from Bishop Butler, one of the great exponents of this view, will illustrate this point. "Nothing," he says, "can be more evident . . . than that, exclusive of revelation, man cannot be considered as a creature left by his maker to act at random . . . :but from his make, constitution, or nature he is in the strictest sense a law to himself. He has the rule of right within: what is wanting is only that he honestly attend to it." The broad drift of this is plain: man's subjection to moral laws, to injunctions and prohibitions which set a standard of right and wrong conduct, is founded on facts to be met within man himself, in his psychological constitution. And this, we shall see, entails a view of the naturalness of the moral order radically different from, and more complex than, the one we have hitherto considered.

I shall be concerned in this essay mainly with this last view; and once again, we shall not understand it unless we consider it in relation to the views to which it is opposed. Traditionally, it is a middle-of-the-road position, the resort of those who are unwilling to subscribe in ethics to what I may call transcendentalism on the one hand and skepticism on the other. By skepticism I mean the view that binding moral duties have no manner of real being: the belief in them rests on misinterpretation of the facts. By transcendentalism, I shall now mean jointly the theological and conventionalist and also the intuitionist views previously distinguished. By contrast with the view I wish now to consider it is justifiable to group them together, for in spite of their opposition to one another they retain some crucial characteristics in common. This may not be immediately apparent. But, in fact, all three are agreed on the externality of moral demands to man: they resemble orders, or claims, made on him from some external source. Moreover, both the purely theological view and its intuitionist opponents are agreed that the source of these orders is beyond nature in at least one sense: it is wholly beyond the sensibly given and accessible only by special cognitive means, either by faith or by a privileged kind of intuition. Now, both transcendentalism and skepticism are typical features of man's view of morality; in fact, the one has often provoked, and is always apt to provoke, the other. The rule of transcendentalist ethics in whatever form tends to end in a crisis of moral skepticism; and the doctrine that morality is founded not simply on nature but on human nature must be understood as the recurrent attempt to meet this crisis.

It is necessary, therefore, to mention the main reasons for the vulnerability of all forms of transcendentalist ethics to skepticism, for they reveal the weaknesses which an alternative theory would have to meet. One reason is in the special claims which transcendentalist ethics make for the possibility of moral knowledge. Whether such knowledge is made to rest on faith or on a special kind of intuition, it is made to rest on some supersensible, and in a sense therefore, 'nonnatural' source of information; and that there are these peculiar sources is not sufficiently evident to everyone to exclude the doubt that our so-called moral duties are not merely specters seen by fanciful minds in the dark. But even granted their existence, there is another difficulty concerning their *bindingness*. We are asked to think of moral duties somehow as orders or demands from without; and this raises the awkward question of people's reasons for complying with them, especially when their inclinations and interests are opposed. We say, people have a reason when something in the thought of an act, some anticipated property or effect of it, has the power to make them do it; and we assume that without this people cannot be expected to act, let alone act against their inclinations which are the impulses which already possess them. But it is plain, when a person is *ordered* to do a thing, this is still quite different from his having a motivating reason for doing this same thing: the one is logically separable from the other. No matter if Jones orders Smith to turn down his radio; this does not in itself seriously bind Smith to do it; and no more would any transcendentalist system of moral imperatives in itself be a system of seriously binding obligations. Acquired habits of obedience, or the fear of external sanctions, may conceal this weakness from the ordinary man. But one day someone will notice it; and then it is not far to conclude that the so-called bonds of morality are shams; that they are not only doubtful as regards their existence, but that in any case they are in themselves not seriously bonds at all. And if this is so, why should not everyone do as he pleases?

I hope this will help to show why so many moralists, from the Stoics to Hugo Grotius, Pufendorf, and Bishop Butler, have attempted to seek the foundations of morality elsewhere. It will explain why they sought an alternative to the theological and conventionalist views of the moral order, views which plainly invite skeptical attack; and also why they evolved a view of morality with its foundations in human rather than in some supersensible 'external' nature.

The question is: shall we fare better if we seek them there? The traditional argument runs, the facts here speak for themselves. Suppose people followed the moral skeptic and discounted duties in all their externalist interpretations. Even so, they would not find themselves freed from obligations in *every sense*: something would continue to demand that they should do some things and not do others; and this remaining authority would be in *their own thoughts*. People need only reflect on their prospective acts and consider what they would entail: what it would be to break one's promises, to ignore the laws of the State, to disregard the interests of others, to neglect oneself. It will then appear that these thoughts have a power, contrary to their inclinations, to deter them from some acts and to impel them to others. According to most exponents of the view, it is the relation of acts to the promotion of social good, and the good of the agent himself, that lends the thought of them this power to impel or to deter. According to others, the matter is more complicated; men have also an innate capacity to value honesty or fair dealing and to disvalue perjury or injustice as such and apart from their consequences, and likewise many other things. But all are agreed on this: if only people were first to *contemplate* what they are about to do, these thoughts would provide them with motives, contrary to their inclinations, to forbear some things and to do others. And there would be something special about these motives. They not only impel, but in a peculiar way they compel: they not merely prompt, but *dictate*. They furnish, therefore, what deserves to be called an inner sense of obligation, of 'ought' and 'ought not'; and as the proximate cause of these motives is reflection they may be called rational motives and the obligations 'dictates of reason'. The skeptic's denial of binding duties in their transcendentalist interpretation cannot therefore rid man in some other sense of the conflict between duty and inclination; this conflict remains, transformed only from a conflict between man's will and outside claims on him to a conflict within his will itself.

Now, if true, this view is more likely to support the objective existence of a binding moral order against skepticism than the view that morality is founded on some esoteric 'nature of things and situations'. For the foundations of the moral order are here conceived as 'natural' in a more familiar and less dubious sense of the term. For one thing, what are here called 'natural' obligations would in one sense be facts of nature in their ordinary empirical meaning. To perceive them would require no special powers of intuition. Again, what is here meant by 'obligation' or a 'dictate of reason' is 'naturally' binding, that is, binding in the only way in which it makes sense to say that men *can* be seriously bound. For there is no need here to ask for a motive; in fact, to do so would be logically absurd. We only say here people are under obligations to actions when we mean they have, contrary to their inclinations, a specially compelling or deterring motive for doing or not doing them. It is tempting, therefore, to conclude that the view that morality is founded on human nature amounts to this: man's subjection to duties is a datum of his inner experience like *any other psychological fact*, a fact which the skeptic can be invited to verify by using his ordinary powers of reflection and self-observation.

But to say this would be too simple. There is a difficulty in describing a dictate of reason, as here used, as in all respects an ordinary fact of nature like any other psychological fact, an emotion or inclination. There is a sense in which we would contrast emotions or inclinations, as belonging to the 'natural' man in us, with a 'dictate of reason' as not belonging to the 'natural man' in quite the same sense; and this makes it necessary to specify more carefully what is meant by saying that the moral order is founded on human nature. Bishop Butler, for instance, was aware of this difficulty, as, implicitly, were most exponents of the view, and an explanation is not far to seek. The point is that a 'dictate of reason' is conceived as an impulse which would arise only *if people reflected* on their projected doings or omissions: and an impulse like this we do not meet in our experience except by our own concurrence, by exerting ourselves mentally. But our own mental exertions we do not regard as, in the ordinary sense, a 'fact of nature'. We use this word only for occurrences which we do not hesitate to regard as causally conditioned by an indefinite series of antecedents: and we hesitate to regard our own active mental life in quite this light. The whole of it as we live through it, and when we review it always at least part of it, is not viewed as related to a chain of antecedent causes; in whole or in part it invariably appears as having its first beginning in and with our active self. We cannot, therefore, without violating language, call our own active mental life a 'fact of nature' like any other, nor what would exist only by its mediation. And this is the case with a 'dictate of reason'. As it would have no being except on condition of our own and seemingly free concurrence, it would not be altogether a 'natural' or psychological fact like a stab of pain or a fit of jealousy. Unlike them, it would be a datum of inner experience sought out and evoked by ourselves and not simply incurred. It has, therefore, been rightly felt that to speak of morality as founded on human nature is to use 'nature' in a specially broad sense; not indeed for anything that lies *beyond* experience, but for experience as including what is felt in spontaneous activity, what results from it, and what is purely of its own or sensibly given; that is, in a sense which allows us to say also, using the word more narrowly, that morality is founded on what in man is 'nature' and what is not 'nature' but mind. In this sense 'natural obligations' used to be spoken of as 'dictates of reason and nature'.

Besides this, 'natural' as applied to the foundations of morality has traditionally some further connotations. It also means 'transparent to reason' or 'explicable'; and in this sense, with the partial exception of Bishop Butler, 'naturalness' is also usually attributed to the moral order both in its essence and in its content. That man is subject to moral dictates is not a brute datum; it is claimed it strictly follows from his being a creature of both appetite and reason. Equally, the whole matter of his duties, it is assumed, can be derived from some simple and ultimate data about him; from his dispositions to value social good and his own and from the effects on social and private good of his actions. These data are said to entail all his duties toward others, the State, and himself; they can, without difficulty, be deduced from them. And last, not only is the moral order 'natural' in this sense of being explicable in terms of other simpler facts, but these facts themselves are said to be, in still another sense, 'natural' to man. The possession of reason, and of dispositions to value good, is of his 'nature' *as constituting his formal essence*; so that, when he acts in accordance with rules resting on these foundations, he will be fulfilling what he essentially is or has been cut out to be.

So much in explanation of what may be called the 'classical doctrine' that morality is founded on human nature. What, then are its merits? I think its attractiveness as an antidote both to a dubious transcendentalism and a frank skepticism is beyond question. Its insistence on the inwardness of some sense of obligation, and on its foundations in the conative and rational properties of man, has a ring of truth. Nevertheless, as an account of what moral belief and moral talk are all about only few today would be ready to defend it. On the contrary, it is not too much to say that the wholesale rejection of this point of view is one of the few points of agreement between the conflicting schools of contemporary moralists.

What prevails today is a transcendentalism clinging, for what it is worth, to the external existence in some supersensible 'nature' of moral demands on man and a rising skepticism which denies to moral obligations any objective being. 'You ought', according to the logical positivist, states no moral truth but simply expresses the speaker's feelings or will to persuade; and 'I ought', I suppose, comes to something like saying to oneself "Gee up." Existentialists like Sartre are similarly disillusioned. "If God does not exist," Sartre writes, "everything is permitted, and hence man is deserted, as neither *in* himself nor *outside* himself can he find anything to hold on to; he nowhere meets values or imperatives to justify or excuse anything he does." Between these extremes the traditional third way of the classical doctrine has come to be regarded as naive and outmoded.

There are reasons for this, partly in the temper of our age, partly in the insufficiencies of the traditional expositions of this doctrine. None of them can stand up to present standards of analysis. The language is confused; the terms are undefined; there is a naive trust in the simplicity and permanence of human nature; a faulty psychology; a misplaced confidence in the powers of reason and observation to settle moral issues with ease, with no less facility, at least, than scientific issues. Moreover, toward the end of the eighteenth century the classical doctrine suffered a misfortune. It was both improved and mangled by Kant, who, in an attempt to revise it, refined its form to the point of squashing its life. Nevertheless, I venture to say, the reaction against it has gone too far, with the uncomfortable results we are witnessing. This is not the place to explain this at length, but I shall offer the outlines of a defense.

II

At heart, I think, the 'classical doctrine' rested on a simple truth. Man might be stripped of everything he ever believed about moral restraints; he would still, in his constitution, find impediments to acting quite at random. For there is in him what might be called a 'natural machinery for self-control' which rests on the capacity of *forethought* causally to control volition. It is commonplace that a man who foresees the nature and consequences of his actions will tend to refrain from some to which he had been inclined and to do others to which he had been indifferent or averse. However, this mechanism is conceived too simply, as was done by the Greeks and is done again today by some logical positivists, if control by *forethought* is equated simply with control by *knowledge or belief*. In order to evoke a conative response, knowledge of fact about future acts requires more than a suitably disposed recipient; it also needs being mentally rehearsed, dwelled upon, chewed over in various ways. The so-called 'guidance of conduct by reason' involves processes both of exploration and of evaluation of fact; and the latter, though also 'rational', are not processes of cognition but of mental presentation or attention. They are 'thinkings of', not 'believings that', and only in conjunction with them can knowledge of fact be said to be able to control volitions.

Before I go on I had better elucidate this last point. It can be illustrated by the observation that ignorance of fact is not all that people plead in extenuation of omissions. A man who has failed to act on his doctor's information that an operation will restore him to health—which is what he desires—may plead, "Of course, I knew, but I never took it in properly; I never actually put it to myself and let it sink in that to do the one would implicitly also be achieving the other which I desired." Here the fault is ascribed not to ignorance of fact but to *obtuseness*, to the lack of appropriate rehearsing of what was known, a rehearsing which may be called, as it would direct the desire for an end to the means to it, *directive* evaluative thinking. Again, the same man, though impressed by what he has been told, may yet be put off by the anticipation of expense and discomfort; and in extenuation he may plead here: "I knew what would be involved, expense and discomfort on the one hand, cure on the other; but I never properly *contemplated* these conflicting implications *alongside each other*; so I failed to give *due weight* to the curative effect." Here we may speak of the absence of proper *selective* evaluative thinking. And again, there is a third plea of this sort. Our man may say: "I knew the operation would restore my health, but at the time I felt indifferent to that; I never troubled to *envisage* 'getting well' as such an end for me; and yet, had I done so, I would have been roused from my apathy." Here the fault is ascribed to a failure to evaluate, by means of imaginative presentation, the potential attractiveness of an end in itself: a failure, we may call it, in *elective* evaluative thinking.

In this sense, then, we may speak of a 'natural machinery for self-control', provided always we understand it to consist of the control of volitions by both processes of exploration and evaluation. It is a machinery in virtue of which humans tend to live on two levels of volitional consciousness and to experience conflict between them; the level of their immediate desires and the level of what, under the influence of forethought, their desires would become; and in this the classical doctrine claims, and I think with some justification, are the foundations of a species of knowledge which is doing the direction-giving work commonly attributed to *moral* knowledge. For a man aware of the possible clash between his immediate and his 'rational' impulses or motives may with good sense inquire before acting: "Would I still want what I do want, or still not want what I am averse from, if I first stopped to explore and to evaluate the facts about it?" And having done so he may come to judge: "These are the facts and, if I contemplated them, they would provide reasons, and, on balance, compelling reasons, for me not to do the one, or to do the other." The function of such inquiry and judgment would be to organize and assist the working of the 'natural machinery'. "Would I still want if . . . ?" will organize the quest for the facts about the act possibly relevant to a change of practical attitude; for without the facts there can be no answer; and again, it will organize experimental evaluative thinking in order to elicit what responses a *viewing* of the facts would entail, i.e., if they were *envisaged* as possible ends in themselves, or as means to ends already desired, or as rivals conflicting with one another. The result would be a knowledge of rational motives acting as a potential impediment to action from inclination; and even with nothing else to 'hold on to' but knowledge of this type humans could be said to possess, in virtue of their very constitution, some specifically direction-giving knowledge.

However, even if this be granted, this cannot be the whole story. For the really disputed question is: Has any of this a bearing on *morality*, on the direction of conduct by moral concepts? Here the classical view was that it did, in fact that the inevitability of some moral order for man was entailed by it. And precisely this the critic denies. No doubt forethought can *prompt* by raising new impulses or motives. But so far this is not to mention any moral concept. 'I ought' (or 'you ought') is different from 'I (or 'you') would want if I (or 'you') first stopped to think'. The one has a normative and coercive connotation which the other has not. Now the classical doctrine had not quite overlooked this point. Forethought, it had been implied, may not only prompt but *dictate*. It may raise motives of a special forcibleness. But, it must be admitted, the grounds for this assertion had not been satisfactorily explained, even by the few who made the attempt. And according to the modern critic this failure is not accidental. There is no bridge that leads from any kind of 'I want' to any kind of 'I ought'. To maintain there is involves the so-called 'fallacy of naturalism', the error of trying to reduce what belongs to a uniquely ethical species of discourse to some wholly other, nonethical and psychological one. Moral discourse either is about something untainted by reference to anything psychological, or it is about nothing at all. Nearly all modern moralists regard this as axiomatic.

And yet at first sight the classical doctrine seems plausible enough. If a person of sympathetic dispositions thinks that an act of his would hurt the feelings of another, and distinctly envisages what he is thinking, it seems natural for him to say: "But, then, I *can't* want to do this," and the 'can't' seems to express some special compellingness of the deterring motive. This point is even more evident in the use of 'I ought' within the context of prudence. For we speak of dictates of prudence no less than of moral dictates. We say, reluctantly, we ought to do one thing on account of some other we desire; that we *must* will, and not merely *would* will, the means as we desire the end. Many of the 'natural obligations' of the classical doctrine were of this form: that we ought to act sociably if we want others to do likewise or be temperate if we desire our own good. And, indeed, who would say he would *want* to stop smoking if he counted the cost? Though some may say, if they counted it, they 'ought', or as it were, '*would have to want to*'. What, then, is involved here in the transition from the weaker 'I would want' to the stronger 'I would have to' or 'ought'? I think Kant is the only one to have seen correctly what this is. According to him, when we say we 'ought', in the prudential or moral sense, we say we have, contrary to our inclinations, not only a rational but a *rationally necessary* impulse or 'will' to do something, which I broadly take to mean this: 'Necessary' is what no trying will alter, however often repeated; 'rationally necessary' what would not be so altered by 'reason', by appropriate mental operations. A both rational and rationally necessary 'willing' would then be one to satisfy two conditions: that someone would own it if he used 'reason', that is, foreknowledge and mental rehearsing (in our case about his ends and the means toward them); and moreover, that no further use of 'reason', however often repeated, would alter it. And this is meant by a 'dictate of reason': an impulse or will to action evoked by 'reason' and not only casually so but in accordance with a principle of sufficiency; one which derives a special forcibleness from having the formal characteristic that no further testing by 'reason' would change or dislodge it. And such an impulse will not unnaturally present itself with the normative and coercive qualities of an 'ought'. We don't always say that, in reason, we *would have to will* things for the sake of others which we desire; more often we say simply we *want* to do them for this reason. We say only, we would have to will them when, though knowing what they would lead to, we still don't want to do them; and this tends to happen when some aversion to the means stands in the way of a ready contemplation and evaluation of what is known. It is here that it becomes proper to ask: "But the facts being what they are, would I not 'in reason' have to will what in fact I don't will?"; and it is because of the contrariety of our inclinations that here we wish to be assured that in reason we not only would will it but could not get out of willing it. This conviction here thus confronts us both with an ideally inescapable objective and with an incipient impediment to acting as we please; it confronts our operative motives with the knowledge of another which, if we exercised 'reason', in this case our capacity for directive evaluative thinking, would supersede them; and the logical force of saying "I would have to will" seems precisely that which belongs to saying "I ought" or "I am obliged."

I think then, the classical doctrine was right in speaking of dictates of 'reason', fully intelligible in terms of the 'natural machinery of self-control'. For the conception of a rationally necessitated willing is nothing other than that of a willing informed by the ordinary powers of self-control exercised not just casually, but carried to an *ideal limit*; and our judgments about this will express, though never the certainty, but some positive likelihood that a willing of ours would conform to this formal standard of perfection. These judgments inform, or remind us, of *something about ourselves*, not, indeed, of a *given*, but of an *ideal* attitude toward an act. Their characteristic function for the direction of conduct is that they organize in a principled manner the quest for practically relevant knowledge about the world, and for its conative evaluation. They are thus ultimately about a species of psychological fact, i.e., conative responses, but not about them as they actually are, or normally tend to be, but about them as, in ideally defined conditions, they would be. Discourse of this kind is thereby marked off from the range of discourse which psychology as a science normally and appropriately regards as its own.

In fact, such discourse is as little about 'purely' psychological fact as is discourse about material objects. But like the latter it may be said to be about some ideal construction out of psychological fact. As the one is about sense-experiences obeying rules of connection only approximately exemplified in actual fact, so the other is about conative responses evoked and tested in accordance with a principle of sufficiency only approximately exemplified in our actual procedures of evoking and testing them. 'Ought' discourse has therefore an irreducible subject matter of its own: but this does not here commit us to saying, any more than in the case of 'material object' discourse, that this subject matter is 'simple' and 'unanalyzable', or that its nature is grasped by the exercise of a special faculty of 'intuition'. What needs saying is that the concept of 'ought', of a rationally necessary motive or willing, is not purely empirical, but has a nonempirical, or a priori, constituent. Experience teaches us about impulses and motives, about mental operations which tend to change them, and about such operations carried to the limit of their de facto effectiveness, i.e., to the point at which further repetition is in fact found to make no further difference. But experience does not teach us about any case of such operations carried to the *ideal* limit of their possible effectiveness, i.e., to the point at which no further repetition, *however far it be carried, would make any difference.* And yet, when we seek to elicit what we ought to do, this is the standard to which, by repeated acts of exploration and evaluation, we seek to approximate. A concept like 'rational necessity', like that of a mathematical point, has no instances which completely exemplify it. Such concepts, we say, are 'purely intelligible'; their object can be 'thought' or 'conceived', but not viewed or perceived. We call them a priori precisely because they have a use prior to and independent of preexisting and intuitable instances which would adequately exemplify them. In fact, such concepts acquire a determinable use only if their object is being created for them by being defined as the logical product either of a system of axioms or of the carrying out of some rule of procedure; as, in order to give a use to 'rational necessity', we have to lay down and define a procedure of repetitions from whose application, if carried far enough, it would in principle result. But though this would make 'ought' a concept with a nonempirical, or a priori, constituent, this would not make it so in the nowadays accepted sense of the intuitionist moralists. For they hold what, I think, is not only mystifying and false, but inherently self-contradictory: that 'ought' is a nonempirical, or a priori, concept, but not because it contains an element which is purely intelligible and determinable independently of experienced instances of it, but because it is derived from and relates to intuitable instances of something first met in some special 'nonempirical' experience, or 'experience in a wider sense of the word'.¹ The epistemological fallacy of this view lies, I think, in the tacit assumption, characteristic of the epistemological 'realism' of this school of thought, that if a term does not denote some fact met in ordinary experience, and therefore seems nonempirical, or a priori, it must, if it has a use at all, denote some 'fact' met in some 'extraordinary' experience, as if there could be no concept of anything without a corresponding 'idea' of it. But on this showing, 'ought' could not be called an a priori concept in the sense in which a priori is contrasted with a posteriori, i.e., what is determinable prior to experience with what is determinable only by reference to some experience; nor, in fact, need every term, in order to have a use, denote something intuitable, or completely intuitable, in some experience. That 'ought' is a nonempirical, or a priori, concept is agreed. That therefore it denotes the object of 'nonempirical' experience is, to say the least, a non sequitur.

However, at this the critic will put forward new objections. He will say this may account for the prudential, but still not for the moral 'ought': and he may add that in the matter of distinguishing between these two the classical doctrine had been hopelessly and significantly confused. Hobbes, for example, did not hesitate to describe as moral precepts 'dictates of reason' which enjoined the civic virtues as means to the desired end of self-preservation. This pitfall, no doubt, must be avoided. But I think it can be; and it will then be seen, the principles of the classical doctrine also yield what has the form of a 'moral ought'.

We must ask here: why do we consider prudential obligations nonmoral, for example, that 'I ought to save today as I want to be secure tomorrow'? Some people say, because they are derived from private good as an end; but this cannot be the point. 'I ought to save as I *ought* to care for my future' also has private good as an end, but has a 'moral' flavor; and 'I ought to save as I *want* to make national saving a success' is derived from public good as an end, but feels 'nonmoral'.

---

1. A. C. Ewing, *The Definition of Good* (New York: Macmillan, 1947), p. 38.

The fact is, we call prudential obligations nonmoral not because they are derived from private good as an end, but from this end when it only happens to be desired; and we call 'nonmoral' all obligations of this form whatever their ultimate end. The reason is that these are obligations only in a restricted sense: they are often inconclusive, and never obligations through and through. They are *inconclusive* when they leave a further question open: whether, namely, they are derived from a permissible end, i.e., not from one which ultimately we ought not to pursue. And even when derived from a permissible end they could still not be called obligations *through and through*, for they would not in turn be derived from an end which we ultimately ought to, but only from one we already want to, and may, pursue. What then, by contrast, do we call a 'moral ought'? I think, one which is *formally conclusive* and an 'ought' *through and through*. A moral obligation to save would be derived from another ultimate 'ought', whether from that we ought to care for our own good or that of others; and principally the moral problem is in the choice of such ultimate ends, ends which, when actually they are not desired, we still ought to pursue for their *own sakes*. And beyond this it relates to something more: that when ultimate ends conflict, one of them ought *absolutely* to be pursued: that is, in the circumstances, in preference to everything that otherwise ought to have been done, and regardless of anything that otherwise ought to have been avoided. This last feature gives to a 'moral ought' its peculiar finality.

Now, it seems evident to me, the principles of the classical doctrine must also give rise to obligations of this form; and this even if, as the classical doctrine implied, our particular obligations were all derived from an ultimate concern for private and social good. For this alone would not make them all obligations prescribing means to what people already want. Not everyone *capable* of concern for his own good or that of others will therefore always *be concerned* about these ends. Often he only would, as I said before, if he evaluated them by distinctly envisaging them in their nature. This is why people, disposed to seek their own good, may know the better and desire and do the worse, and why people, disposed to regard the good of others, and knowing their need, may remain indolent. They are not lacking in knowledge, but they don't imagine; they think in symbols, but they don't mentally cash their meaning. And, for them, the pursuit of their own good no less than that of others will 'intrinsically' become an obligation, using the term again for what 'reason' would 'dictate'. For, indolent though they are, it would be true of them that, if they rehearsed the thought of these ends, they would and could not but will them. Kant rightly insisted on the propriety of speaking not only of a derivative or 'hypothetical' rational necessity for people to will ends for the sake of their desired consequences, but also of an 'unconditional' necessity to will ends for their own sakes. Kant went wrong, I think, only in claiming that the necessity for a person to will ends in themselves could be known by 'pure reason' and that its validity was independent not only of any concern of his for some other end, but no less of his psychological capacity to feel concern for the end itself. For to say that, in reason, a person would will an end in itself is to say (as far as I can see) that the thought of it as such would *cause* him to pursue it if he mentally rehearsed it, and whether this would be so or not is a matter of psychological fact; nor is there another way for a person to elicit whether this would be so save the experimental way of testing his own responses in accordance with a principle of sufficiency, or in the plain man's language, of 'conscientiously searching his own heart'. The classical doctrine was here nearer the truth when it made 'reason' the basis of obligations to promote the good of others, or one's own, only in relation to a being with a natural disposition to attach value to these ends. Kant rejected this view in search of a basis for intrinsic obligation more certain than the limits of man's psychological constitution can provide; he was looking for universality where the classical doctrine could offer only a high-order generality. But in thus founding intrinsic rational dictates on pure reason alone he disregarded what Aristotle knew, that 'the intellect alone can move nothing'; and he made the concept of these dictates an empty form without a clue to any intelligible procedure by which to give it content.

Nor, of course, should Kant have equated the notion of an 'intrinsic' with that of an 'absolute' or 'categorical' rational necessity. That someone ought to pursue some end merely considered as such does not settle whether he also can, or ought to, pursue it in the circumstances, everything considered; and the concept of an 'absolute' or 'categorical' rational necessity, i.e., of a 'moral ought' proper, applies to him. This concept denotes that a person would will an end and could not by reason get out of willing it if appropriate control operations were carried to their *formally complete* limits, i.e., if he also conscientiously explored the relevant circumstances, the means toward the end, the consequences entailed by it, the alternatives to be given up for it; and, again, if he conscientiously evaluated the end not only in itself, but also comparatively, by envisaging it along with all these implications. Admittedly, an 'absolute' dictate of reason in this sense will again express no more than the necessitation of a person's will by the systematic use of his powers of self-control, relative to his conative dispositions; and the judgments about it will again not be a product of 'pure reason': they will be neither demonstrable nor self-evident, but arrived at by factual observation and inquiry, by 'heart searchings', and by the probable inference that these processes were carried to the limit of their possible effectiveness. And some may feel this is still not enough to accord to them the name of 'moral duties'. But for this I see no reasonable grounds. Such dictates have the all-inclusive form and, when they conflict with people's inclinations, the normative and coercive qualities we associate with a 'moral ought'. And, in fact, I cannot see for what more clinchingly prescriptive and incipiently persuasive anyone *could* be asking who wanted control over what he does. I should hold there could be nothing 'more' that would not be demonstrably something 'less'. For let someone ask for 'more' and, for instance, say: "It is not enough for me to know what reason would dictate me to do; I must also be assured of God's will in the matter." There would surely be no point in his making this claim unless he thought that the will of God would, if known and considered, be a factor, and, maybe, the decisive factor in determining his will. But for anyone who thought this there could be no dichotomy between an absolute dictate of his will and reason and the dictates of God. For he could not say 'reason' bade him to do an act *everything considered* before he had considered the will of God in the matter; and when he had, what would be the clinching piece of practically binding knowledge, would not just be that God willed him to do it, but that he would have to will it, given his concern for the will of God, and God willing it. In a critical and reflective being all practically relevant considerations must terminate in a decision concerning his own rational willing, everything considered. And as long as this question is considered as settled with regard to a course of action, no further question with regard to this same course of action of a practically relevant kind can, in logic, be at issue.

I conclude, then, the case for the classical doctrine is substantially sound. If all else 'fails', there is some order of obligations which by their very nature and condition men are bound to incur from within themselves: they need only try to act quite at random; they will soon enough discover good enough reasons in their mental and bodily constitution and in the average conditions of social life to make it imperative for them to be temperate rather than self-indulgent, faithful rather than treacherous, sociable rather than grasping and aggressive. Sometimes, these imperatives will be 'nonmoral' in form: they will prescribe the adoption of means to ends which people already want and may pursue. It is an error to think that all situations inflict the full weight of a moral obligation. But sometimes they will be imperatives through and through, and they will prescribe to people the adoption of means to ends which intrinsically, and in the circum-

stances absolutely, they ought to pursue. The fashionable dilemma
between transcendentalism and skepticism in ethics is therefore un-
real: it rests on the false antithesis, raised in our time to an unchal-
lenged and stultifying dogma, that moral discourse is either about
some esoteric moral facts, untainted by any contact with the psychology of the human will, or that it is about nothing at all. It seems
time, in the name of sanity, to protest against this.

Before I conclude, I must raise one further point. The classical
doctrine has also some characteristic weaknesses. There is no space
left to discuss them, but the impression I have given would be misleading if I did not indicate what they are. Principally, they lie in the
contention that it is transparent not only that man is cut out to live
by some moral order, but also what the content of this order must
be: that all duties have their psychological basis in one or two ultimate
dispositions; that they must be the same for all men; that experience
and reflection will easily teach us what they are. Some of this would
not follow even if we could accept the simple psychological premises
of the classical doctrine. The effect on social and private well-being
of a great number of our actions is notoriously hard to measure; and
this must make choices uncertain and hazardous and dependent in
some measure on personal flair and idiosyncrasies. Nor can it be assumed that all men are equally disposed to make the same choice
between some measure of private good and the good of others. Any
personal decision of some complexity will illustrate this point. I need
only refer to the case cited by Sartre, in support of his negativist thesis,
of the student faced with the choice of remaining with his mother,
whose whole life is wrapped up in his, and of joining the Free French
abroad, with the incalculable chances of ever getting away and doing
any good. A case like this must be the despair of anyone who believes
that either moral problems have a plain solution or none at all. But
beyond this the situation is more complex still. For the basic dispositions for private and social good of the classical doctrine, even if
granted, are not the only ones to be reckoned with. There are also
acquired value-dispositions, dispositions to value or disvalue modes
of behavior on their own account, and quite apart from their effect
on social or private good; they are imparted by society, family, and
early experiences. Some of these dispose to behavior also beneficial
in its effects on private or social good, as to truthfulness, justice, or
faithfulness; but others also to behavior that no longer would have
these effects, or never had them, as is shown by a study of social
customs, or of the neurotic trends the psychologist claims to have
discovered in what he calls the 'superego'. If, then, it is a question for
people to decide what they ought or ought not to do, these dispositions

may be the first data for their evaluations. They may determine in the first place what, on contemplation, they would find they had to will, or could not will, and what in preference to what else. And to some extent, as these are the first data they may also be the last. The consideration of consequences, of the effects of acts on private and social good, will also play a part. But the notorious difficulties in assessing these effects, together with the difficulties involved in breaking down ingrained habits of evaluation, will often make it inevitable that people's acquired dispositions should remain preponderant in their moral decisions.

But this must seriously modify the traditional picture of the transparent rationality of the content of the moral order. Not only will even the ideally correct moral decision contain a personal element which deprives it of claims to *universality*; not only will there be serious limitations to the resolution of moral disagreement between people *differently conditioned*; but more than this, in a crucial sense men's 'natural obligations' will tend to be far from 'natural' to them. There is no guarantee that when men do what their given value-dispositions and the range of their knowledge make it rationally imperative for them to do, they will also act 'naturally' in the ultimate sense in which this term was used by the classical doctrine: that they will in fact do only what their *innate* value-dispositions would make it imperative for them to do, and what would in this sense fulfill the nature or essence of their being. An operative moral order, natural to man in this sense, is not a fact. At best, it is a goal and a hope, at worst a mirage. We can seek to approximate to it by learning from experience; by studying and remembering the effects of actions on social and individual well-being, by developing our powers of imaginative insight and presentation, by allowing what we have learned to break the hold of ingrained habits of valuation. But we are unlikely ever to reach this goal; nor, had we reached it, would we *know* we had.

[10]

Morality, Self, and Others

I

In: And how can you say that I never had a moral education? As a child, I was taught that one ought not to maltreat other children, ought to share one's sweets with them, ought to keep tidy and clean; as an adolescent, that one ought to keep one's word, to work, to save, to leave off drink, not to waste the best years of one's life, to let reason govern one's emotions and actions. Nor did I simply learn that one is *called upon* to act in these ways by paternal authority and social custom on pain of censure. I learned to appreciate that one *ought* to do these things *on their merits*, and that what one ought to do on its merits does not depend on the requests or enjoinders of anyone. The facts in the case themselves make one liable, as a reflective person, to act in these ways of one's own accord: they provide one with choice-supporting reasons sufficient to determine one if one knows them and takes diligent account of them.

Out: I know you were taught all this. But why did your teacher say that you ought to act in these ways?

In: Why? For very cogent reasons. My tutor was a student of the Ancients. The moral man, "the man of practical wisdom," he kept quoting Aristotle, "is the man who knows how to deliberate well about what is good and useful for himself." And surely, he would say, you can see for yourself: if you don't act sociably, who will act sociably toward you? Uncleanliness breeds disease. Without work, how are you

Reprinted with permission of the publisher from *Morality and the Language of Conduct*, ed. Hector-Neri Castañeda and George Nakhikian (Detroit: Wayne State University Press, 1963), pp. 25–66.

to live? Without savings, what about your future? Drink leaves one a wreck. Indulging one's sorrows makes them worse. The wasted years, one day you will regret them when it is too late. People who cannot govern themselves are helpless before fortune, without the aid and comfort of inner strength.

Out: And so you think that you had a moral education? Let me tell you, you never even made a start. For what were you taught? That there are things that you ought to do or to avoid on your own account. But one does not learn about morality that way. What one *morally* ought to do is what one ought to do on account of others, or for the sake of some good state of things in general. Now had you been taught to appreciate that you ought to keep clean so as to be pleasing to others, and that you ought to do what moral custom requires for the sake of the general good, then, and then only, would you have learned the rudiments of moral duty.

In: Very well, my upbringing was too narrow. One would hardly be a human being if the good of others, or of society at large, could not weigh with one as a cogent reason for doing what will promote it. So one has not fully learned about living like a rational and moral being unless one has learned to appreciate that one ought to do things out of regard for others, and not only out of regard for oneself.

Out: No, you have still not got my point. I am saying that only insofar as you ought to do things—no matter whether for yourself or for others—for the sake of others, is the reason a moral reason and the ought a moral ought. Reasons of self-regard are not moral reasons at all, and you can forget about them in reckoning of your *moral* obligations.

In: But this seems artificial. A moral education surely should teach one all about the principles of orderly living and the reasons which tell in their favor. And if there are also perfectly good personal reasons which tell in their favor, why suppress them? To be sure, in talking to people in ordinary life, we do no such thing. If they say, "Why ought I to act sociably?" we say "For the general good as well as your own." If they say, "Why ought I to be provident?" we say, "For your own good as well as that of others." In short, we offer mixed reasons, and none of these reasons can be spared. One ought not to lie because this is a good social rule, and equally because the habit of evasiveness is destructive of oneself as a person. And one ought not to take to drink or indulge one's sorrows, or waste the best years of one's life primarily out of proper regard for oneself, much as there may be other-regarding reasons as well. If morality were all social service, and one had no moral responsibilities toward oneself or toward others, the moral inconveniences of life would be far less than they are. So

I don't see the point of saying, "But one has no *moral* commitment to do anything except insofar as one ought to do it on account of others." To say this seems like encouraging people not to bother about doing things insofar as they ought to do them only for personal reasons, as after all this is not a moral ought.

Out: But one does not speak of a moral duty to do things for one's own sake. If one ought to save in order to provide for one's own future, one regards this as a precept not of morals but of prudence. It would be different if one ought to save in order to provide for one's dependents. Moral commitments are those which one has as a moral being, and what makes one a moral being is that one has commitments toward others and does not evade them.

In: Not everyone will agree that as a moral being one has only commitments toward others or that only such commitments are properly 'moral'. The Greeks, for example, took a wider view. For Plato the equivalent of a moral being was the just or right-living person, and of a moral commitment the right and just course—the one which the right-living person would be led to take. And this right-living person was one who would keep himself in good shape as a sane and self-possessed being, and who would do whatever good and sufficient reasons directed him to do. This is why for Plato and the Greeks temperance and prudence were no less among the just man's commitments than paying his debts and not willfully harming others, and why the one was not treated any less as a moral commitment than the other. The Greeks placed the essence of a man as a moral being in his capacity to direct himself on rational grounds; and his commitments as a moral being were therefore all those which he seriously incurred as a properly self-directing being.

Out: Citing the Greeks only shows how distant their concept of morality is from ours. We will not call every rational commitment 'moral' or equate the moral with the rational man.

In: This is broadly so, although not entirely. Our concept of morality vacillates between the Greek and the Christian tradition. We associate 'moral' with 'social' commitment, and the 'morally good man' with the 'selfless man'. But we also speak of man as a 'moral agent', of his 'moral freedom' and 'moral powers'; and here we refer to his whole capacity of self-direction by good and sufficient reasons. One may speak without strain of a personal and a social ethic, and refer to the negligent disregard of oneself as a vice and a sign of moral defect. We call the improvident man 'morally weak', and we call the man who can resist drink in company on account of his health or who sticks to his vocation in adversity a man of 'moral strength and character'. There is certainly little difference in the qualities needed to live up to a social or a personal ought. It takes self-denial to provide for one's future, moral courage to stick to one's vocation. One may show one's mettle as a moral agent here no less than in selfless care for others. There are contemporary moralists who call 'moral' any 'authentic' commitment of a self-governing person, whether its grounds are social or personal. What justifies them is the broader use of the term which is also part of our language and tradition.

Out: And how eccentric this use is. Our very concept of a moral being is inseparable from the notion of submission of self to a good other than one's own. It is not conceivable that a man should have moral duties on a desert island, devoid of man or beast. Would one say that he still had a moral duty to do what was good for him? You may as well go on and say that if a shipwrecked fellow arrived to share his vegetables, it might be his moral duty to let him starve rather than starve himself.

In: The good of others need not always have the overriding claim on one, if this is what you mean. One could say to a good-hearted and weak-willed person, "For your own sake, you ought to stop neglecting your future, even if this hurts others." This would not be a typically 'moral' ought, but one may be giving sound moral advice.

Out: And so, if beneficence had the better of this person, you should call him morally irresponsible and blameworthy. On your showing, he has evaded a moral commitment, and for such evasions one is held morally responsible and liable to censure. But surely, even if I granted your case, one would not call him blameworthy and a morally bad person; as indeed in any case where a person fails to do what his own good requires we do not call him morally bad, but only imprudent, unwise, rash. It is quite a different offense to be slack about brushing one's teeth than to be negligent about providing dentures for others. And this is so precisely because the second is a moral offense and the first is not and because one is blameworthy for the one and not for the other.

In: I agree that there is a difference. One is only called morally bad and is held answerable to *others* for neglecting what one ought to do out of regard for them. And this is understandable enough. After all, insofar as one fails to do only what one's own good requires, the failing is no one's concern but one's own. But then I should not say that such self-neglect was in no sense morally irresponsible and blameworthy. If it does not call for blame by others, it still calls for self-reproach. A rational person is responsible to himself for not being evasive about anything that he is convinced that he really ought to do. And the lack of moral strength and courage in personal matters, although commonly viewed as an amicable vice, is an amicable vice only in the estimation of others since it is not directly a threat to them.

However, we are not making headway. You find it repugnant to call a commitment 'moral' unless its grounds are social and unless its nonobservance makes one liable not only to social censure but also to self-reproach; and so be it. Perhaps our disagreement is only verbal, and despite some misgivings, I am ready to settle for your usage. Let us speak only of a moral ought where one ought to do things on account of others. But let us not be misled. For it still does not follow that if one ought to do things on one's own account, this ought may not still be otherwise functioning *like* a moral ought.

Out: How could it be like a moral ought if it is not a moral ought?

In: Because when one thinks of a moral ought, one thinks not only that its grounds are social but also that it has a special force and cogency. A moral ought commits one in all seriousness and in every way, without leaving any reasonable option to act otherwise. Your view comes to saying that if an ought is to be moral it must satisfy two conditions: it must seriously bind one in every way, and it must do so for other-regarding reasons. On your showing, a personal ought cannot be moral, as it cannot satisfy one of these conditions simply by having personal grounds. But it may still satisfy the other condition and be as cogently binding and action-guiding in its force and function as a moral ought. This is why I can only accept your usage with one proviso: that one may also say that there are other than strictly moral commitments which a right-living person may have to reckon with no less than his strictly moral ones.

Out: Surely you don't expect me to fall for this. When I say, "Don't count the purely personal ought as moral," I am not saying "Count it as well, but call it by another name." My point is precisely that it does not function like a moral ought at all. Personal reasons do not commit one to do anything with the same cogency as social reasons. In fact, in calling them reasons of prudence or expediency, we deprecate them. We regard them as inferior, and often disreputable, guides to action. So I won't let you reduce my position to triviality. That only the social commitments are essentially moral must be taken as implying that only they have the characteristic moral force.

In: I thought that this was at the back of our discussion all along. It usually is so with people who are so insistent on your usage, although part of the trouble is that one can never be sure. First one is told that a moral ought is one that commits one on other-regarding grounds and that a personal ought is not a moral ought *for this reason*. But then comes the further suggestion that it is not only different from a moral ought in this way, but is also otherwise inferior. It gives directives, but directives of a somehow shady kind. One way or other, the idea is that a commitment that has personal grounds is either not properly a commitment at all, or, if one in any way, then one that belongs in some limbo of disrepute. But your argument so far has done nothing to prove this point. From your language rule, it only follows that the personal ought must be unlike a moral ought in one essential respect, but not, except by way of confusion, that it must be therefore also unlike a moral ought in other respects too. You might as well say, "Surely a lay analyst is not a doctor," because one is not a doctor without a medical degree, and take this to be proof that a lay analyst cannot otherwise cure like a doctor either. 'No lay analyst is a doctor' is strictly and trivially true in one way and may be misleading and tendentiously false in another. And the same with 'No personal ought is a *moral* ought'. Your language rule makes this strictly and trivially true; but it does not go to show that a personal ought cannot otherwise be *like* a moral ought by being seriously committing or by taking precedence in a conscientious calculus of action-guiding considerations. My point is that, even if this were so, your appeal to usage cannot settle this matter. Logical grammar can decree that only social reasons are properly called 'moral'. But it cannot decide what reasons can, or cannot, be seriously committing for human beings.

Out: But what I am saying seems substantially true. What one ought to do on account of others is the prototype of the categorically binding ought. Personal reasons have not got the binding cogency of other-regarding reasons, and one deprecates them as inferior and disreputable.

In: And there is some truth in this. Personal and social reasons are not on the same footing in the economy of action-guiding considerations. Personal reasons are very commonly less thoroughly committing, they are often inferior reasons, and not rarely discreditable. But why this is so is a different matter and has not yet been touched on in any way. What is more, personal reasons need not always be in this inferior position. They are often not intrinsically discreditable and become inferior guides to action only where there are other reasons in the case deserving of prior consideration. Take someone concerned for his health, or future, or self-respect. Surely these are respectable aspirations, and there may be things which he ought to do on account of them without violating other claims. His health requires that he be temperate, his self-respect that he live without evasion. Would it not then be positively remiss of him not to act in these ways? If he did not, one would say that he had failed to do what a man in his position really ought to have done, and precisely for the reason which he had. And, if one can say this, what remains of the blemish?

This is why it remains perplexing to me why commitments on personal grounds should be excluded from the orbit of moral teaching, and why modern moralists, unlike the Ancients, should disdain to mention them as an integral part of the moral life. For they may also be cogent and sometimes overridingly cogent commitments to action. And if they are not the whole of morals, why not count them as part of them? For it also seems natural to say that to teach someone all about morality is to teach him about all the valid directives for action; about all those things which he might not otherwise do readily but which, for good and compelling reasons in the nature of the case, he ought to do and would have to break himself into doing whether for the sake of others or his own.

There is, I agree, one tendency to say that the moral man acts in accordance with precepts of selflessness. But there is also another tendency to say that he is the man to organize his life in accordance with all valid precepts. Our disagreement has exhibited the kind of shuttle-service between rival considerations better known as the dialectic of a problem. It may be that this shuttle-service is maintained by a cleft in the very concept of morality. This concept may have grown from conflicting or only partially overlapping observations, which are not fully reconciled in ordinary thinking.

Out: If this is so, I would have to be shown, for common sense still seems to me right in its disparagement of personal reasons.

In: Very well, then, we shall have to consider why personal reasons should function as a less cogent guide to action than social ones. I shall admit that in more ways than one the personal ought presents a special case, but not that it presents a case for disparagement except in special contexts. After this, the question of whether the personal ought is properly called moral or not will appear less important, partly because it will have become plainer why there is a question. Nor shall I try to offer a ruling on this point. With a background of discourse as intricate and full of nuance as in this case, discretion is the better part of valor, and clarification is a safer bet than decision.

II

Whenever one remarks that clearly there are things which one ought to avoid or do if only for one's own sake, someone is sure to say, "No doubt; but any such ought is only a precept of prudence or expediency." It is a textbook cliché against Hobbes that his account of morality comes to just this. And this is said as if it were an obvious truth and enough to discredit all such precepts in one go. This assumes a great deal and settles nothing.

What it assumes is this: that everything that one ever does for one's own sake, one does as a matter of prudence *or* expediency; that there is no difference between these two; that morality always differs from prudence as a scent differs from a bad smell; and that everyone knows how so and why.

None of this will do.

In the first place, not everything done for oneself is done for reasons of prudence. That one ought to insure one's house, save for one's old age, not put all one's money into one venture, are precepts of prudence. But it is not a precept of prudence, though it may be a good precept, that someone ought to undergo a dangerous operation as a long shot to restoring his health rather than linger under a disability forever after.

The point is that prudence is only one way of looking after oneself. To act prudently is to play safe, for near-certain gains at small risks. But some good things one cannot get in this way. To get them at all one has to gamble, taking the risk of not getting them even so, or of coming to harm in the process. If one values them enough, one will do better by oneself to throw prudence to the winds, to play for high stakes, knowing full well the risk and the price of failure. Explorers, artists, scientists, mountaineers are types who may serve themselves better by this course. So will most people at some juncture. Thus, if someone values security, then that he ought to save in order to be secure is a precept of prudence. But that someone ought to stick to his vocation when his heart is in it enough to make it worth risking security or health or life itself is not a precept of *prudence*, but of *courage*.

One says sometimes, "I ought to save, because I *want* to be prudent," but sometimes "because I *ought* to be prudent." One may also decide that in one's own best interests one ought to be prudent rather than daring, or daring rather than prudent, as the case may be. Now, that one ought to do something because it would be prudent is a dictate of prudence. But that one really ought to be prudent, in one's own best interests, would not be a dictate of prudence again. One then ought to play safe to serve oneself *best* and not to serve oneself *safely*.

A dictate of prudence where one wants to be prudent but ought to be courageous in one's own best interests is a dictate of timidity. A dictate of courage, where one feels reckless but ought to be prudent, is a dictate of foolhardiness. Both will then plainly be morally imperfect precepts. But there is nothing obviously imperfect about a dictate of prudence where one ought to be prudent, or a dictate of courage where one ought to be daring. Such precepts seem near-moral enough to allow one to call the habit of acting on them a virtue. The Ancients considered both prudence and courage as moral virtues. Oddly enough, in our time, one is more ready to view courage on one's own behalf as a moral virtue than prudence. It needs the reminder that precepts of self-protection may be precepts of courage as well as of prudence for one to see that any precept of self-protection may have a moral flavor. I think that the dim view which we take of prudence corresponds to a belief that to be daring is harder than to be levelheaded, a belief most likely justified within our own insurance-minded culture. But such belief would have seemed strange to Bishop Butler and the fashionable eighteenth-century gentlemen to whom he addressed himself. Prudence in Butler's time, as throughout the ancient world, was not yet the cheap commodity which it is with us; and the price of virtue varies with the market.

There are other precepts of self-protection which are not 'just a matter of prudence' either. That one ought not to take to drugs or drink, indulge oneself in one's sorrows, waste one's talents, commit suicide just in the despair of the moment, are precepts made of sterner stuff. One wants to say, "Surely, it is more than just a matter of prudence that one ought to avoid these things." And rightly so. The effect on oneself of taking to drugs or drink, or of any of the others, is not conjectural but quite certain. To avoid them is therefore more than a matter of *taking no risks*. Sometimes, when one looks down a precipice, one feels drawn to jump. If one refrains, it will hardly be said of one, "How prudent he is, he takes no chances." The avoidance of excesses of all kinds in one's own best interests is in this class. The habit of avoiding them the Greeks called temperance, a virtue distinct from prudence.

Another error is to equate the prudent with the expedient, and again, the expedient with everything that is for one's own good. To save may be prudent; but whether it is expedient or convenient to start now is another matter. With a lot of money to spare at the moment it will be expedient; otherwise it will not. But it may be prudent all the same. Again, one marries in the hope of finding happiness; but marriage in this hope is not a marriage of convenience. The point is that reasons of expediency are reasons of a special sort: reasons for doing something on the ground that it is incidentally at hand to serve one's purpose, or because it serves a purpose quite incidental to the purpose for which one would normally be doing this thing. One marries for reasons of expediency when one marries for money, but not when in hope of finding happiness. Hobbes said that "men never act except with a view to some good to themselves." This would be quite different from saying that "they never act except with a view to what is expedient."

There is also this difference between the prudent and the expedient: one can speak of 'rules of prudence', but less well of 'rules of expediency'. The expedient is what happens to serve. It is not therefore easily bottled in rules.

The word 'prudence' is used too freely in still one more context. When one wishes to justify the social virtues to people, a traditional and inviting move is to refer them, among other things at least, to their own good. "You ought to hold the peace, be honest, share with others." "Why?" "Because an order in which such practices were universal is of vital concern to you; and your one hope of helping to make such an order is in doing your share." The classical formulation of this standard move is Hooker's, quoted with approval by Locke: "If I cannot but wish to receive good... how should I look to have any part of my desire herein satisfied, unless I myself be careful to satisfy the like desire: my desire therefore to be loved of my equals in nature, as much as possible may be, imposes upon me a *natural duty* of bearing to themward fully the like affection."

Now, it is said again, "So defended, the social duties come to no more than precepts of prudence"; and this goes with the veiled suggestion that it is morally improper to use this defense. But, even if so defended, the social duties are not necessarily reduced purely to precepts of prudence. For they may be recommended in this way either as mere *rules* or as *principles* of self-protection; and as principles they would be misdescribed as mere precepts of prudence. The distinction is this: when one says, "People ought to practice the social virtues, if only for their own benefit," one may be saying, "They ought to practice them for this reason as a *rule*, i.e., normally, as much as each time this is likely to be for their own good." Or one may be saying, "They ought to practice them for this reason not merely as a rule but as a *matter of principle*, i.e., every time, whether at that time this is likely to be for their good or not." And one might defend the adoption of this *principle* by saying, "Because your best, even if slim, hope of contributing to a society fit for you to live in lies in adding to the number of principled people who will do their share each time, without special regard for their good at that time."

Now this seems to me a precept of courage rather than one of prudence. The game of attempting by one's actions to make society a place fit for one to live in is a gamble worth the risk only because of the known price of not attempting it. This gamble is a root condition of social living. One is sure to give hostages to fortune, but again,

what other hope has one got? Hence, if a man practiced the social
virtues, thinking that he ought to as a matter of principle, and on
these grounds, one will praise him for his *wisdom*, his firm grasp of
vital issues, his steadfastness, his courage. But one will not necessarily
congratulate him on his prudence. For many times the prudent course
might have been otherwise. It may be wise to persist in being honest
with cheats, or forbearing with the aggressive, or helpful to those slow
to requite helpfulness; but it might have been more prudent to persist
for no longer than there was requital, or not even to start before
requital was assured.

Now would it be a moral precept or not that, if only out of proper
care for oneself, one ought to act on principles of wisdom and courage?
That one ought to risk life in order to gain it? And, assuming a society
of men acting fixedly on these principles but no others, would it or
would it not contain men of moral virtue? One might as well ask, "Is
a ski an article of footwear?" There is no more of a straight answer
here than there. One may say, "Not quite"; and the point of saying
this needs going into. But it would be more misleading to say, "Not
at all." For it is part of the meaning of 'moral precept' that it prescribes
what a man would do in his wisdom—if he were to consider things
widely, looking past the immediate concerns of self and giving essentials due weight before incidentals. As it is also part of what is meant
by one's moral capacities that one can live by such considerations, it
becomes fruitless after a time to press the point whether such precepts
are properly called moral.

There are, then, varieties of the personal ought, differing in the
considerations on which they are based and the qualities needed to
follow them; and they all seem at least akin to a 'moral' ought in their
action-guiding force and function. But I grant that one does not want
to speak of more than a kinship, and the point of this needs considering. One's hesitancy derives from various sources which have to be
traced one by one.

Some of the hesitancy comes from contexts where one can say
disparagingly, "He did this *only* for reasons of prudence, *only* for
reasons of expediency, *only* for himself." This plainly applies sometimes, but it does not apply always. One would hardly say of someone
without dependents, "He thought that he ought to save, but *only* for
reasons of prudence"; or of someone, "He thought that he ought to
have the carpenter in along with the plumber, but *only* for reasons of
expediency or convenience"; or "He thought that he ought to become
a doctor, but *only* because the career would suit him." 'Only' has no
point here. Why else should a man without dependents save, except
to be prudent? Why else should anyone have the carpenter in along

with the plumber, except for convenience? What better reason is there normally for choosing a career than that it will suit one? On the other hand, there is point in saying, "He held the peace only because it was prudent," "He saved only because it was convenient," "He practices the social virtues only for self-protection." It is plain why 'only' applies here and is disparaging. One says 'only' because something is done for the wrong or for not quite the right reason—done for *one* reason where there is *another* and nearer reason for doing it anyway. Personal reasons are often in this position, and then they are disparaged as inferior. One saves 'only' because it is expedient, if one ought to have saved anyway for reasons of prudence. One holds the peace 'only' because it was prudent when one ought to have done so anyway as a matter of principle and even if it had not been prudent. And one practices the social virtues 'only' for self-protection when one does not *also* practice them for the general good.

The last case is different from the others. Plainly, one ought to practice the social virtues as principles of general good. But on none but perhaps pure Christian principles would it hold, or necessarily hold, that one ought to practice them on this ground unconditionally, however great the provocation to oneself. The case for the social virtues is weakened when the social environment becomes hostile and intractable by peaceable means; it is correspondingly strengthened where they can also be justified as wise principles of self-protection. That someone practices forbearance 'only' as a wise principle of self-protection is not therefore to say that he practices it for a reason which is neither here nor there; but rather for a reason which falls short of all the reason there is. This was, in effect, the view of the old natural law moralists—Hooker, Grotius, Pufendorf: the social virtues derive joint support from our natural concern for our own good and for that of society. Hobbes streamlined this account by denying the second, which provoked subsequent moralists to deny the first. Both Hobbes's sophistical toughness and the well-bred innocence of the academic moralists since are distorted visions which are less convincing than the unsqueamish common sense of the philosophers and divines of earlier times.

III

So far we have met no reason for deprecating every personal ought. Men often have cause to be temperate, courageous, wise for their own good. This is often the only, or the nearest, reason why they should.

It is then pointless to go on complaining, "But they still act so only for their own sakes." 'Only' is a dangerous word.

Even so one feels that somehow a commitment that has only personal grounds is morally inferior. 'One ought to risk one's life in order to gain it' seems near-moral enough. But compare it with 'One ought to risk one's life in order to save others'. This still seems different. And this is so not only because the one has a personal reason and the other has not, but also because where the reason is social rather than personal, the ought itself feels different—more binding, more relentless, and more properly called 'moral' for this reason. The real inferiority of the personal ought seems here to lie in a lack of formal stringency.

There are such differences of stringency between "I ought to save, because I *want* to provide for my future" and "I ought to save, because I *ought* to provide for my children." The first prescribes saving as a means to an end which one *is* seeking; the second as a means to an end which in turn one *ought* to seek. The first therefore commits one formally less than the second. It leaves one at liberty to escape the commitment by renouncing the ultimate end, which the second does not. One may, as Kant did, call the first ought hypothetical and nonmoral and the second categorical and moral on account of this difference. The distinction is made to rest on a formal difference of the binding force and not at all on any material difference in the justifying grounds. The formally 'moral' commitment is to an ultimate end or rule of life and to what one ought to do on account of it in any particular case.

Now the personal ought comes more typically as nonmoral and the social ought as moral in form. One says, "You don't *want* to make your misery worse, so you ought not to dwell on it"; "You *want* to secure your future, so you ought to be prudent and save." One might also say, "You *want* to provide for your children, so you ought to save"; and then formally this too would be a nonmoral ought although its grounds are other-regarding. But this is the less typical case. One is often more grudging about the needs of others than one's own. So there is here less occasion for saying, "You ought to do this on account of an end which you *are* seeking"; and more for saying, "You ought to do it on account of an end which in turn you *ought* to seek."

This typical difference between the personal and the social ought raises two questions: one, whether it is an inherent feature of the personal ought to be never more than nonmoral in form; the other, whether, even if this were so, it would be any the worse as a possibly serious commitment. Both of these positions have been taken. One's own good one always seeks. It is not therefore among the ends which one ever ought to seek in the absence of a sufficient inclination. But with the good of others, or the avoidance of harm to them, it is different. Here are ends which one does not always seek, but ought to seek all the same: ends which one may still have reason for seeking on their own account; which one would be led to seek on a diligently comprehending and imaginative review of them (of what doing good, or harm, inherently amounts to). Only the social ought, therefore, may bind one to the choice of the final end as well as of the means, while the personal ought binds one only to the means on account of an end which one wants already. The personal ought is therefore nonmoral only in form, and 'only' once again signifies a defect. But all this is misleading. One does not always seek one's own good as much as one has reasonable ground for seeking it, and about this I shall say more later. But even supposing that one did, then all precepts of self-regard would prescribe what one ought to do consistently with an already desired end. But they would not therefore be negligible or improper all the time.

It is true that what one ought to do consistently with a desired end need not be what one really ought to do at all. The end, or the means toward it, may prove undesirable on further scrutiny either by reason of what it is in itself or of the special circumstances of the case. I ought to save because I wish for security, and there is nothing inherently wrong with the end or the means, and so far so good. But I also ought to support my mother, and I cannot do both. Then maybe I ought not to do *all told* what otherwise I ought to have done. But in this case, the precept of prudence would have been less than 'only' nonmoral. It would have been invalid all told and countermoral altogether. But surely not every case is like this.

For often there is nothing wrong with the things which one cares for on one's own behalf, and one really does care for them. Even if one had the abstract option to give them up, one has no serious wish to do so. One often does care for one's life or health or career or the regard of others, and one often *may* without violating other claims. And one always *may* care, if one does, for one's peace of mind or self-respect. And so what one ought to do as far as these ends go one really ought to do. Because one wants to live, one really ought to look after one's health. Because one wants to be liked by others, one really ought to keep a civil tongue. Because one wants to live after one's own fashion, one really ought to stick to one's vocation in adversity. Because one wants to be able to respect oneself, or, in Hume's phrase, "bear one's own survey," one really ought to conduct oneself as one thinks that one has good reasons for doing. All these precepts tell one what one ought to do consistently with a personal end which one actually has at heart; and where they hold after scrutiny, they hold no less validly and conclusively than any fully 'moral' precept. The conscientious man would have to take notice of them no less than of the others. They deserve to be called 'semimoral' at least.

I keep allowing that a distinction remains. "I ought to work hard because I *want* to succeed" is still a different kind of commitment from "I ought to work hard because I *ought* to provide for others." The difference is partly in the end, personal in the one case, impersonal in the other. But this quite apart; there is another reason for the difference. The second ought has a quality of sternness which is lacking from the first, and which is a product of its *form*, not of its *content*. For the second is an ought twice over. It says that one ought to take steps for an end which one ought to pursue ultimately. The first is an ought only once; it says that one ought to take steps for an end with regard to which one is at liberty as far as it goes. So the second ought subjects one to a regimen which is complete. It commits one *through and through*, whereas the semimoral ought does not. And this through-and-throughness gives to the moral ought its notoriously stern flavor. It makes it more imposing and often more onerous. One is having one's socks pulled up all over. And additional qualities are required of one for appreciating it and acting on it: not only forethought and consistency, but also the ability to appreciate an end as committing by reason of its own nature, which, among other things, requires sympathetic understanding and imagination. No wonder that a moral ought inspires those confronted with it with awe. The semimoral ought cannot compete with this, though when it comes to the precepts of wisdom and courage on one's own behalf they come near enough.

However, having given the formally moral ought its due, I want to add that respect for it should be no reason for slighting the other. For in the first place, and as a reassurance to those who regard lack of onerousness as a defect, though the semimoral ought is not so bad, it may be bad enough. How hard it is to pull up one's socks does not necessarily depend on their number; two commodious socks may respond more readily than one shrunken one. One semimoral and one moral case may serve as examples. If one really *wants* to do a thing and do it well, one ought to take trouble. And if one really *ought* to do good to the sick, one ought to telephone and inquire how they are getting on. The first requires a lot: putting oneself into harness, foregoing all sorts of things which one would rather do, particularly at that moment, coping with aches and pains and anxieties, playing the endless game of snakes and ladders with achievement, and yet going on, nursing one's purpose. The second, though in form a commitment through and through, requires nothing but getting up and dialing a number. It may need a great deal not to put things off, not to dwell on one's miseries, not to spend improvidently, all simply because one really ought not to in one's own best interest. The ought that lays down the law on these things may be little imposing in form. But such is the bulk of the stuff which compounds the 'moral' inconveniences of ordinary life. And one also measures oneself and others by the show that is made on this front.

But then it is not the lack of onerousness as much as that of formal stringency that is felt to discredit the semimoral ought. It still is not binding like the moral ought, simply because it is not committing through and through. Moreover, its very subservience to an end which is only desired seems something amiss, as if a man should rather act always for the sake of ends which he ultimately ought to seek, and not just of ends which he happens to be seeking even if nothing is wrong with them.

This sense of guilt about the nonobligatory rests partly on excessive zeal for original sin. What the natural man in one desires never can be quite as it should. It is always "Tell me what you want to do, and I shall tell you what you ought to do instead." But there is also a failure to see that not every semimoral commitment is renounceable at will. Not every situation need confront one with a commitment through and through, and it is improper to demand that it should or to deplore that it does not.

When one ought to do a thing on account of some desired end, then one need not always be at liberty to escape the commitment by renouncing the end. It depends on whether one is free to give up the end itself, and this is not always so. One says of some ends, "If you want to seek it you may, and if you don't want to you need not." There is here no reason against seeking the end, nor reason enough to tell one to seek it in the absence of a desire for it. And one is free to escape a commitment on account of such an end simply by giving up the end. But in the case of other ends one will say, "If you want to seek it you may, but if you do not want to you still ought to all the same." Again there is no reason against seeking the end if one wants to, but here there would still be reason for seeking it even if one did not want to. A commitment on account of such an end one may not escape at will because one is not here free to give up the end. It is arguable whether commitments on personal grounds are not often in this position. One ought to be temperate because one wants to preserve one's health. And although this is a semimoral ought as far as it goes, one need not be free to get out of it at will. For even if one ceased to care about the end, one might still here have reasonable ground for caring, and ought to care all the same.

An ought of this kind commits one on account of an end which one seeks as well as ought to seek. And this makes it like an ought through and through, but still not quite. There can be ends which one seeks and ought to seek. But insofar as one *is* seeking such an end, it is strained to say that one also *ought* to seek it at the same time. One would rather say that if one were not seeking it already, then one ought to be seeking it all the same. This is why, if someone is perfectly willing about an end, a commitment on account of this end would still not for him have the form of a commitment through and through; and this although it is potentially such a commitment and would turn into one as soon as he ceased to be readily inclined toward the end.

The point is that ought applies only where there is a case of pulling one's socks up. The same action may be viewed in otherwise the same circumstances either as one which one ought to do, or as one which one wants to and may do, according to the psychological starting point. One normally wants to have one's breakfast, and one would find it improper to have it put before one with the remark, "You ought to eat this morning." "Why ought I? Don't I eat every morning anyway?" But if one were convalescent, the remark would be in place. Nor would one say to a notoriously indulgent parent, "You ought not to be harsh with your children" (though one might wonder whether he *may* be so indulgent). The remark applies to a parent bad at controlling his temper. If I resolved to become an early riser and succeeded, I might report in retrospect, "For the first month it was a duty, but afterward it ceased to be a duty and became a habit, if not a pleasure."

None of this should be surprising. Ought is an action-guiding concept. It expresses the notion that one is liable to direction by reasons in the case which would motivate one if one gave them due consideration. And one cannot be *liable* to direction by reasons except in a matter of doing what one is not fully motivated to do already. This is why it cannot be an obligation for one to do what one wants to do anyway, much as it might become an obligation for one to do it if one ceased to want to. This is also why, when one really wants to do something, the natural question to ask is not, "And *ought* I to do this thing?" but rather, "And *may* I do it?" or "Would there by anything wrong with it?" or "Ought I perhaps *not* to do it?" One looks for possible reasons against, not for possible reasons for. And what point would there be in doing anything more? When one really wants to do something, one already has, *for* doing it, all the reason one needs. And this is also why one says, "You ought to" to others only when one takes it that there is a case for changing their present frame of mind. But to wonder whether one ought to (as distinct from wondering whether one may, or perhaps ought not to) where one already wants to would be like wondering whether to sit down when seated; and to say, "You ought to" to someone quite ready to would be like advising a sitting man to take a seat. *There is no ought for those blessed with wants which are not wrong.*

One may object: "But surely one can say that everyone ought to do good, and if there were benevolent people this would not make this false." And this is correct, but no refutation. What raises a problem are general statements like "People ought to do good," "One ought to be tolerant." But one may make a general statement without having to specify all the conditions when it shall or shall not hold. One says in general, "Butter will melt in the sun"; and if someone interjected, "But *not* when one has just melted it on the kitchen stove," this would be no rebuttal. "*This* butter will melt in the sun," when I am bringing it dripping from the kitchen, would be different. This particular butter is not *liable* to melt, even though it remains true that butter is. The same with "People ought to do good." This is a general statement, and one need not state the obvious: that it will not apply to someone whose heart needs no melting as it is soft already. Nor does one use 'one ought to' directively to people, except for general purposes of propaganda. 'I ought to' and 'you ought to' are in a logically different class.

One makes general ought-statements about standard ends and practices toward which people commonly have no sufficient inclination. These ought-statements apply particularly to doing things for others and less so to doing things for oneself. And this alone could explain why one normally does not say that people ought to care for their own good. For the question of whether they *ought* to does not here normally arise. They can be trusted with a modicum of well adjustment toward this end—they seek it, and, within limits, they may seek it. Hence, what one ought to do on account of one's own good is commonly a commitment on account of a desired end, much as it might also turn into a commitment through and through with a loss of immediate interest in the end. Nor could one reasonably hope that such commitments were more imposing in form than they are. On the contrary, one may say that the less imposing the ought, the better designed for living the man.

IV

We are nearly out of the woods, but not quite. For the picture now before us still gives *Out* more than he can have. *Out* could say at this point: "By and large you have vindicated me. All your personal oughts are at best semimoral. Only what one ought to do on account of others is in any way like what one morally ought to do. In fact, you have explained why this is so. Men are more immediately and unreflectively drawn toward their own good than toward that of others. So the pursuit of their own good as an end never comes to them as an obligation. But in the matter of considering others they need the full treatment. Here they must learn to care for the end as well as the means, and to care for the end even at cost to themselves. To do what serves social ends therefore comes as obligatory on one through and through. And this is the moral ought, the one that pulls one up without further question all along the line. However, you have convinced me on one point. Personal commitments need not always be negligible or discreditable. Sometimes one really ought to be prudent or courageous in one's own best interest, and the conscientious man ought to take notice of this and to conduct himself accordingly. So in a sense perhaps there is a personal as well as a social morality. But I still insist that the two are not on the same level, that only the social commitments are in every way properly 'moral,' and that only their neglect is a properly 'moral' failing."

This statement calls for two comments. The first is that *Out* is already loosening the hold on his position. He has to speak of morality in a strict and in a broader sense and of the conscientious man as doing his share by both. And this rightly so. By a conscientious person one understands someone who will not be evasive about anything that he is convinced he really ought to do. He is the right-living man of the Greeks whose first commitment is to the principle of self-guidance by good and sufficient reasons. To observe his socially grounded commitments will be an imposing part of his job. But the whole job will be to conduct himself in line with all valid commitments, no matter whether they are imposing in form or not. One may say if one wishes that his properly 'moral' commitments are only those which commit him through and through and out of regard for others. But then it must be granted that there is more to being a right-living person than only observing one's 'moral' commitments and that the neglect of a nonmoral commitment, even if not strictly a 'moral' failing, is nevertheless like one by being the evasion of a known commitment supported by valid reasons.

The second comment is that the case against *Out* needs pressing still further. It is also not the case that only the social commitments are ever fully moral in form. Commitments on personal grounds are less commonly so because of the greater immediate regard which one has for oneself. One's own pain or unhappiness is closer to one than these same states in others. Unless they lie in the future it requires no effort of understanding and imagination to enable one to respond to them. But this immediate regard for oneself has its limits. Men may feel unreasonably unconcerned for their own good as for that of others. Hume rightly spoke of "that narrowness of soul which makes us prefer the present to the remote"; and there are sick drives toward self-effacement and self-denial, so much so that it has been said that "man's inhumanity towards man is only equalled by his inhumanity towards himself." One meets the suggestion that everyone is at liberty to act as he will in the matter of his own life. But it would be odd if in this matter one were not liable to correction from a reflective appraisal of the nature of what one is doing. Men who are separated from their own good as an end may still have reasonable ground for seeking it in the absence of sufficient inclination. Their own good will then become something that they ought to seek and stand up for more than they are wont to or can readily bring themselves to; and to do the things which their own good requires will for them then become a commitment through and through.

It may also be that in a case like this someone ought to stand up for his own good even to the detriment of another. It could be sound advice to say to a woman in strife with herself and tied to a demanding parent, "You ought to consider yourself, and so break away now, hard as it may be on the parent." One is then saying more than simply, "If you wanted to you would have a right to." One is saying, "I know you are shrinking away from it, but this is what you ought to do, and above all else." In form this is an ought through and through, and an overriding one at that, but its ground is not other-regarding. And even true Christian charity might not here prescribe anything different. One cannot love one's neighbor as oneself if one has not also learned to accept one's own wishes as a proper object of respect and care because one's own wishes are the paradigm of all wishes. There is a profound sense in which charity begins at home. For some this acceptance of themselves is hard, and it may confront them with a personal commitment as categorical and as onerous as any. Is this, then, a 'moral' commitment or not? Here language fails one. For the usual conjunction between the categorical and the socially grounded commitment has come apart and turned into a clash. It is to strain the usual associations of language to the limit to speak of a moral commitment to put one's own good before that of another. But the unqualified refusal to call this a moral commitment is strained too and may be tendentiously misleading. For apart from not being grounded in regard for others, such a commitment may be precisely like the typical moral commitment in its cogency, its form, and its action-guiding relevance.

There is still another type of case. One's own good comprises not only one's states but also the possession of oneself as a mind. One cannot earnestly wish to lose hold of oneself, to be reduced to a shaky mess when in trouble; one needs to be in control and to be able to cope with whatever may come. And this preservation of oneself as a capable ego is also something that one may find that one ought to care for when one is too driven or despondent to be inclined to care for it. Kant spoke of the duties of self-perfection, the commitments which subserve the protection of one's rational nature; and he did not hesitate to include them among one's moral duties along with the social ones. And this quite consistently so, for here is a concern for oneself for which one has reasonable ground though one is not always ready for it by inclination. Moreover, this type of personal commitment is morally relevant in a special way. For among the duties of self-perfection is the conscientious man's commitment to live without evading any issue—to seek out and weigh what cogent reasons would lead him to do, and to submit himself without self-deception or evasion to their determination. One cannot derive that one ought to live in this manner from one's special obligations toward others. For one may never duly confront any of one's special obligations unless one is already willing to live that way. All principled conduct which is reasoned practice and not just well-bred habit turns on this commitment as its pivot. It involves the acceptance of the principle of nonescapism as an overall rule of life. And this commitment has the most intimately personal ground. It rests on an individual's inmost concern to preserve himself intact as a living and functioning self: mentally in possession of himself and of his world, able to look at himself and what he is doing without having to hide himself from himself. The penalty for slighting this need is his undoing as a person.

And now is one still to say that only what one ought to do with a view to the good of others can have the *cogency and force* of the 'moral' commitment? The claim has been further reduced. Only most commitments which are committing through and through rest on other-regarding considerations. There can also be such commitments which rest on personal considerations, and they may on occasion take precedence over one's social commitments. And there is one commitment whose ground is intimately personal and which comes before any other personal or social commitment whatsoever: the commitment to the principled mode of life as such. One is tempted to call this the supreme moral commitment, but if no commitment may count as 'moral' unless one has it on account of others, then the commitment to the practice of nonevasive living cannot properly count as a 'moral' commitment at all.

That the social commitments make up the bulk of the formally imposing ones is, of course, a fact which one has no reason to deny. The good of others is the standard case of an end toward which men commonly find themselves less drawn by inclination than committed to on due reflection, through the exercise of understanding and imagination. But it illuminates the logic of the case that this is so as a matter of fact and of none else. Suppose that we were made the opposite of the way we are: that we were concerned about the good of others as immediately as we are now concerned about our own, and were concerned about our own good no more readily than we are now about that of others. Then the whole moral machine would be working busily in reverse. The bulk of the formerly imposing duties would be those which prescribe the subordination of our excessive regard for others to a proper regard for ourselves. Morality, in effect, would no longer serve primarily an order of mutual consideration, but the protection of the individual from being overwhelmed by his social sentiments. Nietzsche's transvaluation of all values was the claim that the hidden facts were such as to make this morality's real task. "Men are too weak-minded to be self-seeking." Their besetting vice is morbid pity, a guilty fear of their own wishes, self-hate, and resentment against others under the guise of concern. The moral machine needs putting into reverse.

I am not saying with Nietzsche that it does, though it may well with some. My point is rather to insist that a morality, if by this we mean a reasoned body of action-guiding principles and commitments, is always a morality for someone; and a morality for humans is one for humans. This is why in our morality, and in spite of Nietzsche, the socially grounded commitments have a special place. They are, even if not the only, the standard case of what reflective human beings meet as committing through and through. But this is so because men are what they are and their situation is what it is: because they do not live alone; because they can identify themselves with the concerns of others and of the communities of which they are members and can care about them; and because they can learn to care as much as they are able to by learning to comprehend. One commonly takes it that materially moral or social reasons are in some measure ought-implying for everyone. And this is fair enough if taken as a regulative principle, or presumption, with a massive, if incomplete, backing in experience. The presumption is that such reasons can be treated as standard reasons; that anyone can be taken to be accessible to them (although to an extent for which there is no standard measure) unless he is willfully uncomprehending, mentally disordered, or immature for reasons of age or cultural background. But there can be no demonstrative certainty of this being so. The case of an otherwise human being congenitally inaccessible to other-regarding considerations may be treated as *incredible*, but not as *inconceivable*.

There is also, however, the suggestion that one means by 'moral' reasons more than this. 'Moral' reasons are considerations of social good which are always binding, and in case of conflict with personal good, always *overridingly* binding on every reflective human being alike. But while one may *conceive* of moral reasons in these terms, there is nothing gained by doing so. For no conceptual gerrymandering can settle what will then be the crucial question, namely, whether what is here termed a 'moral' reason is a concept applicable to human beings; and, if so to any extent, by way of anything but a massively grounded presumption.

One may still say that the social commitments are the only 'moral' ones properly so called. One is then making a *material* criterion a necessary condition for applying 'moral' to a commitment. A 'moral' commitment must not only be validly action-guiding and committing through and through; it must also be incurred on account of others. By this language rule, 'moral' is used to mark off the species of socially grounded commitments from the genus of validly action-guiding commitments in general. That there is this language rule is not disputed. The sole point at issue is that one should not be misled by it. The rule entails that none but the socially grounded commitments are properly 'moral', but only for a reason which does not imply that they alone are seriously cogent, or committing through and through, or that they alone can take precedence in a proper calculus of action-guiding considerations. No answers to the questions, "How ought one to live?" and "What ought one to do?" must be taken as prejudged by the semantic taboo on calling a personally grounded commitment strictly 'moral'. No real-life possibility is excluded by the insistence that a Nietzschean 'morality' would not properly be a 'morality' at all. The question of what can or cannot be validly action-guiding principles and commitments for a reflective and human being is not settled by appeal to a linguistic convention.

V

I have argued that one may say that only the socially grounded ought is properly 'moral', but that, if the only reason for this is semantic, nothing substantial follows. Personal considerations, though not called 'moral', could still be as seriously choice-supporting and binding on one as properly moral ones. But this conclusion may still seem unconvincing. One may object that we simply do not think that doing the right thing by oneself is ever *binding* on one in the same way as doing the right thing by others. In the matter of acting as we ought on our own account we consider ourselves free and not responsible to anyone. But in the matter of acting as we ought on account of others we consider ourselves obligated and responsible to them. This suggests that the personal and the social ought are not after all on the same footing; that the social ought carries with it an added authority which derives from the very fact that it is social, and that this is implied in calling it alone 'moral'.

It remains to be shown that here is another line of argument for the nonformalist, like *Out*, to follow; that this line of argument is indispensable to the understanding of the complex phenomenon that morality is; but that its ultimate relevance must not be overrated.

One may argue as follows. There is one plain difference between ought-abiding conduct in social and in personal matters. Other people have a stake in the first which they have not in the second. Their legitimate interests are involved in our social conduct; they hold us accountable for doing the right thing by them. This applies particularly to those rules and practices which, in a given society, are regarded as the backbone of the social order. Society credits its mature members with the ability to appreciate that they ought to respect these rules for their social merits. If they violate them without valid excuse they act counter to what others have a stake in their doing; and they are made responsible for their conduct. One may ask them to justify themselves, admonish and censure them. And this is why it may be said that the social ought alone is called moral; not only because it is social, but also because it has a special authority. When it comes to respect for social rules and the good of others, society obligates one to act as one ought on pain of moral sanctions. One is here, as it were, doubly bound; by the voice of reason and by the majesty of the law; by the knowledge that one ought to and by one's accountability to others for doing it. None of this applies to one's conduct in the matter of acting as one ought on one's own account. One is not here socially obligated; one is a morally bad and socially guilty person for not acting as one ought.

Contemporary writers like H. L. A. Hart[1] are inclined to make this point more strongly. They suggest that the sense in which social ought-abidance is *obligatory*, and personal ought-abidance not, is the only proper sense of this term. Traditional philosophy, it is said, has ignored that 'ought' and 'obligation' are different concepts. Ought-language is 'teleological'; only obligation-language is 'deontological'. That one ought to do something is to say that it is the 'best' or 'reasonable' thing to do, but not yet that one is obligated or bound to do it. Words like 'obligation' or 'duty' are at home in legal or quasi-legal contexts and apply only to social injunctions or prohibitions. Any other use of them is a philosopher's extension of language, a use which is as unwarranted as it is misleading. 'Duties' are something assigned to one, 'obligations' something imposed on one. Both are liabilities created by a public rule or requirement, or liabilities which one incurs by giving rise to claims against oneself as in giving a promise, or becoming a husband or father. It will then follow that a moral *obligation* can be only a liability created by a social rule or demand on one; and that what makes this liability 'moral' is that its force derives from moral sanctions or from an internalized sense of moral propriety. The definitive authority which one associates with moral injunctions and prohibitions will then derive solely from this source. There may be things which one ought to do even on a desert island; but one is not bound, let alone morally bound, to do them outside a social context which alone can create an obligation.

Here, then, seems to be another way of diagnosing the formalist's error. He assumes correctly that moral judgments have a special authoritative role. And he argues from this that every authentic and definitive ought-judgment is a moral judgment. But it now turns out that no ought-judgment, whether its grounds are personal or social, has the characteristic force of a moral judgment. Moral judgments relate to obligations; ought-judgments only to what is 'reasonable' or 'best'. Even what one ought to do on account of others is a *moral* ought only insofar as one is socially answerable for doing it. What falls within morality is only a segment of ought-abiding conduct. And what segment this is, what will count as *morally* obligatory or permissible, will be settled exclusively by our looking over our shoulders for the frowns and smiles of the social order. I doubt that those who press for a sharp distinction between 'ought' and 'obligation' would wish to go all the way with this conclusion. But this conclusion is implicit and,

---

1. H. L. A. Hart, "Legal and Moral Obligation," *Essays in Moral Philosophy*, ed. A. I. Melden (Seattle: University of Washington Press, 1958), p. 82.

given the premises, not easily avoided. If the conclusion seems extreme, the question is, why?

There is rarely smoke without a fire: social ought-abidance plainly is of social concern, and blame and admonition have a place in it. Equally plainly, personal ought-abidance is treated differently. Our evasions here count as amicable vices and not as moral turpitude. We may take the censure of others amiss and require them to mind their own business. And the same with their admonitions. To say "you ought to" to another is always a kind of interference; and the propriety of *saying so* (as distinct from having a judgment about it) varies with the case. Ought-judgments and ought-speech, ought-judgments and judgments of blame or of praiseworthiness have different and variable functions. Again, the language of 'ought' and 'obligation' is infected with these distinctions. There is a sense in which obligations are social liabilities, and moral obligations such liabilities as are morally sanctioned. In this sense one has no obligation, moral or otherwise, to do the right thing by oneself. Nor has one, in this sense, a moral obligation to do everything that one's social conscience may tell one to do. Society requires only our conscientiousness in standard situations; it treats deeds which only an exceptionally sensitive regard for others would prescribe as acts of superarrogation. To devote one's life to the care of lepers is praiseworthy but 'beyond the call of duty'. But, true as this may be, this fashionable observation also shows the limitations of the view. We do not conceive of moral obligations as dependent only on social requirements and their external or built-in sanctions. Saints and heroes go beyond these in what they judge they must or ought to do. And it would be farfetched to say that, when they follow their judgment, they are not doing what they think is their duty. 'Duty' and 'obligation' are not words unequivocally tied to the socially obligatory.

Nor is the 'morally permissible' tied only to the socially welcome. There may be occasions when someone may validly judge that he ought to put his own good before that of another. Here others may not readily welcome his ought-abidance. They may have a stake in discouraging it and be tempted to censure. But, granted that one accepts the authenticity of his judgment, one will here forbear censure and consider him morally justified. The measure of moral justification is here his conviction that he ought to. But it is well to note how this case puts the social orientation of our moral thinking under stress. The upright deviant from social norms and interests is not judged 'morally bad', but not 'morally good' or 'praiseworthy' either. We have to grant to others, as we must insist on for ourselves, that conscientious ought-abidance is the supreme moral rule for any agent in the situation of choice. But, socially, such conduct need not be an unmixed blessing. And if we may not condemn it on moral grounds, we need not bless it either. 'Moral goodness' is a term of appraisal so geared to socially welcome conduct that not every morally *correct* choice makes one a morally *good* man.

There seems to be, then, a sense in which 'ought' and 'moral obligation' are not sharply separable; though there also is another in which they are distinct, and in which social ought-abidance has the added force of an obligation. How, then, do these two senses relate to one another? The question may be answered by considering the view that what gives to the social ought the force of a special *obligation* adds significantly to its action-guiding authority. For while this view is correct in one way, it is false in another. While social ought-abidance is required of us socially, we are surely not bound to it *only* on this account. The social ought differs in this respect from the obligations created only by law or custom. One has a legal obligation simply by being required by an appropriate public rule. But with the things which one ought to do on social grounds this is not so. What is here socially required of one is moral conduct: conduct in line with what one ought and can be reasonably expected to know that one ought to do. The very requirement presupposes that one has already an antecedent obligation to do it, insofar, namely, as one knows already that one ought to do it.

This would have seemed plain language in the past. What, then, is at issue in debarring us from using it? The traditional philosopher may have been guilty of an unidiomatic extension of language in speaking here of an antecedent commitment or obligation. He may well have made light of the common or garden use of these terms for a liability created by an external rule. But sometimes an unidiomatic extension of language is less misleading than a narrow insistence on linguistic propriety; and if there is cause for complaint here the cure seems worse than the disease. The traditional philosopher wanted to bring out that if a deliberative person ought to do a thing he is to this extent also bound to do it *in some manner*. He is facing, if not a conventional, then a 'natural' duty or obligation. And this extension of language has a warrant. Where one has an obligation or commitment to do something one is up against a characteristic constraint or limitation of one's freedom to act otherwise. And some language is needed to make the point that the demands or assignments of others are neither the only nor the most decisive form in which this constraint can be incurred.

A person who is obligated to do something is under a constraint which is not purely psychological or physical. He need not feel impelled to do it, he is not made to do it by main force, it is not causally impossible for him to act otherwise. The constraint is conceived as latent rather than actual, and as arising not from causes, but from reasons. The situation has features which *tell* for or against some action: they need not determine a person's choice, but they would if he knew them and took careful account of them. A deliberative person who can appreciate that he has such reasons will meet in them a latent limitation of his freedom to act otherwise. Obligations in the common or garden sense are a special case of this. One meets a constraining reason in a social rule or demand on one which one can ill afford to ignore. Such obligations are imposed on one from without. The rule or demand issues from others; their insistence is the feature in the situation which supplies as well as creates the reason which limits one's freedom of action. But not all liability to direction by known reasons is like this. There are choice-guiding considerations which are not first imported into the situation by others with a view to direct one: they exist and can be found in the nature, effects, and implications of actions and principles themselves. A deliberative person need not wait for others to bring them to his notice; nor in being guided by them is he doing their bidding. That he is up against such reasons for doing things is equivalent to saying that he ought to do them, of his own accord and prior to being asked. This is why one may speak of a 'natural obligation': of an *obligation* because a person is up against a latent limitation of his freedom by reasons; of a *natural* obligation because the limitation is the work here not of *anyone*, but of reasons to be found *antecedently in the nature of the case*.

Where one *ought* to do things on account of others, one is therefore *socially obligated* to do only what one has an antecedent natural obligation to do already. One is answerable to others, as someone against whom they have legitimate claims, precisely because one ought, and can know that one ought, to give them consideration to begin with. And this is why one's answerability to them cannot here significantly add to the weight and authority of one's commitment. It may do so de facto. When a person hesitates to do what he has no doubt that he ought to do, the reminder that he is accountable to others is a potent consideration. The mere thought of incurring recrimination and blame evokes apprehension and guilt. But these are not considerations to increase the force of a moral commitment de jure. A reflective person has no need of coercive reasons for acting as he ought. He does not require the fear of blame as a reason for not evading his own better judgment. And this is also why the absence of coercive reasons, where one ought to do things on one's own account, or on account of others, but beyond the call of conventional duty, could not allow one seriously to breathe a sigh of relief. Whatever one judges that one seriously ought to do, whether the reasons for doing it are ultimately social or personal, whether one is socially blameworthy for the omission or not, one is sufficiently committed to do and responsible to oneself for doing unasked. It is inconsistent with the concepts of mature moral thinking to keep looking for the differentia of the authority of the moral commitments in one's social answerability for observing them.

VI

I am saying "with the concepts of mature moral thinking" advisedly. For the complex fabric of moral thinking contains still another notion of the moral bond. And the view that moral commitments have a special authority which derives from the sanctioned demands of the social order keeps drawing support from it. In fact, here is the primary concept of the moral bond, the one from which it derives its name, and the one which comes first, not only in the history of the race, but also in that of the individual. For as one grows up this is what happens. Father says, "Don't lie, don't be slovenly." Mother says, "This is what father says." The world says, "Don't be promiscuous." Father says, "This is what everyone says, this is also what God says." Father also says, "Do what God says," and, he says, "God says, 'Do what father says.'" Here is a mixed barrage of requests made on one or reported to be made on one. They specify what one is to do or not to do. They come from 'out there', though their precise imponent is obscure. They are addressed to one not without heat and are backed not by main force, like the law, but by moral suasion—smiles or frowns, approval or disapproval, the promise of bestowing or the threat of withdrawing love. And in these requests everyone first meets the demands of 'morality'. They are the first model for the notions of 'moral law' and 'moral duty', the first standard of 'moral right' and 'moral wrong'. They create the moral obligations in their primary sense: as restrictions on one's freedom of action by the 'mores' or 'manners' of a social group. These obligations are like the legal obligations in being barriers against license maintained by social consensus for the protection of the social order. They differ from them only by the kind of sanctions employed and by the absence of institutional procedures for their promulgation, codification, and administration.

Confusion keeps arising from the complex relations between the primary moral bond and the commitments of a reflective person by cogent considerations. As one's understanding develops one becomes acquainted and learns to live with both, yet without learning to keep them distinctly apart. One's moral commitments, in the mature sense, may oblige one to defer to the same rules on which the mores insist. In fact, this is how they come to be called 'moral' commitments. The notion of the natural moral commitment arrives on the logical scene when it comes to be understood that a person who can use his own judgment does not need the insistence of the mores to defer to the rules which they prescribe. There are reasons why he ought to do so unasked, and, if not, then there are reasons why he ought to defer to other rules more adequate to the underlying social purposes of the moral code. This is how the word 'moral' is transferred from the one level to the other. The commitments of a reflective person, by social considerations especially, are called 'moral' because they incorporate and supersede the obligations by the mores in their role of protecting the social order. Social reasons become 'moral' reasons, and the powers of mind and agency on which unforced self-direction by reasons depends become 'moral powers' on account of their continuity of function with the purposes of primary morality. But these new connotations are acquired at the loss of others. The new-style moral commitment is no longer a creation of the social order. To call it 'moral' is no longer to imply that its *authority* depends on the apprehension of guilt for the violation of a public rule. It is 'moral' as backed by considerations which, while prior to the demands of primal morality, are favorable to its purposes; and it has authority if and when these considerations prove cogent on a due appraisal of the case.

This is how the word 'moral' acquires its multiple associations. Such notions as the 'moral order', or 'moral rule', may all be viewed in *two ways*: as a body of rules or a rule publicly maintained by moral force; and as a rule or a body of rules which the members of a group ought, and can be expected to know that they ought, to respect unasked. Each time, the moral commitment to defer to the rule may be said to arise from the 'requirements of the social order'. But the ambiguities of this expression easily pass unnoticed. In the one case, the commitment arises from what the *will* of society 'requires', i.e., insists on. In the other, it arises from what the *needs* of society 'require', i.e., causally presuppose for their satisfaction, and from what a due appraisal of these needs 'requires' one to do, i.e., provides one with telling reasons for doing. Both notions are settled parts of ordinary thought, in which the mind moves hazily from viewing the morally right or wrong as being so by a rule whose violation makes him socially guilty to viewing it as being so by a rule to which he ought to conform anyway. Moreover, the primary associations of 'moral' are so ingrained that it is hard to appreciate that there really is a level on which public demands and the apprehension of incurring social guilt are irrelevant to the authority of a commitment considered as 'moral'. There is a standing temptation for the philosopher no less than for the ordinary person to import the quasi-legal features of the primary model into the mature one and to expect them to persist where they no longer have a place.

What furthers confusion is that even in the mature perspective the action-guiding role of the mores is not entirely superseded. There is a presumption (of which one can make too much as well as too little) that a rule strongly insisted on by the mores will also have valid prior reasons in its favor. And there is ground for caution in pitting one's own judgment too readily against the presumptive wisdom of the moral code. A commitment to a rule of the mores on this ground is still, in a way, created for one by the moral code. But there is a difference. The existence of the moral code is here no longer the *ratio essendi* of a moral commitment viewed as primal. It is rather that the moral code has become the *ratio cognoscendi* of a moral commitment on the level of maturity. A moral education is commonly a training in the mores as a first guide to what one is to do or not to do. But it will be a moral education in quite different senses, depending on whether one is introduced to the moral code simply as a body of morally sanctioned demands, or as a first, though by no means the last, ground for the determinations of mature moral thinking.

I have argued that the mature moral commitments are incurred through the unforced appreciation of cogent reasons in the case. Their authority owes nothing to the coercive moral pressures. They are roughly called 'moral' because they are commitments which supersede the primary moral law in its action-guiding role. But the question of why and when they strictly deserve this name cannot well be settled.

We are inclined to conceive of morality by the joint application of two criteria. 'Moral' principles commit one in a special and cogently authoritative manner; and they commit one in this manner to conduct which is, or is held to be, socially desirable. This concept is applicable well enough to primary morality. The primary moral law (on its own level and by its own means) supplies an authoritative rule of life which obligates everyone alike, and in the social interest. The coincidence between rules with moral force and in the service of social ends can here be counted on: it is contrived, albeit unwittingly, and where it is wanting it can be mended. One can define morality, on the primary level, as authoritative action-guidance whose function is to regulate the social order. But morality, on the mature level, is less well-conceived in this way. There are difficulties in uniting the authoritative and the social associations of 'moral' in one concept.

It is plainly not the principal function of mature morality to protect the social order, if by the 'function' of a practice is meant the reason why it exists and is carried on. The commitments by cogent reasons in the case are not imposed on one from without for social ends. One incurs them, if through anyone's doing, through one's own: as someone willing to seek direction from the counsel of cogent reasons. The involvement of human beings in this practice is personal: it turns on their stake in the kind of self-preservation which requires that one should be able to bear before oneself the survey of one's own actions. Responsibly reason-guided and ought-abiding living exists, in the first place, for the sake of sane and ordered individual being, and not for the regulation of the social order. Nor is the coincidence between ought-abiding living and the social interest axiomatic.

The fact—which traditional moral philosophy seems almost to exist to dispute away—*is that primary morality has no unequivocal successor on the level of autonomous choice.* The 'moral law' (whether the actual law of the tribe, or the ideal law that would best suit its needs) has no identical counterpart in a 'law of our own nature'. It is true that the commitments by noncoercive reasons (like the primary moral law) supply a *definitive* guide to conduct on their level; and that where they have other-regarding grounds, they are in the *social interest*. But the agreement between the definitive commitments on this level and those typically geared to the social interest is not here guaranteed. The agreement is not contrived; the social order cannot lay down what reflective choice shall bid a mature person do, or for what reasons. Nor is the agreement logically necessary. Valid ought-judgments rest on the backing of choice-supporting reasons: of facts in the case which can dispose those who know and review them in favor of or against the choice. There is therefore no logical limit to what may be a valid ought. The care of others may be a valid ought for one, and so may be the proper care of oneself. Either end may manifestly direct one to seek it on a diligently comprehending view of it. Either, or both, may be valid premises for a particular ought-judgment. One may be conscientiously ought-abiding in serving one's community, or in seeking personal salvation behind the walls of a Buddhist retreat. Considerations of prudence and wisdom may relevantly add to the reasons why one ought to practice the social virtues, along with the reasons of humanity and compassion. What is judged a valid ought, on a due appraisal of the facts and their force for one as deciding reasons, may have all manner of grounds; it may protect individual as well as social needs; it need not be the same for everyone alike. Nor need every ought be an ought for one through and through in order to be a seriously cogent ought, and among one's responsibilities as a right-living, reason-guided person. The ought-judgments which are formally imposing and backed by materially moral considerations are the standard case for human beings of the formally imposing ones; but they are no more than a species of the broad genus 'definitively action-guiding ought-judgments'.

Is one to say, then, that the mature moral enterprise is the general practice of conscientiously ought-abiding living? Or that it is only the part of it which is socially beneficial and a matter of active social concern? Are the mature moral commitments those which *formally*, or only those which *formally and materially*, continue the job of the primary moral law? Usage here leans uneasily either way. That man is a 'moral agent' with 'moral freedom' is associated with his power for responsible self-direction. 'Moral strength' or 'moral weakness' are terms which relate to the exercise of this power. But the 'morally good man' connects with the 'selfless man'. The 'moral' commitments of a mature person are conceived as essentially self-incurred through the responsible exercise of his moral powers and also as grounded in regard for others. There are those who insist that mature morality is socially beneficial ought-abidance: that language prescribes a material as well as a formal criterion for the use of 'moral'. There are others who will call 'moral' any definitive and 'authentic' commitment of a self-directing person, whether its grounds are social or personal.

Here is a semantic issue which it is far more important to understand than to take sides on. For whatever one says—whether it is the more consonant with ordinary language or not—must be semantically disquieting. Usage (at any rate, current English usage) backs the nonformalist more than the formalist. The mature moral commitments are those to conduct which is of social concern: they are properly called 'moral' *as they supersede the primary moral law in its social role*. This usage is unexceptionable as long as its implications are faced. The *moral* and the *definitive* commitments on the mature level need not then coincide. One must grant that 'morality' on this level is demoted from its accustomed place of being the sole and final arbiter of right and wrong choice. This is why, much as the nonformalist has semantically a case, the formalist has one too. He is opting for the other horn of the dilemma. The moral commitments on the mature level are *those which supersede the primary moral law in its role of supplying an authoritative and supreme rule of life*. And this rule is in the definitive— but not necessarily only materially moral—commitments which a reflective person incurs on a nonevasive appreciation of all the reasons in the case; and, in the last analysis, in his first commitment to the 'authentic' way of life itself.

If both alternatives are repugnant, it is because both fall short of expectations. The unequivocal successor to the primary moral law should be a commitment by noncoercive reasons, manifestly binding on everyone alike, to give precedence always to the claims of beneficence and the requirements of social living. But there is no warrant for assuming such a commitment on the level of autonomous choice. The rules of language cannot furnish it any more than pure reason or intuition. The hard fact is that the rational and autonomous mode of life overlaps, but no longer necessarily coincides, with the moral mode of life as conceived from the point of view of the social interest. The autonomous agent can be a debatable social asset. It is vain to expect morality on all levels to do the same kind of job as the institution of the law. The concept of morality itself bears the accumulated scars of conceptual evolution. Its multiple associations are a bar to summing it up in any one way.

[11]

Morality, Form, and Content

I

Contemporary moralists are concerned with morality as a practice, enterprise, institution. Their interest is in part polemical, in aid of freeing the concept of morality from formalistic impoverishment. The impoverishment is found in the view, held by existentialists, or such noncognitivists as R. M. Hare, that the content of morality is logically neutral. Moral practice, on this view, is in response to moral demands, ought-judgments, and choices; and moral demands are 'moral' by virtue of their formal character and role as action guides. They prescribe authoritatively, so as to settle the question for choice. It follows, or so it is said, that morality may be in its content the practice of anything whatsoever, not perhaps in actual fact but as a matter of logical possibility. Yet objection is taken to this implication. The demands of morality are not commonly taken to be content-neutral. They are thought to connect more than contingently with regard for the good of others and their rights. The classical moralists sought to vindicate such commonsense convictions. The question is on what terms, if any, this can be satisfactorily done.

Contemporary writers (Kurt Baier, Stephen Toulmin, Kai Nielsen, G. J. Warnock) frequently seek the remedy in conceptual considerations. Formal force and cogency are not sufficient to make a directive 'moral'. A directive will count as moral only if its content is social, and this is necessary as part of the grammar of the term. Reflection on morality as a practice or institution of life, and the role of moral precepts in it, is said to confirm the social content of 'the moral'. Moral practice typically supports social cooperation and betterment. This

[232]

contribution is by definition its 'function', its characteristic achievement, if not its end or goal. No wonder the contingency thesis is counterintuitive. Moral precepts are those which guide socially good practice. Their meaning must reflect that of the practice to which they are a guide. We have it logically certified that the morally imperative and the socially good will stay in harness.

The trouble with this view is that it wins too easily. The original problem, the relation between what a person may confront as cogently mandatory and the social, is left untouched. The thrust is rather to dispose of it as a substantive problem within morality by assuming that the ordinary grammar of 'moral' sanctions an exclusive and unequivocal association of 'moral' with 'social' practice. I don't think that this assumption can be sustained. The natural associations of 'moral' connect with both the 'social' and the 'mandatory'. Neither criterion is easily surrendered, nor, as needs showing, are they easily combined into one workable concept.

It is plain that morality will necessarily be social if one is prepared to treat 'social' as *both necessary and sufficient* for the use of 'moral'. Moral practices, then, are defined as socially good practices: doing the moral thing as a matter of doing what is socially needed or beneficial. Whether moral practice in this sense is also practice in which it is *mandatory* to engage, however, will then be a logically open question. "Why be moral?" and "Is there any serious commitment to be moral?" may be asked after the question, "What would be the moral thing to do?" has been answered. And this is in order if 'doing the social thing' and 'doing the moral thing' may be taken to mean the same. But plainly this is to *revise* the common concept of the 'moral' rather than to *characterize* it. By a 'moral' practice we do not mean simply a 'socially good' practice. We at least also imply that the practice in question is one that it is, in some special sense, mandatory for one to engage in. There is a morality only when there are practices that are not optional.

At most, then, the ordinary concept of the 'moral' connects both materially with the social and formally with the mandatory, and, if anything, I should say, somewhat more closely with the latter than with the former. The primary association of 'moral' is with practice under the rule of the mores, mandates created by customary social consensus and with a compelling authority derived from the sanctions of disapproval and censure. That a practice is enjoined or prohibited in this special manner is here the primary reason for calling it 'moral'. The morally taboo is that in which society has a traditional stake and which it backs with moral force. But the stake of society here is not necessarily founded on considerations of social utility, or of them alone.

Our conceptual proclivities may be different when we move from a morality of the mores to the concept of a reflective morality practiced by autonomous persons of their own accord; indeed, the differences in our conception of moral practice on the one and the other level should put us on guard against generalizing about the necessary and sufficient conditions for the use of the term. There are strong inclinations on the level of reflective morality to build into the concept an orientation toward social good. We think of 'moral' considerations, reasons, and motives as other-regarding ones. But here too our associations tend in the other direction as well. A reflective morality is conceived as practice which the due exercise of knowledge and reflection makes mandatory by making it reflectively compelling. In fact, we should also here like to say that 'reflective morality' is the term for a practice which, while under the authority of reason, also supports social good overridingly. But it is precisely on this level that a concept which answers to both the formal and the material criteria turns out not to be workable. We cannot readily conceive of an autonomous moral enterprise that would necessarily and exclusively be under mandates with a social content. Nor could we *make* it an exclusively social enterprise by way of a stipulative definition without mutilating other parts of our common understanding of it.

More needs to be said on these points.

II

Let me say first that there are reasons, some better and some worse, why it may seem that morality could well be conceived as a practice under authoritative mandates overridingly partial to social good. It may not be appropriate to define *institutional* morality (practice under the direction of the mores) strictly in this way, but, following a suggestion of William Frankena's, one may plausibly want to call it a morality only if, at least largely, it was practice guided by socially protective precepts. Some social content would here be necessary if a practice, and the code that informs it, is to count as 'moral'; but not every moral precept which was part of the code would have to be social.

Whether plausible or not, however, the main point of interest here lies elsewhere. *Institutional* morality is, in its nature, a practice which is under mandates because social consensus and sanctions *make* it so. Its mandates issue from human words and deeds; they are manipulable, wittingly or unwittingly, to serve some chosen end. Hence it is at least intelligible how there could be an *instituted* moral practice, *formally* mandatory and social in *content*, to which alone the word 'moral' would properly apply. Social consensus could create such a practice by exclusively giving the backing of moral sanctions to precepts in the social interest.

Some contemporaries believe that *autonomous* morality can be conceived along similar lines. We think of it as practice in response to ought-judgments, prescriptive judgments made by individuals and functioning as action guides independently of and prior to the demands of the social mores. Once again, one may think here of guidance by such judgments as by mandates *issued*, only not now by the mores, but by individuals to other individuals or to themselves. And, if so, the model of moral practice as something contrived for the sake of some socially good achievement can also be applied to autonomous moral practice. We then think of it as in response to *performatory utterances* whose role is to enjoin and which are called 'moral' for enjoining the socially beneficial. Familiar talk about the 'function' of moral discourse, principles, and action guides has a place in this frame of reference. Moral ought-judgments issue mandates. It is in their nature to be usable as tools for promoting a chosen end. Autonomous morality becomes the offspring of prescriptive language used in the social interest, a practice of 'oughting' ourselves and others into doing the socially cooperative thing.

But surely one should recognize that this model of moral practice as *contrived* by mandates issued has no place on the level of reflective morality. A voluntary practice under reflective ought-judgments is under directives which are independent of and prior to the *say-so of anyone*, whether of others or of oneself. The question here is not '*Who* makes it?' but '*What* makes it that I ought to?'; and what makes it that I ought to are the merits of the case, the sufficiency of choice-determining reasons that the case can be judged to present. One might, as Hare does, make allowance for this and remain a prescriptivist. 'I ought to' and 'you ought to' are then prescriptives, but with the special role of making only *reasoned* prescriptions, commendations to choices made only with the nature of the case duly before one. A practice under ought-judgments is here under the twin direction of the imperative 'choose x' and the implied judgment 'x would be well chosen' (or 'there are choice-influencing reasons enough for choosing x'). The model of choice guidance by mandates issued will still apply here but more now in form than in substance. Ought-judgments commend, but only what deliberation vindicates as commendable; and whatever this will amount to becomes a logically open question. A practice under reasoned prescriptions can no longer be designated at will to espouse some preselected cause or other. *It is logically designated to espouse whatever cause that diligent deliberative scrutiny will back most.*

My own view is briefly that a reasoned choice view of ought-judgments would do better without even the trimmings of prescriptivism. One will then say that 'I ought to' is primarily choice-guiding, not by expressing a fiat or self-command vis-à-vis choice-supporting reasons, but by embodying the judgment that one is faced with such reasons and is, as a duly deliberative person, under a liability to determination by them. And likewise, that 'you ought to' is primarily choice-guiding, not by being a 'telling to' but by being the submission made to another that he is under such a liability and can judge of it for himself. The illocutionary force of 'you ought to' is admonitory more than prescriptive, and the directive import of an admonition is in the reminder rather than in the reminding. In any case, ought-judgments will embody the directively relevant claim that the nature of the case itself, prior to anyone's say-so, would dispose and direct a comprehending person to act in some way, and sufficiently or authoritatively so, if all that could bear on the choice as a reason, including the intrinsic nature of the ultimate ends and consequences involved, had been duly taken into consideration. The crucial formal distinction between an institutional and a reflective, or autonomous, moral practice will then be unambiguously clear: the first is under the direction of what is *made* mandatory for one by the will of others; the second under the direction of what no one, including oneself, can *make* mandatory, but one's own reflective judgment alone can *show* to be mandatory, or reflectively compelling, for one.

And this is why the concept of an autonomous morality as a practice formally under the reflectively mandatory and yet materially in support of social good is in trouble. For no coincidence between the reflectively mandatory and the socially good can here be gainsaid. There is *logically* no telling what considerations may or may not turn out to be choice-supporting and reflectively compelling for otherwise equally deliberative persons. Social considerations are plainly not exclusively ought-implying; some things which one validly ought to do concern the care for one's own proper good. Nor are social considerations as such necessarily ought-implying, let alone always so, when opposed by contrary considerations. It is a reasonable presumption that thinking human persons will be accessible to the force of such considerations, and often, even if not always, overridingly so. But it is not analytically true, nor, as there once was the temptation to say, true a priori as a matter of intuitive self-evidence, that they must.

It follows that one cannot have an applicable concept of *reflective* moral practice in the same way that one could have one of its *institutional* counterpart. The concept of an institutional moral practice under authoritative and overriding mandates in the social interest has a referent in a practice which at least could be of our own making. But the concept of a reflective practice called 'moral' because, in being in response *to* the reflectively mandatory, it is also always *of* what is socially good would have no referent in anything that could be sufficiently counted on to exist. There seems to be no way in which, in the concept of a reflective morality, the two customary criteria for 'moral' practice could be preserved without stress. We may preserve 'mandatory' and conceive of it formally as the practice of reflective persons under the judgment of what they ought to do all told; or preserve 'social' and conceive of it as only that part of their practice under ought-judgments which would be materially based on social considerations. But there is a price to be paid on either side. To make it analytic that reflective moral practice is of the reflectively mandatory leaves it logically open whether, or how much, it will also be of the social. To make it analytic that it is of the social leaves it logically open whether, or how much, such a practice will be mandatory. The first is the formalist's option, the second the nonformalist's. Each will understandably have its pull, and neither is likely to satisfy.

I do not think that the stress between these conflicting pulls can be completely resolved. But more can, and must, be said about the problem of at least somehow bringing them under one roof. Autonomous morality is a complex enterprise with distinguishable aspects. It can be viewed as an action-practice under reflexive action commitments and also as the practice of deliberative persons under a reflective conduct commitment to subscribe to rational self-guidance. I shall argue that a social orientation is conceptually more properly associated with autonomous 'moral' practice under the one aspect than under the other.

III

Let me first say something about a case for nonformalism which has a good part of ordinary thought and language on its side. Even granted that a rational agent can find himself under formally valid and cogent commitments based on personal considerations, commitments to personal ideals, to providence, temperance, or self-reliance, one is still reluctant to count them as among his *moral* commitments. It feels natural to reserve 'moral' to ought-judgments which are justified by other-regarding considerations, by reference to social needs and interests, to the life or happiness of other persons. Language tends to treat 'moral' considerations as considerations of this kind. And this is why, it is argued, it cannot be an open question whether there can be reflective moral commitments on nonsocial grounds: the rules of language leave no room for 'private enterprise' (Philippa Foot) in the matter of determining what considerations can be morally ought-implying. Moral choice settles what one ought to do from the moral, i.e., broadly social point of view; 'doing the moral thing' is strictly a matter of doing what it would be reflectively committing from this point of view to do.

By this language rule, 'moral' is used to mark off the species of socially grounded commitments from the genus of a person's reflective action commitments in general. And this use has a point because it serves to mark a substantive distinction. Reflective commitments based on other-regarding rather than on purely personal grounds will be to practices in which the social order has a stake. And society will, legitimately, hold the autonomous agent answerable for their ready recognition and observance. The failure is treated, like a violation of a rule of the mores, as an offense sanctionable by moral censure. The same does not apply to failure to be ought-abiding in personal matters. Such violations do not count as moral turpitude; one may criticize the agent as morally weak but not censure him as morally bad. To reserve 'moral' to the social commitments is to emphasize the special answerability to others to which autonomous agents are subject, as members of a social community, in the matter of taking notice of them.

One should not therefore boggle at this use. It is a settled part of speech; it does an indispensable delineative job. One may object to Hare that not all reflective action commitments may count as 'moral' merely because they are formally well founded. This is not to say that a rational person may not also find himself under reflective commitments not based on social grounds. But there is no objection to calling them, however formally valid and cogent they may be, technically 'nonmoral'.

All the same, the implications and limitations of this use should also be in the open. Reflective moral practice, as just defined, is not necessarily the *whole* of the action-practice to which a deliberative person may find himself cogently committed, nor necessarily even *part* of it. It is not necessarily the whole, for he may also find himself under technically 'nonmoral' commitments; and it is not necessarily even part of it, for it is not necessary (much as it would be incredible) for social considerations to be reflectively committing at all, let alone to be so always overridingly. The 'moral' judgment that guides moral practice, in the nonformalist sense, is only the judgment of what, if anything, one ought to do 'from the moral point of view'. It does not settle what one ultimately ought to do, from every point of view and everything considered.

It follows that the contingency problem from which we started is still with us except for a change of notation. Practice under *moral* commitments has become necessarily social, but the practice of a rational person under his *cogently reflective commitments* is no more necessarily social in content than before. And this will be cold comfort for anyone who seeks to be reassured that there is, on the level of reflective choice, more than simply a contingent connection between the authoritatively (rationally) committing and the socially good, corresponding on this level to the connection between these two which the mores can contrive. The nonformalist lets us speak of this with less seeming paradox. We don't have to say that the practice of *moral agents* need not be social, but only that that of *duly self-guiding rational agents* need not be so. The underlying assumption is that a clear-cut divorce of the 'moral' from the 'rational' agent is possible and that it is conceptually unproblematic that the 'rational' need not be 'moral' and the 'moral' not be 'rational'.

I wish to argue that, although this divorce is possible, it is not possible *exclusively*. For there is a sense in which we connect the *duly self-guiding agent* precisely with the *moral* agent; and, indeed, here not with the agent who does the social thing when he ought to, but with the one who engages, and finds himself committed to engage, in the entire enterprise of seeking and receiving guidance from the judgment of what he validly ought to do, whether on materially 'moral' or 'nonmoral' grounds. Autonomous morality in this perspective seems to consist of the effective engagement of moral agents in a certain practice, a 'moral' practice of self-determination under ought-judgments whatever they lead to, rather than in an action-practice under ought-judgments with a preselected content. And it is noteworthy that it is only in this perspective that we can hope to accommodate one more crucial part of our common thinking about morality, namely, that it is engagement in the practice of something that is *invariably mandatory*, no matter what, in whatever life situation anyone may find himself. Moral practice, if conceptually tied down to social service, cannot, as we shall see, foot this bill.

IV

The crux of the matter is, as Plato and Kant knew full well but we seem to have lost sight of, that the moral achievement of an autonomous person is not exclusively in his actions. He finds himself called upon to *do* certain things, but also, in doing anything, to *conduct* himself in a certain manner. What he does may turn out right, though the conduct from which it is issued was faulty; or his conduct was faultless but failed to issue in the right actions. There is a difference between 'being moral' and 'doing the moral thing'. The one is a matter of one's strategy in guiding one's choices and dispositions to action; the other of the action achievement which results from such a strategy. How one is to *live* as a moral person is one question; what one is to *do*, morally speaking, is quite another. The difference is apparent in the answers that intuitively come to mind: 'Living as one ought to' connects with 'living with integrity', 'responsibility', 'as someone who can own his own actions', 'who can bear his own survey'; and it connects with this as naturally as 'doing the moral thing' connects with 'doing the social thing'. Moral significance attaches to both; and both connect with our concept of morality as an autonomous enterprise. We think of this enterprise as social action-practice under reflective commitments and also as a lifestyle under a primary commitment to deliberative rectitude in choice.

The distinction is apparent even if one took it that moral practice was solely under reflective social commitments and simply asks for the presuppositions of such a practice on the level of autonomy. The answer is that such a practice would presuppose persons of a certain disposition, persons who will take voluntary guidance from what they judge, prior to anyone's say-so, that the social and other considerations in the case would make it compelling for them to do. We have to count on them as conducting themselves as thoroughgoingly deliberative persons; and in counting on this, we shall broadly count on two things: that they will, of their own accord, give timely and honest consideration to the social and other implications of their actions and of their choice-determining force for them; and that, if need be, they will yield to this force in the face of contrary inclinations.

The point is that we treat people's success or failure on these counts as the measure of their conduct achievement as autonomous agents. The avoidable failure to recognize the relevant facts in the case and their ought-implying relevance is viewed as a moral defect; equally so is the failure to bring oneself to do what one acknowledges that one ought to do. There is moral merit in acknowledging one's reflective commitments both in judgment and in deed and the more so when their acceptance required winning out against inner resistance. In fact, whether the honest acknowledgment or the observance of a reflective action commitment is concerned, what is treated *as the core of the moral conduct achievement is the same*. Such commitments are by facts in the case which the agent, who will recognize them, will appreciate and experience as choice-determining for him insofar as he squarely reviews and acknowledges them for what he knows them to be. Such confrontation of directively relevant, even if unpalatable, belief or truth is the condition both for appreciating the force for one of the reasons in the case and for, if need be, taking them to heart in practice. 'Being moral' or 'living morally' relates to a practice of voluntary self-direction by the nonevasion of directively relevant truth, a practice of self-transcendence by giving directively relevant truth efficacious entry where, from the point of view of the wants, habitual attachments, aversions, and fears in actual possession of oneself, it is unwelcome. An autonomous moral agent is a person who can, and will, direct himself in this manner. I like to say that he is a person who conducts himself with *deliberative rectitude*.

Although this moral agent is plainly a relative of Kant's man of 'goodwill', I should not like him to be viewed as more than a distant cousin. It is absurd to think of the moral agent as doing whatever he does, whether brushing his teeth, embracing his sweetheart, or volunteering for the bomb disposal squad, from the reasoned conviction that he ought to do it. One need not, and cannot, bring oneself to do, from the sense that one ought to, that which good habits and sound or innocent inclinations lead one to do anyway; and the issue for deliberation, when there is one, is not here whether one ought to, but whether one *may* do these things, without some countermanding 'ought' in the way. But it is not absurd to think of the moral agent as living on the alert, like a responsible driver, for the situation that calls for a thoroughgoing review and choice, and, when necessary, not evading the lesson of such a review in what he does. Hence my own preference is for saying, more broadly than Kant, that the characteristic achievement of the autonomous agent is to conduct himself *with due care for keeping his action dispositions and actions reflectively right*; and there are more ways than one to display such care. One who goes through his daily routine, mostly following habit or inclination, need not be lacking in such care, provided that he was *entitled to take the rightness* of his ordinary doings for granted; and it would be enough of a test for this that he had not failed on appropriate earlier occasions to check out the principles on which he was acting, or to notice something notably deviant about the present case. Nor is one acting without due care in doing something one wants after having simply checked out that one *may* do it, in response to certain qualms, in whatever way aroused, about a possible issue. The heroic virtue of Kant's 'goodwill' will then be the most provoking and onerous case of 'taking due care', the one where, in order to keep one's action dispositions right, one has to confront them, in judgment and deed, with the corrective force of what one's best reflective judgment would bid one to do.

It needs to be added that 'conducting oneself as a moral agent', either meritoriously so or at least without moral blemish, is not only distinct from 'doing the (socially) moral thing', but is also not otherwise necessarily connected with it. The mark of the formally moral agent is that, one way or another, he is responsibly self-determining, and this is to say that he does not fail in the ready appreciation and observance of *anything* he can validly judge that he ought to do, whether for social, or personal, or religious reasons, or whatever else. The evasion of directively relevant truth in any department of life counts as moral defect and lays one open to legitimate self-reproach; its nonevasion, in combat with inner resistance, counts as meritorious and as a sign of moral strength and character. Indeed, it will not tarnish one's quality as a responsible moral agent even if one opts against doing the socially moral thing in the name of some personal ideal of self-fulfillment, or in the interest of survival in a hostile world, provided that the option has been exercised in full face of the alternatives, or at least did not derive simply from the evasion of them. Such a choice would have the merit of moral strength, provided it required the recognition of the overriding cogency of the self-protective and, maybe, for others, hurt-implying considerations in the case. In fact, the acknowledgment to oneself of one's desires or needs in a case like this may be as much a part of living with rectitude as is the concern for keeping these desires within rational bounds. The autonomous person lives with due care for making his action dispositions reflectively right; and although this would involve, with the classical tradition, keeping them under the check of reason, it may also involve, with the more recent tradition of Nietzsche or Freud, liberating them first from the crippling effects of rationally unfounded but socially or psychologically induced fears of admitting that one has them.

Such choices can properly be said to result from a responsible 'moral' judgment, and in fact, this use, and not the use of the term for what one ought to do from the (socially) 'moral point of view' is the more natural and familiar. The 'moral' judgment is here that by which moral agents settle the question for choice in a formally sufficient and morally blameless manner. It is the judgment, as Butler thought of it, which adjudicates between the freely acknowledged claims of self and those of others, between conflicting and each prima facie ought-implying, or permissible, considerations in the case. On this showing the judgment about our action commitments from the '(socially) moral point of view' is improperly equated with the 'moral judgment', the judgment that alone can function as the ultimate arbiter of right or wrong choice.

The question arises why living with rectitude should, along with acting beneficently, count as 'moral'. Without doubt, we treat the former as a moral virtue and as, in some way, *the* moral virtue par excellence. Plainly, then, we judge that this is how one ought to live and that this has the very *force* of a moral 'ought'. If so, this is the crucial counterexample to the view that nothing may count as moral unless its content is appropriately social. Moral conduct practice is not social action practice, not being primarily an action-practice at all, but rather a lifestyle of managing one's action output and keeping it uncrippled and self-acceptable. Nor could the good social consequences of such a lifestyle be its primary recommendation. Much as it may have them, they are not its necessary or most telling effect. The effect which is of its essence, rather than being on the agent's deeds, is on the agent himself. A thinking person can ill afford to have a will apart from or against his own better judgment. The evasive withholding of directively relevant truth from oneself undermines the fabric of one's being as a functioning mind. The habit of giving it entry and scope so as to monitor one's action-dispositions vitalizes and keeps one intact as a person, as the owner of what one is doing, capable of viewing oneself and one's actions without self-rejection or repression. This was Plato's insight in resting the case for righteous living on its quintessential contribution to personal good, on what right living 'invariably does to its possessor'; and this not because the good of others could never be the ground of a rational commitment, but simply because the basic commitment to right living had a more intimately personal ground.

If, then, the commitment to rectitude counts as 'moral' and, in some way, as the *moral commitment par excellence*, this can be only on account of its *special committingness par excellence*. And there is good reason for this. A thinking and willing person depends for the continued possession of himself as a functioning conscious being on living with comprehension rather than eluding it and on being able to do so in full face of his object strivings and the state of himself and the world resulting from them. If he has a stake in persisting as a mind he must live with due care to keeping himself self-acceptable; and this would be a reflective commitment that is *indefeasible and comes before any other that he might incur*. One may justify anything but the escape from reason by pleading the special circumstances of the case. One may say that one ought to be tolerant or keep one's word, but not necessarily at any price, and only after taking everything else into account. But to say that one ought to live self-acceptably but not necessarily at any price, and only after taking everything else into account, makes no sense. For this commitment is to living compatibly with doing whatever, as sufficiently mindful, one would rather do, with its cost in the case already counted and discounted. Here opposition can come only from one's unreasoned preferences. And they cannot invalidate a reasoned preference to the contrary, one whose exercise will as well grant one the prize of one's maintenance as a self, able to identify and reidentify with its own will and actions without need for self-reproach or self-forgetfulness. If there is a commitment to living self-acceptably, it would have to be the one reflective commitment that holds strictly 'categorically'; not by just holding '*all told*' but by holding '*no matter what*'.

I said before that morality *as a social action practice* cannot qualify as the practice of something that is mandatory *no matter what*. Autonomous morality, as a conduct practice or lifestyle, satisfies this condition. It is the only available candidate for morality as the practice of something to which there is a *perfectly invariable commitment*. 'Why be moral?' is not 'Why be social?' It is primarily 'Why live non-evasively?' at any time and before anything else. There must be something amiss in contemporary moral philosophy if it blithely takes for granted that 'Why be moral?' and 'Why be social?' are the same question.

V

It remains to pull the divergent strands of this essay together. There was the view that *morality*, and autonomous morality especially, being essentially practice of what is reflectively *mandatory or permissible*, must be logically neutral in content. And there was the reply that attention to the conceptual connections between 'moral' and 'social' will dispose of this contention. I said that, although this move has a point, it wins too easily; and only a little more needs saying to summarize how this is so.

The root of the trouble is that the grammar of 'moral' connects both with 'mandatory' and 'social' and that, on the level of reflective morality, these criteria come apart with no more than the chance of an uneasy truce between them. One cannot unequivocally characterize the autonomous moral enterprise as having or not having an essentially social role, nor can one say unequivocally that 'moral' in 'moral commitment' entails either 'social' or 'categorical' or both. The reason is that, inescapably, there is both a personal and a social dimension to our concept of the autonomous moral enterprise, and the grammar of 'moral' shifts with this shift of perspective.

There are reasons for thinking of autonomous morality, or in Butler's phrase, "the moral institution of life," as in the first place a human conduct practice under a primary and intimately personal commitment to deliberative rectitude in whatever one decides on or does. Morality, in this sense, is not primarily or exclusively a social enterprise; social betterment is not the principal reason why one is committed to it. The autonomous moral agent, much as he deserves respect, need not always meet with social approval or encouragement. If his rectitude is not in question, one cannot blame him, but one need not love or encourage him. The fanatic may be blameless, but one may fear him and guard oneself against him. Being morally blameless is no conclusive defense against being burned at the stake.

But we may also think of autonomous morality in its social aspect as that part of the practice of formally moral agents which is under reflective commitments to action in which the social order has a stake and for the discharge of which they are answerable not only to themselves but to others. As language has it, the strictly 'moral' commitment in this perspective is the social commitment; 'doing the moral thing' is 'doing the social thing'. The 'moral' ought-judgment is here the judgment of what one ought to do from the social point of view. Of moral action-practice one can say here that it has an essentially socially protective role. The 'moral' in this sense, however, is not necessarily mandatory or reflectively overriding. It may, but it need not, issue from that moral conduct practice to which the rational agent has a first commitment and from which whatever he may validly *do* will derive.

This leaves the question whether, in the end, we must not side with those who insist that reflective morality, as above all a practice which is formally rational, must be conceived as essentially neutral in content. And, with all, the answer to this should still not be an unqualified 'yes' or 'no'.

It certainly seems *more than just contingent* that autonomous morality should be practice under the foundation commitment to rectitude in choice. It would be odd to say that for thinking beings there might *just as well* be no such commitment; that evasion, escapism, or the steady pursuit of the not self-acceptable might turn out to be an equally legitimate, if not mandatory, lifestyle. This oddity does not, I think, amount strictly to logical impossibility. Rational agents are not committed to deliberative rectitude by definition. They would not be so committed if self-obliteration by slow self-disruption were their final aim, and such sickness unto death cannot be ruled out. But then it cannot lightly be countenanced either. That conscious being shuns its own extinction is as deep a trait as the will to life. We may find it unbelievable, even if we cannot take it to be impossible, that a thinking being, who does not repudiate life itself, should disavow, in a cool hour, any commitment to living compatibly with rational self-maintenance. If the foundation commitment of autonomous morality is not a logical truth, one may at least expect it to be the near inescapable conclusion of reflective judgment.

But what, then, about the connection between the conduct practice of formally moral agents and the socially or materially moral? I have urged that this must remain a logically open question. Whether, and to what extent, social considerations can be expected to have committing force for nonevasively deliberative agents has its proof not in logic but on the testing ground of deliberative experience. But, once more, this should not be taken to imply that moral conduct practice might *just as well* issue in socially inconsiderate as in socially considerate actions. That it might, one cannot treat as *inconceivable*, but still as *incredible*. There is a justified presumption with a massive, even if incomplete, backing in experience and in the standard conditions of interpersonal living, that reflective human agents are accessible to the force of other-regarding considerations. And one might well elevate this presumption to a regulative principle of moral judgment to the effect that one ought to treat unresponsiveness to social and humane considerations as always in the first place a sign of a breakdown in comprehension and deliberative rectitude, rather than as evidence of an ineradicable otherness in the other person's nature. The adoption of such a principle would be justified by a confluence of reasons: by the fact that social unresponsiveness is, more often than not, found to be selective (the concentration camp guard who brutalizes Jews and dotes on his wife and children); that in clinical experience it typically connects with personality disorganization; and that its origins in an incapacity of the mind or a congenital lack of heart are in no one instance conclusively decidable. There would be a pragmatic justification for the principle of imputing an Eichmann's or Himmler's disdain for human life and suffering as such to some deep-seated defect in their deliberative probity, rather than 'excuse' it as caused by some innate otherness of their natures.

To make the connection between moral agency and sociability more than just contingent by way of a regulative presumption is still to keep it synthetic. In a sense which is not obfuscating, it is to make it synthetic a priori but to stop short of making it analytic and conceptual. There is one further small step, however, which might contribute to peace with the conceptualist. We might build our regulative presumption into our concept of autonomous morality. We shall then say that to speak of autonomous morality implies that it is the practice of thinking human agents, under a first and intimately personal commitment to deliberative rectitude in conduct, who may also be counted on, by a regulative presumption, to be accessible, to a degree which has no precise measure, to the force of social and humane considerations. A concept of the 'moral institution of life' with the two basic criteria of the 'moral' thus uneasily united seems the most that is applicable to the human condition.

[12]

Moral Perplexity

Every age has its moral perplexities, but our own seems to have more than its share. And this is not only so because the old days are always the good old days, though there may be something in this too. But it is fair to say that there is less agreement and more uncertainty about moral matters today than, let us say, in the late nineteenth century. There is more dispute about the rights and duties of parents and children, of husbands and wives, of individuals and the state. There is a rejection of ready-made rules, and, generally, an air of unsettlement.

And there is something else too, namely, a sense of uneasiness about the fact that we are so divided and unsure. We are used to believing that there is a right and wrong about choices and ways of life, and that right thinking, here as elsewhere, can discern truth and dispel error. But now there are not a few who feel that this view itself is on trial. What is added to our moral perplexities is perplexity about morals. People put this by saying that there is some radical error in the traditional view that 'reason' can solve moral issues: according to some that 'reason ' can solve them at all, according to others that it can solve them unaided by religion. There was a time when Immanuel Kant could speak of the two great certainties, the starry heavens above us and the moral law, known by pure reason, within us. In our time both of these seem to be fading into the nebulae.

Such views are a measure of some people's bewilderment, but they need not be correct as a diagnosis. And one may look at the situation

Reprinted with permission of the University of Chicago Press from *Ethics* 66 (1956): 123–31. Copyright © by the University of Chicago Press.

more soberly. Because one may say: There is after all no more to the moral condition of our time than could be expected from its character generally. Ours is a time which requires adaptation to big changes all-round. What were sound practices of public finance yesterday are so no longer today; and why should the same not apply to what used to be sound moral practices? Moral codes are rules of thumb for the advancement of individual and social welfare, and as they have been learned they may have to be unlearned. Consider our views on the relations between men and women. At a time when women have careers, when technology changes the economics of the household, medical science the care of the body, psychology our knowledge of mental hygiene, some traditional rules must lose their point, and new ways have to be evolved. This may not be easy and uncontroversial. But it involves none but practical problems. And there is no need for taking the birth pangs of adaptation for the crack of doom.

So one may have different views on the causes of our perplexities. One may attribute them simply to the complexities of a time of change, or to deeper causes, to errors or confusions about right thinking in moral matters. And what I want to discuss are these different diagnoses of the situation.

I might say straightaway that I think that our troubles are both on the practical and on the deeper philosophical level. And this should not be surprising. One cannot doubt that our time is setting us problems for conduct to which we have no ready answers, or which the answer of the past will no longer fit. And it is quite a usual feature of the growth of thought, whether in science or elsewhere, that with big new questions to solve one also has to query what sort of questions these are, and how to solve them. And this is why philosophical questions come up, because philosophy deals with the logic of questions. I might say here, by the way, that philosophers are much misunderstood people. They are either looked down on or admired more than they should be, much as a foreigner in conservative English society. Philosophers have not got a secret key to solving problems at which others fail. Their job is rather to assist question-solving when it gets bogged down in confusion about the questions and about the answers which they permit. This is why there is not really a separate animal in the academic zoo called 'philosophy', over and above such creatures as history or physics or economics. Philosophy sits on all thought rather like the shell on the back of the tortoise; and where the tortoise goes there it goes, and as long as the tortoise keeps going it keeps going.

And now let us get on with the job. And here let me say first that not all moral disagreements lead to philosophical worries. Moral disagreements may have different origins, and this is the first point which we must note.

Many of them are simply about the best means toward achieving good ends. Take two parents who are disagreed on the upbringing of their children. Both will think that they should further their good, but one thinks that disciplinarian methods are right, and the other that they are plain wicked and wrong. This would be simply a dis-agreement about the means toward an agreed end, and, though there may be snags in practice, it is not in principle hard to solve. The facts about child development should decide who is right. And if there actually is much disagreement and uncertainty about this matter to-day, we may lay this at the door of a new science of infants still in its infancy. And many moral disputes are like this one. A dispute about the wrongness of gambling could be resolved by studying the effects of gambling on people's daily lives. The social effects of ownership will be relevant to disagreement about the right to property. And one could easily multiply examples, so much so that one may come to think that all moral disputes are of this kind. People have said: There is one ultimate end on which agreement can be presupposed: that, above all, we ought to do most good and least harm all-round; and all moral disputes are simply about the best means toward this end. And without doubt it would be a comfort if this were so. Because then, in the last resort, we could solve all moral problems with the aid of science. Psychology, medicine, sociology, economics tell us the story of what leads to what, of the effects of bashing children, of gambling, of private ownership. These sciences would then be our proper advisers on all matters of right and wrong.

Unfortunately this is too sweeping. And it is too sweeping because not all moral disputes arise from disagreement about the best means toward agreed ends. But before I turn to this, let me say that one may also easily underrate the importance of this view. Moral codes, like institutions in general, tend to settle in fixed grooves. We develop a jealous attachment to them. And when one feels most defensive about them, this is often the very moment for revising, "in a cool hour," as Bishop Butler said, what good or harm they really do. And to consult the findings of science at this point will not come amiss.

But, as I say, science cannot help us all the way, because there is another area of moral dispute which relates not to means but to ends. And let me first introduce this area, and then consider how it raises problems.

It seems so natural to say: There is one ultimate end, 'above all, do most good and least harm all-round', and on this we are agreed. But, for several reasons, this is far too simple. For one, the formula is too vague. It says we ought to promote people's welfare. But when does a man really fare well? There are many constituents of a good life: freedom from want or fear, health and leisure, justice, freedom of self-expression. And not all of these can be realized to the same extent at the same time. One may have to choose between the one and the other, as, for instance, between economic security and freedom from restraints. So it follows that 'do most good and least harm all-round' does not really relate to one ultimate end but to a family of such ends; and that there is a question for deciding in what order of priorities these ends should be realized.

Moreover, even if we are agreed on how to do most good all-round, can one really assume that everyone must be agreed on this as his first aim? I don't think that we can just presuppose this. Someone might come along and say: "Why this at all? Why concern myself with general good instead of my own?" And this raises the problem of convincing him in some way that the furtherance of general good is an end that he ought to make his own. So *the* ultimate moral premise may be a matter for dispute; and unless there is a way of supporting it, the whole edifice of obligations based on it will fall apart.

And, finally, it is also too simple to say that doing most good all-round is what everyone ought to attempt every time and above all. Because there are at any one moment many claimants for a good turn, and one cannot satisfy them all: there are ourselves and others, our children, parents, our group, the present generation and the next, and there is the good of mankind at large. We think that we have some obligation to further most good all-round, but that we have also got special obligations toward those near us, and that we have some rights ourselves. So, once more, there may be situations for choice: where we have to decide which of two conflicting ultimate claims should come first. Remember our example about the upbringing of children. Few parents will dispute that their children's good is their concern. But *how much so*, this is already another matter. It may be true that infinite patience will rear children free of hate and aggression. But to do so to perfection may also consume the time and energy of their parents. How much of their own lives, then, should parents make over to their children? This is no longer a question of means to ends. It is quite a different sort of question, one of deciding between legitimate and conflicting ends, of how to distribute one's good turns.

And now let us look at the moral perplexities of our time again. It is pretty plain that our major worries are in this area of ultimate ends and of decisions between them. There have been times when these issues were more concealed by a general consensus of opinion. But in our own time, all the devils of dissent and disorientation seem to be let loose. A Nazi will allow that the good of his children is his responsibility. He will allow high priority to the good of his group, far above that of his parents or friends or of any single individual. But he will deny that the good of other groups is his business; and nothing will persuade him of a right for everyone to be treated humanely. A pacifist will put the preservation of human life before everything else. A Communist will put social justice and economic security before freedom of decision or thought. And he will be far more ready than a liberal individualist would think right to sacrifice the good of the present generation to that of the next. These are all differences about moral premises. And when people apply these premises to daily life, then quite different choices will become right or wrong for them: with the effect that, as we are all in this, we become targets to one another of disapproval and dismay. Everyone feels that the other is wrongheaded beyond comprehension; and opportunities abound for feeling this way.

I said before that perplexity about morals is one of the signs of our time. It is the area of dissent which I have just indicated which is mainly responsible for this. Because dissent about first things raises the question of how to settle it. And on this question we find ourselves in a dilemma. As I said, everyone feels that the other is wrongheaded in placing his priorities where he does. And if the other really is wrongheaded, then there must be a right and a wrong in these matters, and a way of showing what it is. But, in practice, is there such a way? There are few who have not at some time tried and failed. We all know how disputes about first things begin in argument only to end in recrimination; and it is where words fail one that one resorts to bad language. But surely words should not fail one here. If the other is wrong, then there should be a way of putting him right. We have been taught, and believe, that by using 'reason' we can put him right. But, as reason is understood, it does not seem to work.

And this is how the philosophical issue has come to be raised. Persistent failure at solving a problem suggests that one has got the wrong measure of it: that one expects too much or the wrong things. So out of the trials and tribulations of our daily experience we are being made to ask: "How can one decide the rights and wrongs of ultimate choices or ways of life at all?"

I must say a little about contemporary trends in response to this question. The keynote, as one would expect, is skepticism of reason. But different conclusions are drawn from this. A very fashionable view is to say that we fail to convince each other only because there is nothing to convince each other of: there just is no arguable right or wrong of ultimate choices. To some people independence ultimately matters more than security and to others not; to some the good of their children is far more important than personal achievement and to others less so. And this is all there is to it. There is no saying that one choice is more 'proper' or 'rational' than the other. There is no disputing of ultimate tastes. And the reason given is that if there were it should be possible to prove to people that they ought to choose one ultimate course rather than another: one should be able to offer a reason for this. And in the nature of the case, this is impossible. First things, like liberty or doing good to others, one values for themselves. And one cannot give people a reason for valuing things for themselves or for valuing one of them more than the other. Because the only reason for valuing things in themselves is in what they are, and if people don't want them knowing what they are, there is nothing to tell them that could convert them. Hume once said that "it was not against reason to prefer the scratching of my little finger to the destruction of the whole world." For if you asked "and why not?" there is nothing one could say. So in the matter of ultimate choices we must tolerate, or may bash, each other, but we must not be perplexed at making no headway with arguing.

One may find this 'solution' a little hard to take, if not its tolerance too complaisant to tolerate. And let me say that its logic is not as strong as it sounds. It is possible that one ultimate choice should be more right than another even if there is no argument from which to prove this because not all truths are known by a formal proof. One does not prove by argument that it is raining outside, one just goes and looks. And, maybe, that some ultimate choices are more proper for a human being than others is also something which everyone just has to see for himself. Supposing that one said: "You may not feel this now, but if you thought, you would not have it in your heart to stand by while others suffer." I cannot prove this to you, but it may be true of you, and you would be the one to check on it for yourself. And by saying that one ultimate choice may be more 'proper' or 'rational' than another, one may just mean this: that it would recommend itself more than the other to a human being who was thoughtful and sincere.

In fact, the main European tradition in ethics is built on a conception like this, and great hopes for a universal and objective ethics used to be pinned on it. Man, it was said, has the moral order in his own nature because he has both a social nature and can reflect. By reflection he can put it to himself what it is to do good or harm; his social nature enables him to respond to these ideas. So when guided by reflection any human being will find the obligation to doing good and not doing harm in his own heart. The right order of choices is laid down for all in their own natures, plain for everyone to see who will trouble to look into himself.

I am referring to this root conception of our ethical tradition because, as we are looking at contemporary trends, it is also under fire today. Its most challenging critic is Jean-Paul Sartre, the French existentialist. Sartre's ideas developed during the war, when Frenchmen were up against having to choose between collaboration and resistance, and where anyone might be in the sort of conflict which Sartre reports of one of his students: should he stay with his widowed mother whose life depended on him, or join the Free French in an uncertain gamble on doing some good for an anonymous cause? Here was the typical challenge to moral thinking: to solve conflict about ultimate ends and ways of life. And, according to Sartre, none of the traditional formulae will stand the test. Should the student do what will cause most good all-round? The calculus is impossible. And even if possible there would still be the choice between causing most good all-round and protecting his mother. Would it help him to consider which choice would be more right by being more properly human? Again, the formula is too wide and vague to meet the concrete case. Human nature is not uniform and fixed enough to allow expression only in one choice and not in any other. The conception of the human heart as a book of rules prescribing the same for all, if only consulted properly, is a metaphysical fiction. Should he then seek guidance from his personal feelings, scrutinize his motives, and decide on that which in truth matters to him most? Sartre will not let him have this way out either. One cannot ask: "Is it more proper for *me* to protect my mother or my country?" any more than one can ask: "Is it more proper for a human being to protect his mother or his country?" And one cannot ask this because it is an illusion that by reflection a man could find out about his true feelings so as to guide his choice by them. The only proof of one's true feelings is in the acting. One only knows oneself by what one has decided. And, therefore, in the situation of conflict *there is no known guide to turn to*. Man, Sartre concludes, is "deserted," he must choose in darkness, he must opt for his ultimate goals in default of any knowledge of a better or worse. All the consolation he has is that in freely committing himself one way or another he is not drifting but exercising his human power of cutting the Gordian knot.

This doctrine destroys the illusion that in every complex situation there is one choice which, for everyone alike and quite unmistakably, is more properly human than any other. But, if it has a point here, it does not stop at this. For it goes on to deny that not even in any more personal and more fallible sense could our ultimate choices be guided by any conception of a better or worse. We cannot wait to see on which side our Gordian knot is buttered. Moral thinking in the past was naive and hopeful enough to think that we could. But the conflicts of modern man have found this out.

One need not follow Sartre all the way, as we shall see in a moment. But even so it becomes clear that right choices of ultimate ends may often have no sure guide in reason. And not everyone will, like Sartre, accept this with stoic pride as the cross of human freedom. So it is not surprising that the present should show one more trend. The trust in reason as a guide to conduct has historically succeeded the view that reason in morals requires the backing of religion. The emancipation of morality from religion on the contemporary scale is a product of recent history. And now that the limits of reason have become more apparent, there are also voices which cry "we told you so." That reason fails us does not mean that there is no right or wrong for human choices; but it shows that we have forgotten to look for instruction in the right place. The true lesson of the present is that we must go back on the divorce of morals from religion.

And with this, the picture of the philosophical situation is complete. Skepticism of reason is its keynote. And if it leaves us with a problem, it is the problem of reassessing what part reason can play.

I should like to say some more about this. And I shall begin with a word about the last view, that return to religious authority is the key to the situation. This is a wide topic, and I cannot do it justice here. All I want to say is that in my opinion this solution would be no cure-all. Because morality, as we understand it, is logically independent of religious authority. And if the skeptics were right, and there were no better or worse in ultimate choices discernible by 'reason,' then religious authority could not mend things either.

Because how could any authority settle that well-doing is the right, and harm-doing the wrong, choice for a human being? One may say: "But if God says so, surely this should settle it." And, in a way, this is fair enough, for believers at any rate. But we must be clear about the sense in which this is to be taken. For some people will mean by this: "God settles the matter by *saying so*, by *commanding* us to choose in these ways." But this would not be to settle the matter in the required way. It might make people do good or avoid harm in obedience to an order. But it could not produce the conviction that this choice was a morally right one or produce actions which could be called 'moral' because they flowed from this conviction. Because one understands by a morally right choice one which is justified purely on the merits of the case and one which one makes independently of anyone's 'say-so.' And one understands by moral conduct, conduct which is quite unforced from without, coming purely from the inner conviction that the action is right for one in itself. God's command as such, therefore, could not do in place of rational conviction of right or wrong. Morality, as we understand it, still stands or falls on the possibility of arriving at such a conviction independently of any authority.

But if it is said that, "if God says so, this should settle it," one may also mean something else: that what should settle it is that it is *God* who says so, rather than God *saying* so. For one will then be saying: "If God has given the command, then one must take it that he is commanding the right thing; and it is reasonable to take one's instructions from a superior being." And this would be fair enough. But, again, this is not a view which could do in place of an ability on our part to arrive at rational convictions. For, in the first place, it would presuppose that we can form these convictions. We could not even conceive of God as telling what ultimate choices are right for us unless we knew what it was like to distinguish by ourselves between a right or wrong choice. So if skepticism of reason were correct, this view of how God could support us in our ultimate choices would fall to the ground too. And, in the second place, God's support here could not replace independent thinking as much as one may hope. Because the divine rulings tend to be general, as general, in fact, as the general enjoinders to doing well or dealing justly, which one thinks have a plain support in reason too. And, like them, they still leave us without a sure guide when it comes to complex cases: to a choice like that of Sartre's student or to a problem like deciding on the right measure of liberty or social justice in the institution of a given society. Moreover, as the philosophers and divines of the eighteenth century used to stress, without the recourse to 'right reason' and independent moral thinking, there would be no check on the interpretations of the divine will by fallible human minds.

I do not therefore think that, if skepticism were right, the return to religion, even if possible on a wide enough scale, could provide enough of a remedy; nor that our present bewilderment is, in the first place, due to confusions about the right place of religion in morals. The crucial question remains that of skepticism of reason. We must ask: How far is it really justified?

Skepticism often comes from the disappointment of misplaced expectations. There is no comfort in anything, because nothing is good enough to replace the lost hope. And Sartre's views illustrate this. He finds that there is no *sure* way of choosing between one's mother and one's country. So he concludes that there can be *no* way of choosing anything rather than anything else. But this is precisely what does not follow; and the truth, as I see it, is rather that the power of thought to guide ultimate choices is a matter of degree. Some of them are plainly right or wrong—for anyone who deserves the name of a human being. One would have to be a fiend not to have it in one to see that some thought must be given to the good or harm of others. But when it comes to concrete cases, and to matters of conflict, then the big certainties begin to evaporate. How *much* of one's own life is one to give to others? How *much* is one to prefer independence to security? How *much* the good of humankind to that of one's group? These are issues of a different kind, and this must be acknowledged. One has not got enough ground here for saying that only one choice and no other could be right for everyone who is properly human. But nor could one say that every natural basis for a better or worse choice has gone, but rather that the basis for choice has become more personal. One may still make these choices judiciously or not, be guided in them by impartial reflection and honest self-scrutiny, or follow one's blind leanings. For these are qualities of mind on which judiciousness in choice depend at all times. In hard cases they cannot be exercised easily; but this is not enough for saying with Sartre that there is no guide in them at all. If there is not always a choice which is the *one* that is properly human, there is always a properly human way of making one's choices.

We keep confusing ourselves when we call this the way of 'reason', and this confusion accounts for much of our disorientation. The point is not that the right choice may not be called the one 'guided by reason' but that 'reason' may mean so many things. 'Reason' makes one think of calculation, of deduction, of learning from experience. But the reason which can guide ultimate choices is none of these; and one draws attention to this when one says that 'the good' need not be 'the clever'. The 'reason' of the clever finds out about things unknown. But everyone knows what it is to do good or harm; and if people fail to take notice, then this is not for lack of knowledge. And yet one may say, if loosely, that it is for lack of 'using reason'. Because 'using reason' may also mean 'reminding oneself of what one knows already', 'putting it to oneself clearly, vividly, and without reserve'. And the properly human choice is the one which is directed by such reminders. In a thoughtless frame of mind one may not mind hurting others; if roused, one may even enjoy it. But if one reminds oneself, sympathetically and plainly, of what doing harm does, one will find that one's own nature will not let one. One finds that harm-doing could not be one's choice as a reflective and normal human being.

And the same principle applies to the more tricky choices between ultimate alternatives. I should say that even with as trivial a choice as that between lambs fry and Wiener schnitzel, one is not condemned, as Sartre will have it, to choose in darkness. Even here one may choose rashly or considerately, with one's eyes open or not, in order to elicit which alternative would truly deserve priority for one. And to choose considerately would here mean making quite clear to oneself the nature of the alternatives before one; presenting it to oneself that having the one would be forsaking the other; and eliciting one's response to the thought of still opting for the one even in full view of thereby sacrificing the other. A choice so determined will be the one more truly proper for one than any other; one which I can defend to myself and others; one to the thought of which I can hope to return ever afterward without self-reproach. And to choose between one's mother and one's country, between independence and security, between one's own good and that of others, is only harder and beset more by inner conflict, but in principle no different. Here, too, it is a matter of distinguishing between one's immediate leanings and the well-considered order of one's priorities: the one which sincere reflection on the competing alternatives would show one to express one's true evaluation, the one again with which one could afterward hope to live in peace.

But I want to emphasize that these cases also show more clearly what diverse qualities of mind right choice requires. Philosophers' talk about a simple and unique faculty of moral intuition has here done much to befog the truth. There is not one faculty, there are many qualities of mind which must cooperate. One must have experience of what one is choosing between. One cannot choose well between independence and security any more than between lambs fry and Wiener schnitzel if all one knows is the basic meaning of the words. One must know the savor of living the one as one must know the savor of eating the other. Experience of life and the chance of living it as well as the enterprise to seek it are conditions for making right choices. The real worth of things must be explored; it cannot be deduced. And with big issues like freedom or security this is just the difficulty. We cannot vary the balance of a social order just for the sake of deepening our experience, and if we put our money on trying the one, we easily destroy our chance of trying the other, perhaps even our fitness to try it. This is why it has been said that freedom is more easily lost than gained. Moreover, our own experience is not always enough. To be clear about the good or harm of others, one requires imagination as well, the ability to put oneself into the other fellow's shoes, to extend one's sympathies from the familiar to the unfamiliar by noticing a human being behind the curtain of color, age, class, and distance. This ability, as everyone knows, is not easily exercised; and failure to exercise it lies behind many of our disagreements about the ethics of group relations in the international field. (Though, I should hasten to add, not of all.) And then again right choice requires still another quality of mind. For in order to present the issues to ourselves effectively, we must also be able to relive in the imagination what we know already. One may know of three thousand flood victims and feel no compunction to help because, as Arthur Koestler once said, "statistics don't bleed"; and, one might add, not *unless one makes them bleed*. And, finally, merely to put the alternatives before one, as when one is choosing between oneself and another, may still not be enough—because one may also do this either halfheartedly or without reserve, with or without self-deceit. And only if done without reserve will one's proper choice come before one. Now one may follow custom and call this the 'choice of reason'. But, then, let us be quite clear that moral reason is not that of the scientist or mathematician, whose 'reason' has in our time become the paradigm of all reason. One's proper choice is not found under the microscope or by calculation, but it can be found; and not by the exercise of one special faculty but, rather, by the whole man testing *himself* out against an *objective* view of the issues for choice.

I shall only say a little more by way of a summing up. I hope that I have shown why contemporary skepticism goes too far. It is not true that Sartre's student had nothing to guide him. It was up to him to be judicious about his choice or not. True enough, no one else could have *handed* him the answer: your conscience cannot tell me what I ought to do. But it is also needlessly tough to pretend that in matters like these there could be no answer, no helpful or critical exchange. One cannot prove how anyone ought to choose, but one need not therefore take everyone else's views on ultimate ends, or ways of life, in silence or leave each other confined to the ivory towers of our private consciences. The outsider may help from his experience to make the issues stand out more clearly; he may work on the other's imagination; he may prompt him to reflect in the right way; he may deflate his self-deceits by a calm "if you seriously feel that way, then go right ahead." One should not think that where there is no argument there can be no conversation.

This applies to small things and large, and our big contemporary disagreements about ways of life are not therefore beyond treatment. We do in fact fail in treating them. But then, rather than blame the instrument, we might blame our tardiness in using it in matters in which our interests, or our conceits, are involved.

But I said before that skepticism comes from the disappointment of misplaced expectations. And skeptical disorientation will remain a sign of our time until we have learned to accept moral thinking for what it is and with its limits. What everyone hopes for as a guide are rules by which to settle all cases, applicable with ease, and in the same way to everyone alike. Instead, what we have available is a procedure, calling on many and fallible qualities of mind; a procedure which yields some broad and fairly obvious answers, but which for the rest leaves us to puzzle things out for ourselves, with a margin for error and disagreement too wide for comfort. It may be that we still have to grow up to learn to accept this for a fact: there is no moral Santa Claus in pure reason.

And let me conclude with one gentle reminder. It would not be fair to blame philosophers or 'sophists' for forcing this recognition on to us. For what is doing it are once more the circumstances of our time, and philosophers are at best their mouthpiece. Our circumstances are complicating the issues beyond the powers of any book of rules. Not every society has to choose between freedom and social welfare as hard as ours. In the days when economic laissez-faire was a working proposition, one could have freedom along with economic welfare without much of a need for choice, or so one could think. But today, with the new means for procuring economic welfare, we must choose. To choose one must think. And even if thinking came to no more than to having a heart and keeping one's head, it would not come to nothing.

PART THREE

REASON AND SOCIETY

[13]

The Age of Reason

I

It was the high hope of the eighteenth century that the growth of science would transform life. Men would rid themselves of squalor, hunger, and disease by their ingenuity and industry. "At last all the clouds are dispelled," wrote Turgot in 1750. "What a multitude of great men in every field.... What perfection of human reason.... Each day adds to the extent of the sciences; the methods are multiplying with new discoveries; the scaffold is rising along with the edifice." And with the growth of science would come the growth of skills. "The arts are but the utilization of nature, and the exercise of the arts is a series of experiments which progressively unveil her." Thus the new learning was to be part of a new strategy of living. Men had been taught to meet deprivation by forbearance and by outlawing wish; they were now to say yes to their wishes and to change their environment so as to give them satisfaction. Here was a way whose ultimate success was thought to be fully in man's reach and one alone worthy of his capabilities.

The age of reason bequeathed this program to the nineteenth century and our own time, and its vitality is far from spent. It is the official doctrine of both East and West; and the formerly quiescent cultures of Asia and Africa are just beginning to pin their hopes on it. But not all is well. At the rate at which discovery and invention are proceeding, the returns for human betterment are not forthcoming. The way of progress seems to aggravate a drift toward evil rather than to be able to arrest it.

Maybe these are only passing troubles. Any way of life is bound to run into rough weather. Maybe also somehow we are falling down on the job for not having taken sufficient measure of its complexity. But there are other voices, too, and they take the portents of the times for the crack of doom. The labors in which we are engaged do not seem to them those of Hercules but of Sisyphus. The failings of the way of progress are nothing passing or remediable. They simply reveal it as pointless or meaningless. For this way of life is powerless to solve the ultimate problem of human insecurity; and no way of life or choice of project that fails this ultimate concern can have worth once it is seen through. The shortcomings of the way of progress, manifest in our time, therefore simply force on us the lesson that it is another God that failed. What, then, is left, if this is so, is another question. Some say, following Kierkegaard, that only the return to a religious and severely acquiescent mode of life can make life meaningful and secure again. According to others, such as Jean-Paul Sartre, the religious hope, too, is vain; and what is left is a heroic defeatism, a dogged participation in labors, known and felt to be forever futile because they cannot solve the ultimate problem of human limitation.

Before such views are taken as seriously as is the fashion, some less extreme possibilities should be ventilated. One need not deny that what I have called the way of progress deserves to be reexamined. The naive hopes that have often been pinned on it have not been fulfilled. But then how much was it ever justified to entertain such hopes? Ever since the way of progress was first enunciated it has been under fire. It was recognized to have defects that belong to its very nature and that unless the right steps are taken to guard against these defects new problems may be created as fast as old ones are solved. According to the thinkers of this group, the growth of science is beneficial only if we know how to control it. To live with scientific progress is a challenge which, given the progress, it is still up to humanity to meet. That this body of ideas exists should be recalled at the present moment. For if the strategy of progress seems to fail us today, the first question, though it need not be the last, must be whether the lessons of its constructive critics in the past have been properly absorbed.

II

The story begins in the eighteenth century with Rousseau's indictment of the very arts and sciences in which his contemporaries were proclaiming their faith. In the two *Discourses*, *On the Arts and Crafts*, and *On the Origins of Inequality*[1] Rousseau compares the scientific intelligence to a dangerous weapon in the hands of a child. With all the powers that it confers, it is futile in the objects it proposes and dangerous in the effects it produces. Man does not need all that his inventiveness makes it possible for him to get. That he lived to invent things shows only that by his inventiveness he has multiplied his wants. What first pleased as a novelty, Rousseau insists, degenerates into a real need till the want of it becomes more disagreeable than the possession had been pleasant. Self-improvement by multiplying the means of satisfaction becomes, in the end, self-defeating; and moreover, it is dangerous by creating new problems and evils. This point is summarized by saying that it destroys simplicity and natural virtue; but Rousseau's understanding of these is not simply romantic and naive. Rousseau's use of 'virtue' is close to that of the Greeks. The *arete* or virtue of a being is measured by its capacity to maintain itself in good repair: a virtuous habit is one that furthers the life and well-being of a creature, vice a disorder that makes it at variance with itself and incapacitated for living and living well. Rousseau thought that scientific progress threatened virtue in the sense of life-preserving habit. The self-created dependence on convenience and luxury was a case in point; and even more so were the social, or unsocial, habits fostered by the multiplication of wants and means and the dependence on them. It is only through technical progress that man is properly thrown into society, that he is committed to the organization of labor, to commerce and exchange, while his cooperative habits become undermined. Being addicted to the fruits of their skill, men become more self-regarding and competitive, while the possession of these very skills makes them more potentially menacing to one another. Hobbes's man of the state of nature is a true picture only of civilized man, who alone had fully acquired the motivation and the power for getting the better of his fellows. Paradoxically enough, only a society of civilized men tends to be mutually destructive. It is this tendency toward mutual destruction which Rousseau brands as unnatural: it shows man at variance with himself, cut off in his mode of living both from a wholesome self-regard and from the exercise of compassion, a life-preserving power which man possesses in his ability to identify himself sympathetically with the needs of others. And so Rousseau concludes that the scientific understanding is the source of all human misfortune: "A thinking man is a depraved animal."

It is common to think of Rousseau as a provincial, who, having been

1. Jean Jacques Rousseau, *The Social Contract and Discourses*, Everyman Library (New York: E. P. Dutton, 1950).

brought up in the small-town and straitlaced environment of Geneva, reacted to the worldly ferment of Paris like an insecure and high-minded adolescent. But there is more than romantic nausea to Rousseau's indictment; nor were many of his observations at all novel. It is important to recall a little of the history of these observations, for Rousseau's significance is not so much in that he made them as in what he made of them.

Much of Rousseau comes almost word for word from the writings of Bernard Mandeville, a Dutchman living in England, whose famous *Fable of the Bees* appeared early in the eighteenth century.[2] Mandeville's thesis was that one could not raise a people into a populous and flourishing nation without the assistance of evil, both natural and moral. The advancement of knowledge on which material progress depends must enlarge men's desires, refine their appetites, and increase their vices. If you would preserve men in their native simplicity, frugality, and honesty you must keep from them anything that might improve their understanding. "If you would banish fraud and luxury and make the generality of people charitable, good and virtuous, break down the printing presses, melt the founts, burn all the books in the island, except those at the universities, where they remain unmolested" (ibid., p. 258). Or, as he says in the poem in which he first expressed his views:

> To make a great and honest hive
> To enjoy the world's conveniences
> Be famed in war, yet live in ease
> Without great vices, is a vain
> Utopia seated in the brain.
> [Ibid., p. 23]

A choice has to be made between accepting the consequences of scientific progress and a consistent and total rejection of the desire for its benefits.

What lay behind this was Mandeville's insight into the new forces that were beginning to shape Western society. He knew that economic individualism, inventiveness in production and commerce, spending rather than hoarding, even spending on such futile projects as wars, or on repairing the calamities of nature such as the great fire of London, would all contribute to employment and the collective accumulation of wealth. His great slogan "private vices, public benefits" anticipated Adam Smith's "invisible hand." It is certain, he says, that "the fewer desires a man has, and the less he covets, the more easy

2. Bernard Mandeville, *The Fable of the Bees* (Oxford: Clarendon Press, 1934).

he is to himself; and the more charity he has for his neighbor, the more he shines in real virtue. But what benefit can these things be of to promote the wealth, glory, and worldly greatness of nations? It is the sensual courtier who sets no limits to his luxury, the fickle strumpet that invents new fashions every week, the profuse rake that scatters about his money without wit or judgment, it is these that are the prey and proper food of a full grown leviathan; or, in other words, such is the calamitous condition of human affairs that we stand in need of the plagues and monsters I named to have all the variety of labour performed which the skill of man is capable of inventing in order to procure an honest livelihood to the vast multitudes of working poor" (ibid., p. 355). Mandeville's concern was to bring his contemporaries to a consistent and unafraid acceptance of a new way of life, to which by their actions he saw them already committed. If people wanted the benefits of the arts and sciences, they must understand and tolerate the diversification of want and ambition and the will to gratification to which their advancement gives rise. They must not want production and cavil at consumption. Nor must they complain that invention and discovery are taking place at all: for the spirit of inventiveness itself is not the product of idle curiosity; it is set in motion by desire for its fruits and an unwillingness to endure suffering and deprivation as in the nature of things. Rousseau said that we desire knowledge only because we wish to enjoy; and Mandeville goes to town on this point: "Hunger, thirst and nakedness are the first tyrants that force us to stir: afterwards our pride, sloth, sensuality and fickleness are the great patrons that promote all arts and sciences, trades, handicrafts and callings" (ibid., p. 366). We must not therefore complain that invention and discovery are taking place if their restless progress can be promoted only by drives which, in our hearts, and contrary to the protestations of some, we have chosen to gratify. Mandeville did not think that men were capable of any other choice, nor did he regret that they were not. He castigated what would be the only alternative strategy of living: one based on self-denial, acquiescence, and the fear of being led astray by our own wishes for satisfaction; and he would not allow that those who profess such views were honest about them. But in any case he took it that the men of his age had made their choice against self-denial; and his concern was to teach them the implication of this choice and that there was no need to get het up about its consequences.

So when Rousseau said that "as the conveniences of life increase and luxury spreads the virtues disappear; and all this is an effect of the sciences and the arts,"[3] he was saying nothing novel. He was only

3. Rousseau, *Social Contract*, p. 164.

accepting what an insightful and outspoken apologist of the new strategy of progress had said already. What made Rousseau original was that, unlike Mandeville, he refused to be reassured. He was more impressed by the unfavorable than by the favorable features of the new way, and he was concerned to show the problematic of living with it.

Mandeville was eager to emphasize its tremendous possibilities for the collective accumulation of wealth. Rousseau was aghast at the psychological unbalance and the corrosion of life-preserving habits of which Mandeville made light. Mandeville's defense of luxury and reckless spending as being good for trade becomes, for Rousseau, "that paradox so worthy of our times." Mandeville had praised the great fire of London for the employment it created all round; those who could rejoice in it far outnumbered the victims. Rousseau objected, "What are we to think of a relation in which every man finds his profit in the misfortune of his neighbor" (ibid., p. 274). Whatever the merits of the economic argument, there seemed to him some deep threat in the principle that collective well-being should be brought about by a form of cooperation which alienated the individual from the natural virtues, as he understood the term. Moreover, given that these evils existed, Rousseau was perturbed by the manner in which they were generated. There seemed to him something of the relentlessness of Greek tragedy about them. There is what may seem the "noble and beautiful spectacle of man trying to raise himself from nothing by his own exertions; dissipating by the light of reason, all the thick clouds with which he was by nature enveloped" (ibid., p. 146); and yet it seems that by his very striving he is brought to naught by the means he adopts to achieve his ends. He is subject to the tyranny of his own understanding. And according to Rousseau, there is a fundamental reason for this dilemma. The progress of our wants depends on that of our knowledge: "We cannot desire or fear anything, except from the idea we have of it." As the horizon of possible achievement is widened we are therefore drawn into making what is possible real. The scientific intellect is the servant of the passions; but it is a servant who by the incessant changes of the fare he is able to provide for his master will never let his master's eating habits settle down to any steady, well-tried, and wholesome routine. The crucial evil that overwhelms men by their own striving for betterment lies in the unbalancing of all ordered purpose. More than anything, it is this threat in the strategy of progress that makes Rousseau conclude that it cannot be accepted cynically or lightheartedly. If anything, it seemed to justify his outburst in the *First Discourse*: "Almighty God, thou who holdest in thy hand the minds of men deliver us from the fatal arts and sciences, give us back ignorance, innocence and poverty" (ibid., p. 172).

But this outburst was not Rousseau's last word, and he would hardly be of interest to us if it had been. The lesson is not that we must return again to the forests to live among bears (ibid., p. 281). Rousseau may have had a romantic longing for this solution; but all his writings after the first Discourse repudiate it. Man cannot at will, he says, reverse the direction he has once taken. It is not only that he has become unfit to subsist on plants and acorns; but the step back would be truly retrograde. By ceasing to use his understanding, man would mutilate himself as a man. In *Emile* Rousseau asks, "Would nature have done better to have endowed man with instinct and made him a fool?" and he answers, "He would be happy, no doubt, but his happiness would not attain to its highest point." If the rational mode of living tends to destroy man, its suppression would only further destroy him. This is why the evils the intellect has inflicted on mankind cannot be healed by destroying the instrument that caused them. We can neither stand still nor go back; so we must go ahead. And in doing so, "we must attack not the instrument, but the hand that guided it." The evil lay in the corruption of purpose by the discoveries of the understanding. But man has not only theoretical understanding, he also has practical intelligence and will; he can be clever in the discovery of means, and he can be wisely self-limiting in the choice of ends. In this is the principle of Rousseau's solution: man can live with the strategy of progress but only insofar as he can *supplement* it with a strategy of controlling it and its deleterious effects; but to the extent to which he fails in this, he will find himself overwhelmed and destroyed. With this conviction Rousseau influenced deeply such diverse thinkers as Kant, Hegel, and Marx.

Rousseau's detailed blueprint of the solution to his problem is in his work on *The Social Contract*. It has often been said that this work is inconsistent with his earlier writings. In them he had complained of the dependence of man on the social order. Here he recommends the total subordination of all to a sovereign who, like the absolute sovereign of Hobbes, may legislate on any matter whatsoever. But the teaching of *The Social Contract* is perfectly compatible with Rousseau's early diagnosis of the ills of scientific progress; in fact, it must be understood as a bold attempt to solve the problem of these ills without taking a retrograde step. When considered from this point of view the teaching of *The Social Contract* has three characteristic features which must be understood in connection with one another.

The first feature has been mentioned. Rousseau requires of all the ready acceptance of the principle of subjection to a common rule; and in this he expresses his conviction that the corruption of purpose which is endemic to the way of material progress must be checked first by *political means*. The disorder is too big a problem to be solved individually. Self-restraint cannot be expected of *one* if it is not incumbent on *all*. There must be a responsible collective organ that is charged with preventing the individual's striving for betterment from getting out of hand. In this emphasis on a *political solution* Rousseau did not stand alone. Hobbes had made the point before him; Montesquieu and the Encyclopedists agreed with him. Rousseau was especially close to Hobbes in regarding it as crucial, and also as involving a concession which human beings will find deeply against the grain and of the need for which one must keep convincing them by good argument. Neither Hobbes nor Rousseau believed man to be a political animal by nature. Only insight into a necessity and not love can persuade them to exchange the free-for-all of being the judges and executors of their own interests for the ready acceptance, for good or ill, of some instituted arbitrator and guardian.

No less important than this point of agreement between Rousseau and others is another one of disagreement. Most of Rousseau's contemporaries, like many of our own, were satisfied to leave political power in the hands of, as it was hoped, a benevolent and enlightened autocrat. Rousseau alone insisted on the principle of total control of this power by the people themselves, ideally exercised by them directly, without elected intermediaries. All that concerns us here is to see how this insistence on democracy connects with his concern for the problem of a feasible strategy of progressive living. The point about the tyranny of science was that "man's noble effort of raising himself by his own exertions" (ibid., p. 146) was frustrated by the unsettling effect on him of his own discoveries. His problem in going ahead was to emancipate himself from this self-created dependence. And although the way to this freedom lay through the acceptance of the restraint of law, this acceptance would only make him dependent once again on one of his own creations if the making of law were not under his control and a matter of his own responsible decisions. So the *political* solution is complete only when it is founded on a *moral* solution, when our practical intelligence, through the restraint by law which we readily impose on ourselves, succeeds in controlling what our theoretical intelligence tends to mismanage. With this view Rousseau is in line once again with many of the democratic thinkers who came after him.

There is still another and third point which is purely Rousseau's own. For there is something conspicuously unshallow about Rousseau's version of the democratic solution. Rousseau never says that this solution *will* work, only that it *can*; and he is so insistent on showing why it might not work that he has provided his later critics with the basic reasons for saying that it can't. The standing danger for any system of self-rule is that the majority decisions may be neither prudent nor fair; that free majority decisions will only perpetuate the disorder they are intended to cure. The practical wisdom of the common man which is made the ultimate guardian of the scientific intelligence may not be exercised, and Rousseau's apprehension about this point was a direct consequence of his apprehensions about the way of progress from which he started. It is the unregenerate victim of this way of progress who needs guidance; and the economic pressures to which he is subject seem to make him least fit to guide himself. The antidemocratic solutions of Hegel on the one hand and of Marx on the other developed from taking up this point. The singular feature of Rousseau is that he fully faced the problem but refused to be defeatist about it. His stand was that legislative constraint informed by the practical wisdom of those over whom it was exercised was the only solution of any real promise. If we choose, it will be within our reach; if we don't, we shall fail. But in the nature of things, there is no other and safer alternative to turn to. The success of living with progress was thus precariously made a matter of everyone's responsibility; but this did not seem to Rousseau a life situation beyond the powers of human beings to endure.

Rousseau has been discussed at such length for one reason—as a reminder of how living with progress may be viewed as a problematic enterprise, which may always prove self-defeating unless kept under control. Rousseau is a key figure in the history of thought for having been the first, and, if perhaps no more than intuitively, the most profound to take the measure of this problem. But others since Rousseau have taken up the same issue, among them the most important and influential, Hegel and Marx. It is not always seen clearly enough how much they are disciples of Rousseau, how much they built on his diagnosis, and, under the influence of new experience, deepened his critical analysis. Nevertheless, neither of them was prepared to go the whole way with Rousseau's solution; and the resulting deep conflicts are part of our contemporary ills.

All that the mentioning of Hegel tends to call to mind is that he was the advocate of a new idolatry of the state. But it is of greater interest to consider his reasons for this advocacy. They are found in his analysis of what he called civil society, the social order of laissez-faire of Mandeville's *Fable of the Bees* and Adam Smith's *Wealth of Nations*. Hegel was sympathetic toward this order. He approved of discovery and invention, economic individualism, and the division of labor, as likely to promote, through the play of the market, the collective accumulation of wealth. But Hegel was also concerned, like Rousseau, about the deleterious and self-defeating effects of this way of life on the psychological balance of its participants. Civil society, he said, shows "a spectacle of extravagance and want as well as of the physical and ethical degeneration common to them both." There is a tendency toward "measureless excess," toward discontent and "moral frustration." "Man expands his desires, which are not a closed circle like animal instinct, by means of his ideas and reflections"; he is carried by them "to a false infinity." What is more, Hegel was no longer convinced that the mechanism of the market was only a power for good. He was aware of the problem of the trade cycle and explained it in terms of underconsumption. "Despite an excess of wealth," he says, "civil society is not rich enough to check excessive poverty and the creation of a penurious lower-class"; consequently, "the important question of how poverty is to be abolished is one of the most disturbing problems which agitate modern society" (ibid., pp. 150, 277). What is more, it is such a problem not only for humanitarian reasons. The problem is created, not by nature but by human actions. It results unwittingly from the sum of individual decisions taken by the members of a market economy. And as the evil is thus avoidable, as caused by the actions of men, the sufferers have a right to see it remedied. "Against nature," Hegel insists, "men can claim no right"; but what society does to them is not misfortune but "injury." Civil society is therefore also threatened by "upheavals arising from clashing interests," by tensions "arising through the working of a necessity of which the participants themselves know nothing."[4] We see here not only Rousseau's account of the negative effects of the unchecked strategy of progress writ large but also, more outspokenly, the complaint that in suffering these effects men are in bondage to their own theoretical intelligence and the effects of it on themselves because their practical intelligence has not yet learned to control a part of themselves. Hegel's famous promotion of the state to the actuality of the ethical idea must be understood in light of this problem. It seemed to Hegel not only that there is wide scope for remedial collective control (Hegel was the first to see that modern society will require not the weak law-and-order state but the strong interventionist state); he also took it that the principle of collective supervision was man's final step in completing the rational mode of life by bringing the unintended effects of the striving for betterment under the deliberate control of the

---

4. Georg Wilhelm Friedrich Hegel, *The Philosophy of Right*, trans. T. M. Knox (Oxford: Oxford University Press, 1945), p. 267.

practical intelligence. The acceptance of the political solution represents man's ultimate conquest of himself.

The Hegelian program is, however, by Rousseau's standards, dangerously incomplete. The Hegelian, like the Platonic state, provides for the exercise of practical intelligence *on behalf of all*; and it confuses this with the exercise of practical intelligence *by all*. The interventionist state always threatens to provide the one at the cost of discouraging, if not inhibiting, the other; and this effect is aggravated if, as in Hegel, the interventionist state is authoritarian as well. Hegel denies that the unregenerate member of civil society is capable of managing the problem of a reasonably prudent and fair-minded democratic control. By Rousseau's requirements this solution is once more defeat: the rational mode of living is no more complete with the tyranny of the state than it is with the tyranny of scientific progress.

And now a few words about Marx. His indebtedness to Hegel is familiar, and as far as our problem is concerned the affinity is so close that I can be brief. In Marx's thinking the problem that Rousseau had raised erupts in its most extreme form. Marx was an unqualified believer in human self-betterment by technological advance and a total unbeliever in the combination of technological advance with economic individualism. His economic critique of capitalism is based on complete rejection of the classical belief in the efficiency of a market economy. But it should not be overlooked that he also followed Rousseau and Hegel in their criticism of the laissez-faire strategy of progress in human terms. Marx's early writings contain a scathing criticism of the claim that the freedom people enjoy in a society based on the money motive and the division of labor can help them to develop into well-rounded human beings. For what rules here is the "egotistic individual," the "individual that is reduced to his own private interest" and "divorced from the interests of the community."[5] Money and material possessions acquire a value far in excess of all other values of art, culture, and education. Money, Marx says, "lowers all other human values; it deprives the human world and nature of their proper value." What takes place is "an impoverishment of personality"; it is as if the involvement in economic competition forced on all a loss of the capacity to be wholeheartedly concerned about anything without the intrusion of economic considerations. The man of civil society, who *seems* to himself to have all the chance of self-development, is in fact a man who, through the organization of society, is corrupted, who is dominated by depersonalizing circumstances, and so is es-

5. Robert C. Tucker, ed., *The Marx-Engels Reader* (New York: Norton, 1972), pp. 7–163.

tranged or 'alienated' from himself. Marx also emphasizes that in the matter of their human no less than of their economic discontents men are under compelling pressures of their own making but not under their own control; and the Marxist solution of the problem by total economic planning has the same ethical twist as Hegel's solution through the interventionist state. The real problem is seen once more as that of man emancipating himself from a self-created dependence. It was with a view to this dependence that Engels spoke of the transition to the planned society as "the ascent of man from the realm of necessity to the realm of freedom" (ibid., pp. 32ff).

Here is once more the political solution. The forces of scientific progress will be mastered only by the *collective* exercise of practical intelligence. But at the same time, as with Hegel, the solution stops short at this point. The story is not completed with the Rousseauean demand that the exercise of practical intelligence *on behalf* of all must be founded in turn on the responsible exercise of practical intelligence *by* all: that only the moral, and not yet the political solution alone, represents man's final conquest of himself. The reasons for this omission are complex and connect with the Marxist doctrine of social determinism. For this doctrine implies that before the communist environment is fully established, man is unregenerate and not fit for self-rule, and that after it has been established, man will be whole and in no need of any rule. The *democratic* state is not possible before the day when the *state* becomes *unnecessary*. Marx, like Hegel, would have no reliance on the powers of voluntary self-limitation in the individual. The disorder of purpose in the individual can be cured only from *outside* himself, either by the force of the state or that of the socio-economic environment. In opting for the force of environment as the ultimate hope, Marx thought that he had turned Hegel upside down. It is not what men are to make of themselves, whether by individual or collective effort, that determines their condition; it is their condition that determines what they shall be. Thus Marx thought that he had stood Hegel from his head on his feet. And so, maybe, he had. But whether on his head or on his feet, Hegel is still Hegel.

III

Enough has been said for the present purpose about the constructive critics of the strategy of progress. There is plainly reason for the contemporary feeling that this strategy is working under stress. With all our know-how, much of our achievement is disappointing; and there seems something inexorable about the way in which our innovations breed new troubles, including the threat of collective suicide. One can understand that there are some who say that our time cannot but cause one to live with a paralyzing sense of futility, fear, and nausea, though it is well to add that, whether right or wrong, not everyone feels himself afflicted in that way.

It was said earlier that there is a modern current of thought to give these signs of the time a more drastic interpretation. They are supposed to reveal to us a stark truth about our entire enterprise, one which its earlier successes have made us miss but which now at last is becoming apparent. The truth is that our disenchantment has no remediable cause but is the proper frame of mind for man, who no longer deludes himself about his existential situation. The delusion was that of the age of reason, that man could hope by intelligent striving to satisfy his urges. But what man craves for essentially, as a conscious mind, is comprehension of the world and his place in it and the continued possession of his own identity; and this craving cannot be satisfied. We shall never know what lies beyond phenomenal reality and our scientific reconstructions, nor can we avoid death. So defeat in what concerns us most is always certain; and before this certainty we are left with the anguished realization that all striving for enlightenment and betterment is reduced to absurdity. Here is the core of the existentialist message. "The world can no longer offer anything to the man filled with anguish" (Heidegger). "Man is a useless passion" (Sartre). "The ultimate is always shipwreck" (Jaspers). "Man's exile is without remedy, as he is deprived of the promised land" (Camus). The rational enterprise is without hope; and this discovery explains and forever justifies despair. If there is any remedy, it would have to be in a complete turnabout, in the total abandonment of what Kierkegaard called the aesthetic mode of life, with its attachment to "relative and transitory values, such as health, beauty, riches, honour, talent and sensual pleasures," and of the ethical mode of life as well, with its reliance on rational self-management; and, instead, in the offering of oneself, with a hope against hope, to a divine mercy. Or, as Sartre insists, there is not this remedy either. Modern man has not even got the comforts of unreason; and in that case the lesson is that we must carry on as we do, for the transitory value of our own conscious existence and power of agency is still with us, yet with a sense of the pointlessness of it all because every choice is possible, and no choice is more valid than any other.

One should not make light of these views. The trust in the strategy of progress has had the effect of diverting attention from ultimate limitations; the addiction to its benefits may make it harder to meet them when more insecure times bring them drastically to mind; and in any scheme of life there must be provision for interpreting and coping with the problems of failure and of death. There seems to me, however, something very lopsided in these views if they are put forward as a diagnosis of the frustrations of our time. If the strategy of progress feels disappointing and even threatening, and more so today than previously, there may be special reasons, the special complexities of our life situation and failure on our part to meet them. It need not all be because of the sudden discovery that the rational mode of living cannot take from us the fear of sudden death and of an end to everything as far as we ourselves are concerned. For this reason, the constructive critics of the way of progress were discussed. For in their views surely may also lie a lesson relevant to the diagnosis of our ills. What these views tell is that there is nothing surprising in situations in which our own striving for betterment seems to overwhelm us with disappointments and unwanted consequences. For they describe this way as a problematic enterprise which only a constant and complex remedial effort can hope to keep on an even keel; and they show that acceptance of responsibility for this effort, and of the hazards in which it involves us, are humanity's price for a fully humane existence. Rather than bemoan the ultimate meaninglessness of it all, it is therefore no less pertinent to ask at what points our strategy of controlling the strategy of progress has run into deep water. And there is much here, too, to help us understand our present situation.

There are two points that stand out, though of course, there are any number. A great deal of the feeling that with all our know-how, if not because of it, we are going downhill in a runaway bus is attributable to the threat of war. But then it is clear that the reason for this trouble is not the strategy of progress as such but our present inability to bring international relations under the protective umbrella of law and order and collective arbitration. Once more, one feels like saying with Rousseau that what we should attack is not the instrument but the problem of the hand that guides it. It is not suggested that it is a cheap failing on our part to be unready to submit to or to arrange for international government. The nation-state is too entrenched to allow for the political solution by which the strategy of progress must be supplemented. So we have to make do with other methods; and that this situation gets us near the brink of disaster gives us every cause for anxiety. But this anxiety is that of those in a storm at sea. It does not prove that ships are no good, though it may keep one on the alert for ways they may be improved.

The other stultifying source of trouble is nearer home. A monotonous daily round, an unlovable physical environment, an anonymous, separated existence seem to be the price technology exacts for multiplying consumer satisfactions of a fading charm. There is a growing problem for many of where, in this self-created desert, to place their attachments. Moreover, the old disagreements on the right strategy of controlling the strategy of progress are still with us. How much is to be given over to collective control, how much is to be left to itself, or to the good sense of the individual? And again, how much can we afford to hamper, or not to hamper, our political guardians by keeping them under democratic control? There was a time when these issues seemed fresh and stark, when it could seem that the balance of argument was clearly in favor of one or the other of these alternatives. But this situation has changed. We may still have decided views; but the margin has narrowed. We have become too clearly aware that there is no perfect solution, that circumstances alter cases, and that with every option we commit ourselves to tolerating some evil. So we seem confronted with the choice between withdrawing from the game and keeping ourselves pure, or continuing to attach ourselves while tolerating imperfections. And a low tolerance for imperfection and lack of certitude seem characteristic marks of those members of the intelligentsia who preach the gospel of nausea. Our big choices today have no *plain* answer in terms of a better or worse; but this does not mean that every answer is as objectively *invalid as any other*. Life may also become pointless when one is sickened by an overdose of perfectionism. But this nausea is not irremediable and, however one may rationalize it to oneself, has nothing to do with the ultimate limitations of life.

I have argued that a sense of the vanity of our striving for betterment may have many causes. I don't wish to say that *among* them is not also a sharpened sense of the fringe of the incomprehensible and the unmanageable which always limits it. And it barely needs saying that this leaves an emptiness beyond, which to stare at is precisely as frightening as it is unrewarding. But what is puzzling is the sudden popularity of the view that it is profound to cultivate this dread and that, because there is no relief from it, all temporal attachments must be equally joyless and vain, except to those who delude themselves. Logic does not support that one can possess nothing without possessing everything. But I once heard it said that, if the second law of thermodynamics were true, then life would be meaningless. And it took me some time to decide what could be meant by this statement. But then, evidently, it was meant that no project can have any point unless its achievement is sure to last. What is unbearable, it is thought, is to have built what one knows will fall down in the end. One can see that this is consistent, given that someone clings so much to the very real wish for perpetuity that nothing short of what will gratify this wish can count for anything. But when a child says, "My doll is broken, so nothing is any good any more," we understand and know how its mood is defeating itself. Everything else seems vain because the child cannot let go of the one object for which striving *is* vain. In the same way, in suffering the loss of someone we love, life seems to become meaningless, for there is no other object like the loved one. A wishful expectation that has been defeated defies logic by cutting one off from all other object-love. And the wishful expectation which the belief in progress had aroused, but as is now apparent, in vain, is that of sheltered security: of a permanent defense that our ingenuity can build against all the threats that derive from the shortcomings of our bodies and minds, our human and natural environment. But some wishes must die if there is to be life, which is sane counsel, and cheap only in the saying. And the answer to the existentialist sickness was given long ago by Alexander Pope, who knew his Mandeville as well as Rousseau did:

> Shall man alone whom rational we call
> Be pleased with nothing if not blest with all.

[14]

Rousseau on the General Will

Few speculative minds have had a more varied influence on political thought than Rousseau. Rousseau championed the individual against the state, the poor against the rich, popular government against hereditary monarchy. He knew also the failings of popular government; he stood for an austere democracy and for the supremacy of the community over the individual. He inspired the moderates and the extremists of the French Revolution and gave ammunition to the liberals, Hegelians, and socialists of the nineteenth century. Liberals have called him an authoritarian, conservatives an anarchist. Many feel that the breadth of his influence has been achieved only by the inconstancy of his views.

And perhaps this charge is not unfounded. Rousseau's ideas evolved. He started as a critic of social abuses in the *Discourse on Inequality*, and turned into the apostle of a new order in the *Social Contract*. This new order was to be political, its principle "supreme power under the direction of the general will." As I shall show, this formula is charged with tension between conflicting ideas, but not entirely because of inconsistency. Rousseau's mind was unusually receptive and synoptic; he saw the human condition not in black and white but through a prism of broken shades. He saw man advancing in technological know-how and social and economic differentiation. The trend, he thought, was both menacing and irreversible; the problem was not to arrest it but to find a new order for us to live with it. In this order there had to be room for many things: for freedom and for discipline, for the good of the individual and of the group, for security of possessions, and for equity. Government under the supreme direction of the general will was the prescription for bringing all these requirements under

[279]

one roof; and at bottom it turned on two assumptions. One was that government was indispensable, the other that, though indispensable, it was only conditionally tolerable. The institution may be either food or poison, and only its control by the general will can make it palatable. The qualification is Rousseau's special contribution. But that he so strongly affirms the need for government must be considered, too. The one should be understood in the light of the other.

His praise of state power in the *Social Contract* is a surprise after his account of it in the *Discourse on Inequality*. There the state was just another product of man's fall from the original grace of the state of nature. Government is a tool for enforcing peace; it evolved when invention and discovery, commerce and industry had made us competitors for possessions and power. But the peace was one to protect wealth and influence, and not all alike. The law enforces an illusory equality, being so framed as "to keep the poor in misery, and to support the rich in their usurpations." The common man everywhere is no party to an institution that requires him to keep the peace but denies him protection. No wonder, then, that the states of Europe were shaky structures. Their authority was limited to their powers of coercion, and they deserved no better.

And yet in the *Social Contract* Rousseau commends the state as being in the common interest, with the poor and the rich equally dependent on it. What is more, this state must be strong as Hobbes had envisaged it earlier, without the diffusion of power of medieval government. The modern state must be a determinate superior, with its own will (the power of decision and command), with executive organs (administrators, judges, and police), and with a preponderance of armed force to give effect to its rulings. It must be a sovereign lawmaker, the final arbiter and enforcer of everyone's duties and rights. The principle of a civil order is that "every right is determined by law"; and this principle requires the "total alienation of each and of all his rights" to the sovereign jurisdiction of the state. The acceptance of this principle seemed to Rousseau, as it had to Hobbes, a condition of survival but no longer for the same reasons. Hobbes saw sovereign state power as the answer to the critical condition of man in a *primitive* state of nature. Rousseau, with more historical insight, sees it as the answer to his critical condition in an *advanced* civilization, intellectually sophisticated, technologically resourceful, competitive, and materialistic. The new situation creates for the rich and the common people a common interest in combining as a *people* for common defense and for the provision of services which, in a complex civilization, only concerted action can provide. There is need for law to curb the social and moral ill effects of a rampant economic individualism and, above all, to provide machinery for settling the conflict of private wills in peace. On the crucial importance of this last point Rousseau is at one with Hobbes. Self-protection by force as a method of conducting intragroup relations is out of date. Instead there must be reasonable protection for all through processes of law, which is what a sovereign legislature is needed to provide. The state, to do justice to all, must have full authority to protect or change the social status quo.

But whereas sovereign state power had for Hobbes been a cure-all, this is not so for Rousseau. The state of the past had been tyrannical and partial; if it is now to serve all, the question remains how to make it safe. Locke had asked this question before by inquiring into the conditions of civil obedience, and Rousseau here follows Locke. His opening question in the *Social Contract* is about the conditions in which state power would be legitimate; who may rightfully exercise it and on what terms. Like Locke, he rejects Hobbes's answer that any sovereign with strength enough to maintain law and order could reasonably ask to be obeyed. But beyond this their conclusions are far apart. Locke's legitimate authority was a public trustee, with an ill-defined popular backing, pledged to support a code of individual rights founded on an immutable law of reason. Rousseau's legitimate sovereign is the general will, the body of the assembled people pledged to use a discretionary power of adjudicating rights and duties expediently and justly.[1] Locke's answer is the commonsense compromise of a man of affairs and a philosopher still moving within a traditional framework of institutions and thought. Rousseau's answer is that of a literary man and solitary observer who uproots every traditional framework in the search for first principles. The mark of both their answers is on nearly every political system of our time.

There are three themes connected with Rousseau's concept of the general will: the first, that the general will is the will act of the assembled people; the second that it is only that will act of the people which is general in its essence; and the third that it is a disposition residing in every people to make laws whose essence is general, and to exercise this disposition in responsible acts of decision. These themes are not well distinguished by Rousseau, which is a major bar to understanding him. But they are plainly there; and I shall take them up one by one.

The first theme is the most conspicuous. By the sovereignty of the general will Rousseau always means sovereignty of the people, though he never means this alone. The general will here is the will act or fiat

---

1. Jean Jacques Rousseau, *The Social Contract and Discourses*, Everyman Library (New York: E. P. Dutton, 1950), p. 19.

which declares what the law is to be and which comes from the joint vote of all or the majority. The general will in this sense is not some underlying group will or striving for some common objective. It is simply a verdict pronounced by a show of hands. In this sense any verdict of the people is their general will, and there is not yet a general will on any matter unless they have voted.

Here, then, is Rousseau's first condition of legitimacy: only the people's law is law. This condition rules out as illegitimate any law proclaimed by a monarch, aristocracy, or leader and even by delegates selected by popular vote. By this principle every government in Europe was exercising jurisdiction without title; and Rousseau insists on this principle, being aware of its implications and its practical drawbacks. He concluded that political units must be small, and large states must be federations of small units. But also he confines direct democracy to the legislative function. Only the "conditions of society" ought to be regulated by the body of the people. The administrative function may be left to the old monarchies, or, preferably, to an elective aristocracy, a select body responsible in turn to the assembled people.

There are historical reasons why Rousseau prefers the direct exercise of the general will to its delegation. The model of the representative system that Locke had championed was the rotten borough system of the British Parliament; the remnants of medieval representation elsewhere in Europe were even less palatable. Whether he would have agreed to representation on the basis of universal suffrage and free competition of opinion, one may doubt, though he might have come around to it as a second best, as he accepted other compromises with reality in his later writings. In any case, whatever its implementation, the main point was the principle that any law not expressly sanctioned by the people themselves is oppression without right. And more challenging even than this principle was Rousseau's defense of it.

Here we must consider how the very need for the state, and the sovereign state at that, presented itself to Rousseau as a problem. For there seemed to him a menace not only in the possibility of abuses but in the very principle of state power. The state as lawmaker is a master that settles our way of life for us; and this conflicts with the need of every man for autonomy and freedom. The problem is therefore "to find a form of association which, while protecting us all, will also leave us as free as before" (ibid., p. 14); and direct democracy was for Rousseau the means of squaring the political circle. One may wonder, however, why he thought so. Rousseau's popular sovereign had discretionary powers over everyone to assign duties and restrict rights (ibid.), to regiment the economy, or to put a ban on luxury and loose living. It was not necessarily confined, like Locke's trustee, only to protecting the individual from arbitrary interference with his person and property.

But then it did not seem to Rousseau that the main threat to liberty lay in the discipline of the law. Discipline is part of living, and Rousseau was more tolerant of it than Locke. In his scale of values, social justice and moral health were more deserving of protection than was elbow room for the economic man. He did not want to see needless interference either; but the crux of the problem of liberty lay elsewhere: not so much in the need for the discipline of the law, but in having any law prescribed for us by the will of another. This had been the way of the traditional state. To the individual it had stood in loco parentis. The individual was its ward as if he had no will and agency and vital stake in the matter of the law made for him. Rousseau's historical genius was in exposing this dependence as humanly intolerable. Control over the lawmaking power was to be our quid pro quo for surrendering to it: the more extensive our need for the regimen of the law in the modern world the more jealously must we guard our autonomy in relation to the making of it. And his reason here is not the more common and dubious one, namely, that the people can always be counted on to be the best guardian of their own interests. Rousseau neither thought that they could not fail nor that a benevolent and efficient leader might not sometimes do better. What was at stake was a principle and not shifting calculations of expediency. The ability and the will to be self-preserving by his own judgment and choice is part of man's natural constitution. The total surrender to the determination of another's will, even if to that of the most benevolent and enlightened prince, involves the abandonment of our own will and power of control; and only an insane lack of due care for oneself could permit such radical self-curtailment. To give up all self-dependence is "to renounce our quality of man"; and "there is no adequate compensation for a sacrifice so complete" (ibid., pp. 8, 9).

Moreover, the role of being our own legislator is not only our ultimate shield against helpless dependence. It also has its own intrinsic rewards. In assuming this role, man is challenged to become morally mature. In legislating with and for all, he is made "to consult his reason before he listens to his inclinations"; "his ideas are extended," his mind is enlarged and refined: he is transformed "from a circumscribed animal to an intelligent being and a man" (ibid., p. 18). The reward of exercising legislative autonomy is a broadened rational self-realization. This dizzy promise has become the prop of classic liberalism, and this may not be all to the good. For of Rousseau's two arguments, the one from the moral challenge of being self-legislative is, though the more lofty, also the less fade-proofed. The wear of exercising the whole man may well outweigh its gratifications; content is found not only on heights of moral achievement; and a comfortable dependence has its temptations. But I think Rousseau saw legislative autonomy in the first place as our last-ditch defense against being at the mercy of others and only in the second place as a source of rational self-improvement. The strength of his case and its novelty rested on the fusion of the two lines of defense into one. Between them they yielded the conclusion that to let the determination of the law slip away from our direct control is unpardonable folly.

Let me now turn to the second theme. It is often felt that Rousseau goes to extremes in two directions at once. No law is legitimate unless the assembly has sanctioned it; and whatever law the assembly sanctions *is* legitimate. His words often suggest this conclusion. We all alienate our will to the verdict of the community. This verdict settles all our rights and duties; the decision of the majority always binds the rest (ibid., p. 106). It is here that Rousseau seems to compare unfavorably with Locke. The surrender to Locke's representative assembly was not unqualified. The assembly had a duty and the citizen a claim to the protection of inflexible basic rights. By comparison, the Rousseauan assembly seems without any code of duty and the citizen without any legitimate grounds for dissent. Whatever the assembly decides is right and ought to be obeyed. At this point Rousseau seems to be at one with Hobbes by simply exchanging the possible tyranny of the majority for that of an absolute king. But Rousseau would not be himself if he meant anything so unqualified. Whatever the general will decides is right and ought to be obeyed, and there is no general will without a majority decision. But then not every majority decision exhibits a will that is general. A decision of the general will must be general both in its *source* and in its *essence* (ibid., p. 29). It must come from the people, and it must be in the common interest. Unless it does both, the law will still not be 'authentic' (ibid., p. 30). The decisions of all will be decrees only to which the name of law is falsely given. They are not then proper acts of sovereignty, and they have force without right. The assembly therefore has a duty, and our allegiance is only to an assembly that lives up to it. Rousseau is clear about this point: "A convention which stipulates absolute authority on one side and unlimited obedience on the other must be vain" (ibid., p. 9). An important difference from Locke remains. The Rousseauan assembly is not bound to operate within a specified code of natural rights. For Rousseau denies that such a code can be spelled out to cover all contingencies. It is bound only by the principle of the common interest. And so, likewise, the citizen's commitment goes much further. His ordinary commitment to accept the majority as the final arbiter on any matter of right is bounded only by the duty of the assembly to use its powers in a principled manner. Rousseau does say that the general will is always what it ought to be. But this is true by definition. The general will is only that joint will act of the assembled people which is directed toward its proper object.

Before being critical of this view we must try to be just to it. That an authentic law must be general in its essence is a broad formula. It means that it must serve the ends of the association, which is "the preservation and welfare of the *whole* and of *all its parts*" (ibid., pp. 290, 303–4). But the formula is far less vague than it is broad, and Rousseau's critics have treated it less than fairly. The formula is taken to imply that the law may prescribe anything expedient for the survival of the group, that the individual is made a pawn of the collective interest; and this is far from Rousseau's intention. He does stress a common group interest more than other political thinkers did. The individual in the modern world depends on organized partnership with others for common defense and cooperative action. In some measure he owes his life and being to the welfare of the whole and has a joint interest with others in seeing it preserved. Hence the law may ask reasonably that all contribute to the common cause; and on this account alone there can be no inflexible rights to life, liberty, and possessions because they would be incompatible with taxation for common purposes and with the exigencies of war. But at the same time Rousseau is always emphatic that whatever serves the preservation of the whole must be done with due regard to the equal protection of everyone. The welfare of each single citizen is no less the common cause than that of the entire state; and it is part of the understandings of the social compact that each may require from the sovereign equal protection with every other. Rousseau is also as sure as Locke that the life, liberty, and possessions of each are legitimate interests. He may even speak of the right of property as the most sacred of all the rights of citizenship. And yet he will not, like Locke, make the protection of property the chief end of government because of his view that "all authentic acts of sovereignty oblige and favour all citizens alike." The emphasis is on *equal* preservation, which implies equitable protection of the poor against the rich. And hence the right to property cannot be unqualified. This point is a landmark in political thought and central to Rousseau: "It is not enough to have citizens and protect them; it is also necessary to consider their subsistence" (ibid., p. 311).

Provision for public wants is an obvious inference from the general will. The most important function of government is to prevent extreme inequality. A graded income tax is more equitable than a flat rate: "He who possesses only the common necessities of life should pay nothing at all, while the tax on him who is in possession of superfluity may justly be extended to everything he has over and above mere necessities." It may be objected that his rank makes him more necessitous; "but this is false: for a grandee has two legs just like a cowherd, and like him again but one belly" (ibid., pp. 321, 22). Rousseau and Locke were agreed that the law should be directed toward the common good. But Locke's concept of immutable natural rights seemed to Rousseau incompatible with this goal. The assumption behind Locke's concept was that some claims of individuals were plainly defensible by good reasons at all times. And this assumption seemed to Rousseau plainly falsified by the unequal and variable conditions of men in society. The worth of everyone's claim to the protection of his property, liberty, or life is a matter for *judicious assessment* relative to circumstances, and not for any inflexible ruling.

Rousseau's difficulty was to replace Locke's code of rights with a formula sufficiently flexible in content and yet precise enough in form to ensure the protection of each. Sometimes he thought that he found this formula in the formal generality of the law. All would be equally protected if the law prescribed the same rights and duties for everyone. But by this principle the rich and the poor would be equally protected by a law against stealing apples and sleeping under bridges (as Anatole France remarked), and a graded income tax would be impossible. And so Rousseau amends this principle: the law may also divide the citizens into several classes according to their circumstances and assign different duties to each, provided it does not legislate for anyone individually (ibid., p. 22). Equality may thus be tempered by equity. And if this raises the question of a rule of equity, Rousseau has an answer. In a famous passage he says: "There is often a great deal of difference between the will of all and the general will; the latter considers only the common interest, while the former takes private interests into account, and is no more than a sum of particular wills: but take away from these same wills the pluses and minuses that cancel one another, and the general will remains as the sum of the differences" (ibid., p. 26). This strange piece of political arithmetic harbors a profound commonsense point. Our private wills and interests clash. The rich want a flat rate of income tax, the poor a steeply graded one. Each, if in the majority, could embody his special interest in the law. Such a law, Rousseau wants to say, would not embody the common interest. For the law to do this, it must split the difference between the majority and minority interests and ask everyone to scale down his own claims to the point at which the care for his own needs and interests becomes commensurate with the care for the needs and interests of all others. The story about the pluses and minuses enunciates a new principle of political decision making: it must be centered primarily on the mutual accommodation of conflicting interests by applying a rule of give and take. There is no doubt that Rousseau oversimplified the applicability of this principle in practice. Rather than whittle down our first preferences, we may have to agree on what for each is a second best. A compromise choice of a party leader must be a second preference and not the halves of the two original candidates combined in one. Nor may it be enough to go splits between clashing wills according to their strength. The weight of the needs behind them must be considered too. Nor is it so certain that there always is enough room for maneuver for a compromise solution. Marx contemplated situations in which there could be irreconcilable class conflicts. At best, the judgment of what is equitable will often be hazardous. And yet, much as Rousseau's formula is inferior to Locke's code of rights in precision, it surpasses it in depth by making the claims of equity coequal with those of personal liberty and property: "The right which each individual has to his own estate is always subordinate to the right which the community has over all: without this, there would be neither stability in the social tie, nor real force in the exercise of Sovereignty" (ibid., p. 22).

We have seen, then, that the rule of the general will does not simply mean that of the majority. The assembly must legislate responsibly; and civil obedience is the result of a responsible assembly. This makes more sense than if the sovereign were simply the popular will; but this view also has its problems. Rousseau's sovereign people are without a fixed code of rules to guide them in doing their duty. They have only a canon of judgment, principles of expediency and equity, by which to judge every time afresh of the balance of rights and duties in the case. The task is such that it can be done better or worse, and at times manifestly so, but never with any certainty of success. And the same hazard applies to the judgment of any minority that thinks itself wronged. Here again Locke's natural rights had chartered the case for civil disobedience, whereas the Rousseauan objector to the law has to rely on the same probable judgment as the legislative assembly. This is why Rousseau never spells out the case for civil obedience; and if his criticism of Locke is correct, for good reason. There are basic understandings between the sovereign and the citizen in Rousseau's scheme, not unlike perhaps the basic understandings between the British citizen and his Parliament. But they can be spelled out only in general and uncertain terms; nor can they be applied, except in always debatable ad hoc judgments.

I shall now turn to the third and last point. Rousseau says that legitimate law can come neither from the irresponsible will acts of the people nor from beneficent will acts of an authority other than the people. The rule of law is indispensable; but only through the responsible will acts of the people is it possible. And this confronts Rousseau with his final problem. He must show that the people can be trusted with the job, for if they could not there would be a dilemma. The rule of law, which we cannot do without, could also not be had, at least on humanly acceptable terms. Rousseau thinks that he can escape the dilemma with an affirmative answer; but the answer is also equivocal. He continues to do what he has done all along: to rub our nose in the ambiguities of the human situation.

What would be needed if the decisions of the people were to be in the common interest? Obviously, intelligence and information. The people would have to be good judges of facts and situations. But before this happened, there must also be a disposition or readiness to seek what is in the common interest in preference to private interest. Such a disposition Rousseau presupposes in all; and it is another aspect of what he means by the *general will*. The general will is here not the common will act which settles what the law is to be. It is rather a constant disposition, attributable to each and all, to make their legislative decisions conform to the common interest. Of the general will in this sense he says that it always tends to the common advantage and that it is indestructible but may be deceived and silenced. About the prospects of it being operative he is of two minds.

Sometimes Rousseau speaks with great confidence. There is the idyll of groups of peasants directing affairs of state under an oak and always acting wisely; the whole people determining for the whole people, being naturally the best judges of their own interests (ibid., p. 102). The sovereign cannot impose any burdens useless to the community; it cannot even be inclined to do so. The majority is always right, and if I find myself in the minority, this only proves that I had been mistaken. But this famous remark is also misleading, for Rousseau adds: "This is indeed supposing that all the characteristics of the general will still reside in the most votes" (ibid., p. 106). The rider shows that the people's voice need not always be the voice of God.

One reason why they may fail is for lack of foresight and information. The public wills the good, but it does not see it. No multitude is enlightened enough to find by itself the right means to its ends. This defect is in the nature of the case, and the assembly cannot solve it except by accepting the principle of legislative leadership. Hence the need for the figure of the legislator. His job is that of an expert, chairman, prime minister, or subcommittee to submit to the assembly reasoned proposals (ibid., pp. 37, 40).

But the majority may also fail for another reason: because it is lacking in goodwill, in a proper readiness to seek what is necessary for the best of all. Its vote may be guided by private and short-term interests. The deliberations of the people often tend to have this fault. When they have it persistently the general will is no longer the will of all; it is silenced; popular sovereignty is discredited, and the end of liberty in sight (ibid., p. 102). But unlike the intellectual shortcomings, this defect of the will is the people's own responsibility. A preference for the common good is necessarily latent in them. It is not uppermost only through their own fault. As a dispositional preference the general will is indestructible; as an operative preference it is problematical.

How does Rousseau support this view? A disposition to seek social good seems to him in the nature of man; and here is his one act of faith. But the nature of this faith must be well understood. The disposition is not in the first place compassion, an inborn love of justice for others. Such disinterestedness, which can be met in man, results from living in society; it is not in this sense that he is "good by nature." The fundamental dispositions are self-protective, "self-love, fear, the dread of death, the desire for comfort." But these aims involve us in the common good rather than separate us from it. The good of the whole, the good of others, and our own good become interdependent as we evolve from the primitive, and perhaps happier, state of nature. And so the concern for the equality of right and the idea of justice "derives from the nature of man by deriving from the preference which each gives to himself" (ibid., p. 29). Although this seems to Rousseau a plain fact, his real act of faith in human nature concerns something else: namely, that man is not so lost and self-destructive a creature that he has not got it in him to will what is necessary to keep himself intact, or at least that he could not will it 'in reason', when considering things widely, looking past the immediate concerns of self, giving essentials due weight before incidentals. The general will, as the spring of legislative action, is thus a latent preference for the common interest depending on our own personal involvement in the common interest; and it is a preference which is rational by being found to be ours if we use our understanding.

It was with this latent preference, and the freedom to exercise it, that Rousseau credited the common man, in the face of the skepticism of his age.

For this "union of interest and justice" on which Rousseau rests his argument he sometimes offers a simple reason. Let the sovereign make only general laws which apply to all alike, then the law which anyone votes for will also affect himself; and such law would have to be reasonable because no one would wish to burden others with restrictions he could not reasonably want for himself. But this, of course, is too simple, and Rousseau knows it. The law may be general in form without affecting everyone alike, especially if it divides cases into classes. Bachelors have little use for a law providing for widows' pensions and the well-to-do for a steeply graded income tax. Here justice would require readiness for give and take and the mutual accommodation of interests which was mentioned before. And here Rousseau has another argument which he bases on the first principles of the social compact. The general condition for accepting the rule of law is that it should give equal protection to all; and we all have an interest in the rule of law being generally accepted. On the other hand, the law obliges only those whom it protects; and so in denying justice to one another we would be destroying the foundations of civil obedience. The rule of law is the rule of peace, and there cannot be peace without justice. But Rousseau is well aware of the brittle force of this reasoning in everyday life. Much injustice can be done before the perpetrator is punished by general lawlessness, born from justified resentment. And at best it would need great wisdom and constant self-reminders on everyone's part to keep everyone alive to the merits of concessiveness. The temptations to partiality in the special case will be ever-present. This is why the early Rousseau spoke of the general will as resting on an act of the understanding, which when it reasons "in the silence of the passions" shows what we owe to others and others to us. He won't have it that this act is a mere "speculative chimera"; but he allows that it requires of each feats of forbearance, especially when the crucial question of the adjustment of property rights is concerned: "There would have to be, on the side of the great, moderation in wealth and position, and, on the side of the lower classes, moderation in avarice and greed"; and some measure of abuse is inevitable. "The social state is advantageous to man only when all have something and none too much" (ibid., p. 22). That the popular will may lose its rectitude, or may never quite achieve it, is endemic to an arrangement under which ordinary men make the law for ordinary men. Sectional and shortsighted interests are always at the point of taking over; and the obstacles to the habit of concessiveness will be the greater, the wider, and the more organized, the more conflicting are the interests. Hence Rousseau's insistence that democracy is incompatible with vast economic inequalities and with the organization of sectional interests in subordinate associations. And hence also his insistence that the

habits of mind on which a healthy general will depends need culti-
vating: a lively sense of the social bond, of the dependence of all on
the whole and on each other; a habit of judiciousness and responsibility to be imparted to all by their early education. This is why Rousseau's *Emile* is the companion volume to the *Social Contract*. But with
all, these are remedies within the system, which the people in their
legislative role would have to apply to themselves. In the last resort,
therefore, the social clock can only be self-winding; and this is why
there is no unequivocal answer to the question whether it can be relied
on to tick. That the general will is indestructible expressed Rousseau's
confidence that man was not so corrupted by original sin as to be
unable to do the necessary for himself when placed in a position of
self-dependence. That the general will may be silenced expressed his
realistic acknowledgment that any job men can do, they can also bun-
gle. The sovereignty of the general will is the only tolerable solution
to the social problem, and it is possible, but only for a people that
elects to be sensible.

This conclusion, along with the rest of the argument, makes the
sovereignty of the general will a solution to the social problem of
modern man as poised between the practicable and the absurd as any
human solution for a human problem can be. There is no complication
which Rousseau will spare us, nor any comfortable illusion he will
leave intact. The pride of the enlightenment, civilization depending
on the advancement of knowledge, and our mastery over nature have
come to stay; but for all we know, we might have been better without.
The state is the age-old instrument of oppression, but we have to
accept it as our savior. We must buckle under to it as the final arbitrator, but it is morally intolerable to do so unconditionally. The sovereign can fail in his duty, but there is no law of reason to tell us with
certainty that he has. The arrangement is humanly intolerable unless
controlled by ourselves, but there is no guarantee that we shall manage
it. And Rousseau was not deterred by this solution. He accepts civilization without denying its discontents. He defends democracy while
refusing to be naive about it. The best he can say for his solution is
that it makes for an emancipated human being and that it is better
for us to live with its ambiguities than to seek refuge in the dubious
comforts of paternalism.

Library of Congress Cataloging-in-Publication Data

Falk, W. D. (W. David), 1906–
   Ought, reasons, and morality.

   Includes index.
   1. Ethics—Addresses, essays, lectures.   2. Reason—
Addresses, essays, lectures.   I. Title.
BJ1012.F35   1986   170   85–22436
ISBN 0–8014–1784–8 (alk. paper)